D0988750

# Reading & Spelling Through Literature

## Book 1

Kathy Jo DeVore

REVISED EDITION

barefoot
ragamuffin
*curricula*

www.barefootmeandering.com
veritas • gnaritas • libertas

Copyright © 2022 by Kathy Jo DeVore. The eBook version may be printed for the use of one household and may not be resold. The print version may not be reproduced.

Clipart images Copyright © GraphicsFactory.com

# Table of Contents

# Part 1: Phonograms & Spelling Rules      15

# Quick Start Guide

*Reading & Spelling Through Literature* (RSTL) is an Orton-Gillingham (O-G) reading and spelling program. This methodology teaches reading through spelling instead of treating them as two separate subjects. Once students are reading fluently, they continue with the spelling lists to learn more advanced words and spelling rules.

The process is quite simple:

- Students first learn the phonograms. Students starting with RSTL Primer learn only the sounds of the individual letters, *a-z*, before beginning the spelling lists. More advanced students will also learn multi-letter phonograms that make a single sound, such as *sh* in *wish*, before beginning the spelling lists.

- Once the student has learned the necessary phonograms for the level of RSTL that you're using, you will begin to dictate the spelling lists to the student. Each word is called out to the student, phonogram by phonogram, while the student writes the word. If the student cannot remember how to write a phonogram, simply remind them and move on to the next phonogram. Words are analyzed according to the phonograms and the spelling rules. The instructions for dictating each spelling word include all of this information, so it is not necessary to know all of this information yourself before you begin.

- Students initially practice reading by reading through the spelling book created through this process. Once students are comfortable with reading the spelling words, they may move on to the stories that correspond with the spelling lists.

RSTL teaches 75 phonograms and 30 spelling rules. With just 105 pieces of information, the majority of words in the English language can be analyzed and explained logically. RSTL takes the O-G methodology and combines it with the *Elson Readers* for reading practice with words that the student has already been explicitly taught.

Each level of RSTL is named according to which *Elson Readers* it includes. The first book is the RSTL Primer, which includes the *Elson Readers Primer*. The second book is RSTL Book 1, which includes *Elson Readers Book 1*; etc. The *Elson Readers* were originally intended for public school use, so if you are primarily teaching spelling, the book numbers are roughly equivalent to grade level—Book 1 for 1st grade, Book 2 for 2nd grade, etc. If you are teaching reading from scratch, begin with the Primer, regardless of age or grade.

Each volume of *Reading & Spelling Through Literature* has three parts:

**Part 1: The Phonograms.** Reading and spelling instruction begins with teaching the phonograms. There are some slight differences between O-G programs regarding which phonograms are taught, each dependent on what makes the most sense to the author. This program teaches 75 basic phonograms. You can download a free set of phonogram flashcards from our site. A set of two-per-page flashcards is also included at the end of this book.

**Part 2: The Spelling Lists.** Dictating the spelling words begins after students know the phonograms, and **Part 2** includes full instructions on how to do this. In the Primer, you begin teaching the spelling words after you've taught the first 26 phonograms (*a* to *z*). In later volumes, it is assumed that children know the additional phonograms taught in previous levels—any previously taught phonogram may appear in any list, and all 75 phonograms are taught in the Primer and Book 1. If you're new to O-G programs but want to start with a more advanced level, never fear! Instructions are included for quickly teaching the phonograms to fluent readers. This is a quick process for students who can already read since they already know the sounds the phonograms make; we're just providing an organizational system for knowledge they already possess.

**Part 3: The Elson Readers**. The spelling lists are arranged around the stories in the *Elson Readers* in order to give students practice reading with words that they have been explicitly taught. Each story corresponds to a spelling list or a series of spelling lists—e.g., to read Story 1, children need to learn the words in lists 1A through 1H. Students may read a story when they have learned all the words in a story and are comfortable reading the words from their spelling notebook. It is fine if they still need to sound the words out, but they should not be struggling.

Following is a more detailed overview of each part. This overview is intended to provide a basic roadmap of where the program is headed. Feel free to skip to **Part 1** and begin teaching the phonograms if you'd prefer; I myself found that I understood O-G better when I jumped in and started doing it, but I do encourage you to first read the section on **Necessary Materials** below. You can return to this **Quick Start** section once you are comfortable teaching the phonograms.

## Necessary Materials

**A place for handwriting practice:** Children learn to both read and write the phonograms in this program, so they need a place to practice handwriting. This can be in a composition book or the optional workbooks, but it can also be on a white board, in a sand tray, or any other method you wish. Instructions are included later in this introduction for adapting the program for a child who is unable to learn to write while learning to read. See the section on **Non-Writers**.

**Composition book or notebook with loose-leaf handwriting pages:** Children will need a place to write spelling words or (for non-writers) to have the instructor write them. Preferably, this will be a composition book. Primary composition books are available that are lined for grades K-2 and are nicely bound already. You can also adapt regular composition books to this purpose, either wide-ruled or college ruled, though the college ruled books work best for primary grade children. See page 25 if you want to see an example of how the various composition books are setup for spelling.

I prefer composition books. However, you can use whatever writing paper you normally use. If you use loose-leaf pages, keep the spelling lists together and separate from other work. Students should read their spelling words for practice, so it's best if they don't have to search for them.

## Part 1: The Phonograms

A *phonogram* is a symbol that represents a sound, so each letter is a phonogram. We also have phonograms that are made up of multiple letters, like *ch*, *sh*, *igh*, etc.

You've probably heard the quote from Canadian writer James Nicoll concerning the English language: "We don't just borrow words; on occasion, English has pursued other languages down alleyways to beat them unconscious and rifle their pockets for new vocabulary." So because English is a tad insane—and possibly violently unstable—we have multiple ways to spell each sound our language makes, and many of the phonograms make more than one sound, including all of our vowels. Step one in the O-G style of reading instruction is to learn the sounds that the phonograms make. RSTL teaches 75 basic phonograms. The basic phonograms are the ones that are most common as well as most likely to be found in words that a beginning reader will encounter.

Students learn the first 26 phonograms—*a* through *z*—before beginning the spelling lists in the RSTL Primer, which is intended for beginning readers. Once the first 26 phonograms are learned, children will begin to learn spelling words, which eases them into reading, one word at a time. They learn which phonograms make up a word as well as which spelling rules apply to that word. This takes place somewhat passively as the instructor dictates spelling words and simply reads applicable rules to the student; they learn many spelling rules through sheer repetition alone. RSTL teaches the other 49 phonograms in the Primer and Book 1 as they appear in the spelling lists—not before. Because of this, students will always have at least one example word to practice that contains the new phonogram. Older students who begin with an advanced level will need to learn all of the phonograms taught in the previous level(s) since any previously taught phonogram can appear in any list.

## Part 2: The Spelling Lists

Once students have learned the necessary phonograms, you should begin dictating the spelling words. This means that you will call each word out to the child, phonogram by phonogram, until they have written the entire word. With O-G, the emphasis is always on the phonograms, not the individual letters.

Full instructions are given in **Part 2** for dictating the spelling words, and the first five lists give explicit directions for dictation, even reminding you to pause while the student writes the word. After that, the more obvious instructions are dropped to conserve space.

## Part 3: The Readers

The spelling lists are made up of some of the most common words in the English language, and they are arranged around the stories in the *Elson Readers*. Part 3 includes the complete text of an *Elson Readers*. Each RSTL level takes its name from the *Elson Readers* volume that it includes—RSTL Primer includes the stories from the *Elson Readers Primer*; RSTL Book 1 includes the stories from the *Elson Readers Book 1*; etc.

The *Elson Readers* include traditional stories, folk tales, and fables; stories about nature and festivals; and poetry, including Mother Goose rhymes and poems by poets such as Christina G. Rossetti and Robert Louis Stevenson. Retellings of old tales have been simplified but not dumbed down. The punctuation and vocabulary have been updated as necessary to suit modern sensibilities and conventions.

Children may read a story when they have completed the corresponding spelling list(s). Each story corresponds to a spelling list or a series of spelling lists—e.g., lists 1A though 1H (80 words) correspond to Story 1; lists 2A through 2B (20 new words) correspond to Story 2; list 8 (10 new words) corresponds to Story 8.

Children should be comfortable reading the words from their spelling notebooks before progressing to the stories. It is fine if children still need to sound out the words, but they should not be struggling—laboriously sounding out each word in a story is no fun for anyone. The child can, and should, practice the words by reading the spelling notebook because comprehension is not an issue when children are reading only single, unrelated words.

Part of the philosophy behind the *Lessons Through Literature* programs is to help children progress in incremental steps. And RSTL is specifically for the purpose of reading *and spelling*. In the early levels of RSTL, the words in the stories have many of the same markings that children are learning to use as they analyze their spelling words. Later volumes will have the phonograms marked throughout to emphasize proper spelling.

## Non-Writers

Some children have problems which prevent them from learning to write, but they are ready to learn to read. My oldest three boys all learned to read without a writing component to their lessons. So, while I do believe the writing helps, I also recognize that it's not strictly necessary to learn to read. I hope these instructions will help you adapt the program if you have a child who cannot do the writing portion.

When you introduce the phonograms, simply skip the writing portion of the lesson. If possible, work on letter formation through air writing or finger tracing the letters. Remember, adding a multisensory component always helps with retention.

When it is time to begin the spelling lists, use phonogram flashcards or tiles; both are available as free downloads from our website. It's important to use something with phonograms, not letters, because we want children thinking in terms of phonograms rather than individual letters. Make sure that you have enough cards or tiles to complete each word in the list. As you dictate each word (explained more fully in **Part 2**), have children identify each phonogram as you call it out and put the phonograms together to form the word. Then, write the word in the spelling book and have the child mark it as much as possible. Alternatively, explain the markings as you make them. Later, have the child tell you how to mark the words.

## A Word About Spelling Tests

This is the only place in RSTL that you will see a mention of spelling tests, and I'm mentioning them here to make one simple request: Please don't do them.

A spelling test has one point and one point only—to inform the instructor of the child's ability to spell words. Please consider that for a moment. Think carefully on this. **A spelling test has absolutely no benefit to the child.**

Now consider that every time children spell words incorrectly, it's another block towards spelling those words correctly. I've heard people make references to this particular phenomenon my entire life, and I've seen it with my own children. It is best to never see incorrectly spelled words, particularly while a child is still learning.

I tried a traditional spelling program only once before discovering the O-G method. My oldest son, in approximately 3rd grade, had a "proofreading" exercise. At the end of it, after seeing words spelled incorrectly, he was no longer able to spell the words that he could previously spell without difficulty. For my very visual firstborn, seeing words spelled incorrectly was enough. So consider that when children spell a word incorrectly on a spelling test, they are using multiple senses. They are seeing the word and writing it down. In practice tests, they have likely spelled the word incorrectly out loud as well. And when they get the paper back, they're told to examine their mistakes!

Everything you hear about multisensory learning works in reverse as well. The brain will ever-so-efficiently store away each multisensory mistake, leaving two or more different ways to spell each word lodged in the brain. And now, the child has to decide between these various versions of the word every single time that word is needed until it has been practiced the correct way so many times that it blots out the misspellings.

For the child who is struggling with spelling, by placing those incorrectly spelled words in the child's mind, the spelling test has actually become a stumbling block to correct spelling. But even the child who has no trouble with spelling has not benefitted from the exercise. And realistically, neither has the instructor! The spelling test is not an accurate indicator of whether students will be able to spell words in their own writing.

Young children who are fairly new readers are still internalizing spelling, from their reading and also from explicit spelling instruction. I leave this process alone to work slowly in the background. I do not test to see if it's working. I cannot. This is the uncertainty principle for teaching spelling: You cannot test how well your young child is spelling without altering the child's ability to spell—and not favorably.

In our household, here's how this plays out: I don't put my children in a position to fail while they're still going through this process. That means that I do not require original written work from my children in the early grades. They do copywork. They do oral narrations, which I write for them. I don't prevent them from doing their own writing, but I never require it. By the time I begin requiring writing from them, when they begin doing their own written narrations and prepared dictations around 3rd or 4th grade, they're ready for them.

## RSTL for Reading and Spelling

*Reading & Spelling Through Literature* teaches reading *through* spelling, so the focus is on how to spell the words from the beginning. That does not mean that this is necessarily how it works in the child's brain, of course. Kindergarteners and 1st graders are *learning* to read and *learning* to analyze and spell words. Some of what RSTL teaches is developmentally inappropriate for children this young to do on their own, so they learn phonograms and spelling rules passively through repetition. And yet, it is always amazing to me how quickly they begin analyzing words as they are dictated instead of waiting for the instructor to tell them how to mark words. In this way, RSTL allows children to learn at their own developmental pace. We keep moving forward, teaching explicitly, and children naturally do more on their own as they are able.

At the same time, it is a lot of fun to ask your six-year-old why *e* says its name in the word *the* and hear them respond, "*E* says its name at the end of a syllable." Just remember that when they do so, they are responding at least partially by rote and may not understand the concept fully yet, and this is fine. So when your child does not know the answer, there's no reason for concern. Simply tell them and move on.

Regardless of whether you are focusing primarily on reading or spelling, for most people, I recommend going at a pace of one book per school year. Each volume of RSTL contains 460-520 spelling words in 46-52 spelling lists. Taking the two ends of that spectrum, here are examples of how that could look over 33 weeks, which allows for 3 weeks for phonogram teaching and/or review:

46 spelling lists over 33 weeks:
Complete 1 list per week for 20 weeks and 2 lists per week for 13 weeks.
Or you could complete 1 list every 3-4 days.

52 spelling lists over 33 weeks:
Complete 1 list per week for 14 weeks and 2 lists per week for 19 weeks.
Or you could complete 1 list every 3 days.

You can see that it is easy to adjust this schedule to your own life by doing two spelling lists on the weeks when you are less busy. And this is a comfortable pace for any age, in general. Always remember that curricula authors speak of generalities; you should adjust for your own child, and your own circumstances, as needed. Use the curriculum; don't let it use you! But for the average person, living the average life, with the average child, this will work well in the average, expected way.

RSTL also includes optional workbooks that give students more practice with their spelling words each week while helping to keep the pace through the textbook slow. With the workbooks, the best option would likely be to complete a lesson—list plus workbook exercises—every 3 to 4 days, then simply move on to the next one.

Alternatively, simply complete one spelling list per week and move on to the next book when you finish. In this way, your student will continue to make steady progress though it will take longer to get through the books. For some families, this will be the sweet spot.

Having said that, RSTL is extremely easy to accelerate. Simply do more spelling lists each week. Traditional O-G programs recommend as many as 40-50 new spelling words per week, even for young children, and this may get young children reading faster. But the slower pace will also get the job done with less stress to both the child and the instructor, in this author's opinion. I have personally used the original version of this program in both ways. I wrote this program for my son who was struggling to learn to read when he was seven or eight. Because of his age, we were both quite comfortable doing up to five spelling lists some weeks. However, more recently when I taught my daughter to read, we normally only did one or two lists per week. I encourage you to find your comfort zone. The important part is to continue working through the lists on a regular basis. Your normal may not look like mine.

## Stay the Course

A new homeschooling mother asked, "Which reading program will teach my child to read?" An experienced homeschooling mother replied, "The third one."

Sometimes, we change curricula because we read new research or we learn new information, so we change to a program that better fits our own educational philosophy. But other times, we simply don't give a program time to work. Learning to read takes time, and it also relies on the developmental readiness of the child. If the methodology behind a program is sound, then there is no reason to switch programs. Reading is hard work and requires lots of practice. Whatever program you use, give it time to work.

Part 1

Phonograms &
Spelling Rules

# The Phonograms

RSTL teaches 75 basic phonograms. The basic phonograms are simply the most common ones that students will find in their reading. This section includes a one-page list of the basic phonograms that can be used as a quick reference page for the instructor. To learn the phonograms, the student will need a set of flashcards. A set of two-per-page flashcards is also included at the end of this book. Free flashcard files can also be downloaded from our website. These can be printed and laminated, or you can use them by simply flipping through the file on a phone or tablet—my favorite method. And unlike a card file, it's (mostly) toddler proof.

One of the lovely parts about learning the phonograms as someone who can already read is that it organizes information that you already know but may have never before put together into a logical system. Of course *a* says /ǎ/, /ā/, /ä/. I had read and spelled words using *a* in those ways for more than two decades before finding a system that organized that bit of information so beautifully. So when teaching a student who can already read, learning the phonograms is more like a review with an excellent cheat sheet than learning from scratch.

For new readers, teaching the phonograms is giving them this information in its most logical, organized way from the very beginning. I think that's a beautiful gift to give a child.

# About Teaching the Phonograms

The name of a phonogram is the sound or sounds that the phonogram makes, not the names of the letters that make up the phonogram. Teaching the phonograms is teaching the sound(s) of each one. The sounds are necessary to learn to read, not the names of the letters, so we want students to think first of the sounds rather than the names of the letters. And we want students to think of multi-letter phonograms as units, not as individual letters.

In some cases, the name of a phonogram includes a phrase to help differentiate one phonogram from another with the exact, or almost exact, same sound(s). The phonogram name—the sound(s) plus any identifying phrase—is what children initially learn to say when they see that phonogram. Here are a few examples. Notice that phonograms appear in italics, *e*, while individual sounds are in brackets: /ě/.

| | |
|---|---|
| *b* | Say: /b/ |
| *e* | Say: /ě/, /ē/ |
| *ck* | Say: /k/, two letter /k/ |
| *ee* | Say: /ē/, double /ē/ |

In the first example above, instead of the letter name *b*, you say the sound it makes. It is important to say only the phonogram sound; remember that *b* says /b/, not /buh/. An internet search will yield audio files of the phonograms being spoken. For *e*, notice that you say both of the sounds that *e* can make, both long and short, rather than just its letter name. The last two examples have additional words to help distinguish them from other phonograms. The phonograms *k* and *ck* have the exact same sound, so saying "/k/, two letter /k/" lets the student know that we are not talking about the phonogram *k*. In the case of *ee*, while it only has one sound and *e* has two sounds, if we didn't add "double /ē/" to its name, dictating this phonogram might sound like we are just saying the name of the letter *e*, so the additional words provide clarity.

Reading & Spelling Through Literature Book 1

A phonogram can make up to six sounds. Sample words are given on the cards as well as on the one-page reference sheet to help the instructor identify each sound, but these are for the instructor, not the child. We do not want to give children extra steps to wade through, like words or pictures, while trying to remember the sounds.

For beginning readers, once the first 26 phonograms—*a* through *z*—are learned, children will begin learning spelling words, which eases them into reading. Older students will need to learn all of the phonograms taught in previous levels before beginning the spelling lists. All 75 basic phonograms are taught in the Primer and Book 1.

Children will forget the sounds, but that's okay. Just keep moving forward, and eventually the sounds will stick. Help them with the sounds when they forget. I do this quickly. If the child hesitates during a review, I say the sound(s); I have the child repeat the sound(s); and I move on to the next phonogram. If a child hesitates while I'm dictating a spelling list, I use the back side of the previous page to write the phonogram quickly for the child to copy.

## How to Teach the Phonograms

Students begin by learning the basic phonograms. For all students, the first part of this is quite simple: Hold up a flashcard with the phonogram on it. Say the name of the phonogram, which includes the sounds the phonogram makes plus any additional information. Have the student repeat the name several times.

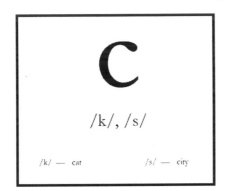

Instructor: /k/, /s/. Say that several times. /k/, /s/.

Student: /k/, /s/. /k/, /s/. /k/, /s/.

Some phonograms are taught with an applicable spelling rule. For instance, English words do not end in the letter *i*, so the phonogram *ai* is "/ā/, two letter /ā/ that we may not use at the end of English words." After a child has learned this well, he can simply say, "/ā/, two letter /ā/," during reviews. Occasionally, ask, "Can it be used at the end of English words?" as part of the review process.

I prefer flashcards that have all of the information on one-side, as in the example. These work best for flipping through them on a phone or tablet (my preferred method). I have not found the additional information to be distracting to my young children. And for older students who can already read, while the information does technically tell them the sounds, there is value in learning the various ways we write sounds.

Ideally, students should learn to write the phonograms while learning to read them. Saying the names of the phonograms while writing them is a tremendous memory aid.

For younger students (ages 4-8), the optional Primer Workbook A teaches the sounds and how to write the phonograms, and it includes phonemic awareness exercises for children to practice with. Review of phonograms already learned is included in each lesson.

Older students who are beginning RSTL as a spelling program can also practice writing the phonograms as a memory aid, particularly the multi-letter phonograms. This can be accomplished on any type of paper you prefer. Our *Handwriting Lessons Through Literature: Primer* can be used for this purpose as well as it teaches handwriting through learning the phonograms and Webster's Syllabary to reinforce proper spelling.

Please see the section on **Non-Writers** in the **Quick Start Guide** if your student cannot learn to write at this time.

## New Readers and Writers

Children who are just beginning to read and write will learn to write the phonograms at the same time. The method is simple and follows a multisensory approach. Seeing, hearing, saying, and doing—these are the basics in multisensory learning. Using multiple senses to learn new information helps the brain process the information, which helps children remember the information better and longer.

• Before moving to the written portion of the lesson, have children practice making the phonograms in other ways while saying the sounds.

This step can be either practically free or quite expensive, depending on your own preferences. My own preferred method is of the "practically free" variety—I simply have them trace the phonogram with a finger—either the large example in the optional workbook or a large example that I have written for them in a composition book that we are using for handwriting.

Some like to start with large motions by having children write the phonograms in the air with their whole arm before moving on to smaller motions by having them use a finger to trace the phonograms. Other methods include using sandpaper letters, blocks, and/or wooden letters to practice forming the letters. These are not necessary, but they can be helpful if the budget allows.

• During the written portion of the lesson, have children say the sound(s) of each phonogram while writing it approximately four to eight times. This can be accomplished in a variety of ways:

• Optional workbook
• Composition book
• Sand tray
• White board
• Chalkboard

## Pace for Teaching the Phonograms

The multi-letter phonograms are taught when they appear in the spelling lists in the first two books. However, for the RSTL Primer, you will need to teach the first twenty-six phonograms—the alphabet *a* to *z*—before beginning the spelling lists. Older students will need to learn all of the phonograms before beginning Book 2 or higher.

I advise spending approximately three weeks learning the phonograms. For older students who are already fluent readers, this would mean five phonograms per day, but learning the phonograms for a fluent reader is more about review and organizing information that they already know, so this pace should be fine for them to learn all 75 basic phonograms. Adjust as necessary for your student.

For new readers, two phonograms per day is a nice pace to learn the alphabet sounds, *a* to *z*. If you prefer to use the optional Primer Workbook A for teaching the phonograms to young students—and I highly recommend the new optional workbook—you can slow down the pace and spend longer on teaching the phonograms before moving on to the spelling lists. Primer Workbook A includes phonemic awareness exercises, handwriting, and built-in review. It also begins teaching CVC (Consonant-Vowel-Consonant) words and silent *e* words that make the vowel say its name. At almost 300 pages, you could easily spend a few months just working on these basic skills before moving on to the spelling lists.

# 30 Spelling Rules

## Vowel and Vowel Sound Rules

1. *Q* always needs *u*, and *u* is not a vowel here.
2. *C* says /s/ before *e, i,* and *y.* Otherwise, *c* says /k/: picnic, picnicking.
3. *G* may say /j/ before *e, i,* and *y.* Otherwise, *g* says /g/.
4. Vowels *a, e, o, u* usually say /ā, ē, ō, ū/ at the end of a syllable.
5. Vowels *y* and *i* may say /ĭ/, /ī/, or /ē/ at the end of a syllable.
6. Vowel *y* says /ī/ at the end of a one-syllable word: by, sky, why.
7. Vowel *y* says /ē/ only at the end of a multi-syllable word: baby, candy.
8. Vowels *i* and *o* may say /ī/ and /ō/ when followed by two consonants.
9. At the end of a base word, /ā/ is usually spelled *ay.* There are ten exceptions when /ā/ is spelled *ey*: convey, hey, ley, obey, osprey, prey, purvey, survey, they, whey.
10. At the end of words, vowel *a* says its third sound: ma, zebra.
11. The *gh* phonograms *augh, ough, igh,* and *eigh* can each be used only at the end of a base word or before the letter *t.* The *gh* is either silent or it says /f/.

## End of Base Word Rules

12. English words do not end in *i, u, v,* or *j,* but YOU and I are special.
13. Phonograms *dge* and *ck* are used only after a single vowel that says its short sound.
14. Phonogram *tch* is used only after a single vowel that does not say its long sound. Phonogram *tch* is the phonogram usually used to say /ch/ following a single vowel at the end of base words, but *ch* says /ch/ after a single vowel at the end of six base words: attach, spinach, rich, which, much, such. Phonogram *ch* is used at the end of base words following two vowels (teach, preach) and after a vowel followed by a consonant (church, bunch).
15. We often double *f, l,* and *s* after a single vowel at the end of a base word. We sometimes double other letters.

## 5 Reasons for Final Silent E

16. (1) The vowel says its name because of the *e.*
17. (2) English words do not end in *v* or *u.*
18. (3) The *e* makes *c* say /s/ or *g* say /j/.
19. (4) Every syllable must have a written vowel.
20. (5) Miscellaneous silent *e* covers all other silent *e* usages. This can include preventing a word that would otherwise end in *s* from looking plural, making a word appear larger, making *th* say /TH/, and making homonyms appear different.

## Affix Rules

21. When added to another syllable, the prefix all- and the suffix -full each drop an *l*: almost, truthful.
22. When adding a vowel suffix, drop the final silent *e* unless it is still necessary according to other spelling rules, such as making *c* say /s/ or *g* say /j/: charge, chargeable, charging.
23. When adding a vowel suffix to a word ending in one vowel followed by one consonant, double the last letter only if the word is one syllable or the last syllable is accented: begin, beginning; worship, worshiping. Do not double *x, w,* or *y.*
24. The single vowel *y* (not part of a multi-letter phonogram) changes to *i* before adding any ending unless the ending begins with *i*: happy, happiness; try, tries, trying. This is because...
25. English words cannot have two letters *i* in a row.
26. To form the past tense of regular verbs, add *ed. Ed* forms a new syllable when the base word ends in *d* or *t.* Otherwise, *ed* says /d/ or /t/.
27. Use *s* to make regular nouns plural and to make the third person singular form of a regular verb. Use *es* after phonograms that hiss: *s, ch, sh, x,* and *z.* Refer to rule 23 when adding *es. Ch* does not hiss when it says /k/: stomach, stomachs.

## Spelling Sh Rules

28. *Sh* spells /sh/ at the beginning of words and at the end of syllables. It never spells /sh/ at the beginning of any syllable after the first one except for the ending —ship: she, fish, hardship.
29. *Ti, si,* and *ci* say /sh/ at the beginning of any syllable except the first one. Look to the root word to determine which one to use: par*t*, par*ti*al; transgres*s*, transgres*si*on; fa*c*e, fa*ci*al.

## Miscellaneous Rule

30. *Z* says /z/ at the beginning of a base word, never *s.*

# 75 Basic Phonograms

| | | | | | |
|---|---|---|---|---|---|
| a | /ă/, /ā/, /ä/ | at, acorn, wasp | n | /n/ | no |
| b | /b/ | but | o | /ŏ/, /ō/, /ö/ | pot, go, to |
| c | /k/, /s/ | cat, city | p | /p/ | put |
| d | /d/ | dog | qu | /kw/ | queen |
| e | /ĕ/, /ē/ | best, me | r | /r/ | run |
| f | /f/ | four | s | /s/, /z/ | sass, has |
| g | /g/, /j/ | garden, gem | t | /t/ | tap |
| h | /h/ | hat | u | /ŭ/, /ū/, /ü/ | umbrella, unit, put |
| i | /ĭ/, /ī/, /ē/, /y/ | igloo, ice, radio, onion | v | /v/ | vowel |
| j | /j/ | jam | w | /w/ | water |
| k | /k/ | kite | x | /ks/, /z/ | fox, xylophone |
| l | /l/ | lot | y | /y/, /ĭ/, /ī/, /ē/ | yellow, gym, sky, baby |
| m | /m/ | mat | z | /z/ | zoo |

| | | |
|---|---|---|
| ai | /ā/ — 2 letter /ā/ we may NOT use at the end of English words | hail |
| ar | /är/ | car |
| au | /ä/ — 2 letter /ä/ that we may NOT use at the end of English words | pauper |
| augh | /ä/, /ăf/ | caught, laugh |
| aw | /ä/ — 2 letter /ä/ that we MAY use at the end of English words | paw |
| ay | /ā/ — 2 letter /ā/ that we MAY use at the end of English words | play |
| bu | /b/ — 2 letter /b/ | build |
| ch | /ch/, /k/, /sh/ | chat, chasm, chef |
| cei | /sē/ | receive |
| ci | /sh/ — short /sh/ ("short" because it begins with a short letter) | facial |
| ck | /k/ — 2 letter /k/ | back |
| dge | /j/ — 3 letter /j/ | dodge |
| ea | /ē/, /ĕ/, /ā/ | beat, dread, break |
| ear | /er/ as in pearl | pearl |
| ed | /ed/, /d/, /t/ | waded, slammed, picked |
| ee | /ē/ — double /ē/ | tee |
| ei | /ā/, /ē/, /ī/ | their, protein, feisty |
| eigh | /ā/, /ī/ | eight, height |
| er | /er/ as in her | her |
| ew | /ö/, /ū/ | dew, few |
| ey | /ā/, /ē/ | they, key |
| gn | /n/ — 2 letter /n/ that we use at the beginning or the end of a word | gnome, sign |
| gu | /g/, /gw/ | guest, language |
| ie | /ē/ — 2 letter /ē/ | thief |
| igh | /ī/ — 3 letter /ī/ | sight |
| ir | /er/ as in dirt | dirt |
| kn | /n/ — 2 letter /n/ that we use only at the beginning of a base word | know |
| mb | /m/ — 2 letter /m/ | comb |
| ng | /ng/ | ding (nasal sound) |
| oa | /ō/ — 2 letter /ō/ | boat |
| oe | /ō/, /ö/ | doe, shoe |
| oi | /oi/ that we may NOT use at the end of English words | toil |
| oo | /ö/, /ü/, /ō/ | food, hook, floor |
| or | /or/ | cord |
| ou | /ow/, /ō/, /ö/, /ŭ/, /ü/ | our, four, tour, famous, could |
| ough | /ŏ/, /ō/, /ö/, /ow/, /uff/, /off/ | bought, dough, through, bough, rough, cough |
| ow | /ow/, /ō/ | plow, bow |
| oy | /oi/ that we MAY use at the end of English words | toy |
| ph | /f/ — 2 letter /f/ | phonics |
| sh | /sh/ | shell |
| si | /sh/, /zh/ | transgression, vision |
| tch | /ch/ | clutch |
| th | /th/, /TH/ | think, that |
| ti | /sh/ — tall /sh/ ("tall" because it begins with a tall letter) | nation |
| ui | /ö/ | fruit |
| ur | /er/ as in turn | turn |
| wh | /wh/ | wheel |
| wor | /wer/ | worm |
| wr | /r/ — 2 letter /r/ | wreck |

# Advanced Phonograms

Advanced phonograms are the phonograms that are uncommon or appear in more advanced words. In addition to the advanced phonograms, some of the basic phonograms have advanced sounds—again, the advanced sounds would be the ones that are uncommon or appear in more advanced words.

Basic phonograms with advanced sounds have an asterisk (*) beside them in the list, and then the advanced sounds and examples follow another asterisk.

Keep in mind that the advanced phonograms are for reference and for students who are already reading and using RSTL for spelling only. I recommend teaching only the basic sounds of the basic phonograms to new readers to simplify matters for them. Older students may learn the advanced sounds of the basic phonograms as well as the advanced phonograms, but keep in mind that many words with advanced phonograms can also be explained with silent letters or as exceptions! You may never feel the need to teach the advanced phonograms at all.

| | | |
|---|---|---|
| ae | /ā/, /ē/, /ĕ/ | aerial, algae, aesthetic |
| ah | /ä/ | blah |
| ai * | /ā/, */ī/, /ă/ | mail, *aisle, plaid |
| au * | /ä/, */ō/, /ā/, /ow/ | pauper, *chauffeur, gauge, sauerkraut |
| ay * | /ā/, */ī/ | day, *cayenne |
| cc | /ch/ | cappuccino |
| ce | /sh/ | ocean |
| cu | /k/, /kw/ | biscuit, cuisine |
| eau | /ō/, /ū/, /ŏ/ | bureau, beauty, bureaucracy |
| ei * | /ā/, /ē/, /ī/, */ĭ/, /ĕ/ | their, protein, feisty, *forfeit, heifer |
| et | /ā/ | ballet |
| eu | /ö/, /ū/ | neutral, feud |
| ey * | /ā/, /ē/, */ī/ | they, turkey, *geyser |
| ge | /j/, /zh/ | surgeon, mirage |
| gh | /g/ | ghost |
| oe * | /ō/, /ö/, */ē/ | toe, shoe, *subpoena |
| ot | /ō/ | depot |
| our | /er/ | journey |
| pn | /n/ | pneumonia |
| ps | /s/ | psalm |
| pt | /t/ | pterodactyl |
| rh | /r/ | rhyme |
| sc | /s/ | science |
| sci | /ch/ | conscience |
| th * | /th/, /TH/, */t/ | thought, them, *thyme |
| ut | /ū/ | debut |
| yr | /ēr/, /er/ | lyric, syrup |
| z * | /z/, */s/ | zoo, *quartz |

Part 2

The Spelling Lists

# The Spelling Lists

The spelling lists are made up of some of the most common words in the English language, and they are arranged around the stories in *The Elson Readers* to give students practice reading with words they've already learned explicitly. The instructor will dictate the spelling words to students, and as students write the words, they will be creating their own spelling notebooks.

The following pages give an overview of making the spelling notebook. You can use whatever writing paper you normally use—we have free writing paper downloads available—or you can purchase a composition book. These are available in the standard wide-ruled and college-ruled varieties. Primary composition books, which are lined for grades K-2, are also available. The examples to the right show how this will look with different types of paper, but remember that the important part is to get the words into the book, not the precise layout of said book. For older students, I do recommend skipping lines between words so that they have plenty of space for markings and so that the words are easy to see and read later.

Here are a couple of pro-tips, as my children would say:

• To line up the words in the second column, simply fold the page in half. That produces a nice line that your students can follow, and students can do it themselves at the beginning of each lesson. Alternatively, simply use one column to avoid trying to squeeze the occasional long word into too small a space.

• If you are on a strict budget, or if you cannot find primary composition books locally, you can easily create one with a college-ruled composition book—stock up during the back-to-school sales when you can buy these for as little as fifty cents each! Use a highlighter to highlight every third line. The highlighted part is where letters like lowercase *a* sit, and highlighting every third line gives you space above for tall letters, like *d*, and space below for letters with extenders, like *g*. You can do this as you go rather than attempting to highlight an entire composition book in one sitting, depending on your tolerance for mundane tasks.

The spelling lists give explicit instructions for both student and instructor—even telling you to wait for the student to write the phonogram in the first few lists. Some instructions are dropped or simplified after you have had a chance to get used to the process. The first word in spelling list 1A is printed on the following page as an example. Notice that instructions written to the instructor are in a different font.

Primary K-2 Comp Book with space for picture

| 1A | |
|---|---|
| bag | rug |
| beg | run |
| big | sun |
| bog | can |
| bug | man |

Primary K-2 Comp Book

| 1A | 1B |
|---|---|
| bag | not |
| beg | note |
| big | mad |
| bog | made |
| bug | kit |
| rug | kite |
| run | hop |
| sun | hope |
| can | cut |
| man | cute |

Altered College-Ruled Comp Book with Highlighting

| 1A | 1B |
|---|---|
| bag | not |
| beg | note |
| big | mad |
| bog | made |
| bug | kit |
| rug | kite |
| run | hop |
| sun | hope |
| can | cut |
| man | cute |

Wide-Ruled Comp Book

| 1A | 1B |
|---|---|
| bag | not |
| beg | note |
| big | mad |
| bog | made |
| bug | kit |
| rug | kite |
| run | hop |
| sun | hope |
| can | cut |
| man | cute |

bag        She put the groceries in the bag.
- Bag. The first phonogram is /b/. Wait while student writes it.
- The next phonogram is /ă/, /ā/, /ä/. Wait while student writes it.
- The last phonogram is /g/, /j/. Wait while student writes it.
- /b/-/ă/-/g/. Bag.
- Instructor: Have the student read the word just as you did, by saying each sound and then saying the word: /b/-/ă/-/g/. Bag. This is always the last step after the student has written the word.

As you can see, the format is simple. Read the word and the example sentence. Then dictate the word, phonogram by phonogram, until the word has been completely written. The instructor reads the word back to the student, first the sounds followed by the word itself, and the student then reads the word back to the instructor in the same way. When applicable, additional information is written in the explanation for the instructor to read aloud; students will learn much of the information through this repetition in each lesson.

Notice that sounds are written between slashes, like this: /b/. Phonograms and letters are written in italic, like this: *b*. All of the sounds are given for each phonogram in the first five lists. After that, just the phonogram is given, and you will need to say the names of each phonogram. The one-page reference in **Part 1: The Phonograms** is handy both while you're learning the phonograms as well as for less common phonograms.

## Analyzing the Spelling Words

Words are marked according to which phonograms they contain and by which spelling rules apply to them. I want to make it clear that neither you nor your student needs to understand these markings before you begin the spelling lists! You will both learn them as you progress through the program.

The following are some of the most common markings used. Again, the words are marked and explained in the spelling lists. These are merely explanations for the markings you will see rather than a list that you need to memorize.

1. Underline multi-letter phonograms. This makes them more visible and shows their connection as a single sound unit.

fi<u>sh</u>

2. When a phonogram does not say its first sound, put a small number above it to show which sound it makes.

<u>a</u>ll

3. Leave a space between syllables. This helps students sound out each syllable individually. It also highlights spelling rules that pertain to syllables.

fi<u>sh</u> <u>er</u>

4. Mark eXceptions, which are phonograms in a word that are not saying any of their regular sounds, with an X. This is handled differently in the Primer and Book 1; see the section **Exceptions, Sight Words, and Lazy Vowels** at the end of **Part 2**.

<u>tor</u> <u>toise</u>

Because numbers 5 through 10 are based on spelling rules, their markings are a bit different than the ones mentioned in numbers 1 through 4. There is a temptation among new users to ignore these markings in favor of the rules taught in numbers 1 through 4. For instance, several spelling rules state that vowels will almost always say their names in certain circumstances, such as at the end of a syllable. In these cases, we *underline* the vowel *instead of* marking the vowel with a number 2. You will grow accustomed to this difference. **The purpose is to help emphasize the spelling rule, that it's not merely some arbitrary time when the vowel says its second sound.**

Some people find it helpful to both underline *and* write the number, and this can be a good strategy if the child needs help remembering which sound the vowel is making, especially at first for new readers. Simply write a small number beside the underline, which will remind the student of the sound while also emphasizing the spelling rule. I will include examples of this in the explanations below. These are not marked in the spelling lists, but they're easy to include if you wish, and they're equally easy to drop when your student no longer needs them. I recommend saying, "Add a small 2 next to the underline to show that the phonogram is saying its second sound."

5. Double underline silent letters. The most common is the final silent *e*. Final silent *e* has different functions, and these functions are often marked and discussed with the word. For instance, type 1 silent *e* makes a vowel say its name, so a bridge is drawn from the silent *e* to the vowel *instead of* writing a number 2 over the vowel. The other reasons for silent *e* are marked with a number beside the double underline and discussed in the explanation. All of the reasons for a final silent *e* are listed in the **30 Spelling Rules** at the beginning of **Part 1: The Phonograms**. Reason 5 is a miscellaneous silent *e*, but the others have specific reasons.

mine        give₂        voice₃        lit tle₄        are₅

6. (Book 1 and up.) When a vowel suffix is added to a type 1 silent *e* word, we drop the silent *e* before adding the vowel suffix. Draw a tiny bridge over the vowel *instead of* a number 2 as a reminder that the vowel says its name because of the silent *e* that we dropped.

bāk er        bāk ing

7. Underline *c* and *g* when they say /s/ and /j/ when followed by *e*, *i*, or *y*. This is a spelling rule, so the consonant receives an underline *instead of* a number 2 over it.

cir cle        gem        OR        cir cle₋₂        gem₋₂

8. Underline a vowel when it says its name at the end of a syllable. This is a spelling rule, so the vowel receives an underline *instead of* a number 2 over it.

me        OR        me₋₂

9. Underline *i* and *o* when they say /ī/ and /ō/ when followed by two consonants. This is a spelling rule, so the vowel receives an underline *instead of* a number 2 over it.

colt        OR        colt₋₂

10. Underline *y* when it says /ī/ at the end of a one-syllable word or /ē/ at the end of a multi-syllable word. These are spelling rules, so the vowel receives an underline *instead of* a number over it.

sky        can dy        OR        sky₋₃        can dy₋₄

## Dictating the Spelling Words

Full instructions for dictating the spelling words are right in the spelling lists. In the first few spelling lists, you are even instructed to pause while the student writes the word. Some of the instructions are simplified in later lists to save time and space, but for those first few spelling lists, I've tried to provide instructions that are detailed enough that anyone can do this simply by reading and doing each bullet point.

**It's important to note that this program is built upon repetition and practice.** Applicable spelling rules are given with the spelling words. Over time, instructor and student will both learn these rules just from hearing and saying them so often during spelling dictation. So please don't skip a reference to a spelling rule just because you have already read it once in the lesson. This is to ensure that as your child drifts off to sleep at night and you whisper, "Why do we underline *e* at the end of *the*?" they will sleepily reply, "Because *e* says its name at the end of a syllable."

## Reading the Spelling Words

Children should read their spelling words frequently. That means daily at first. For new readers, their spelling notebooks give them a place to practice reading their spelling words in isolation; they don't have to try to remember the context for the word they're reading or fit all of them together into a cohesive whole. They only have to read and understand one word at a time.

But reading their spelling words is useful for older students as well, particularly those who have had difficulties with reading and/or spelling. Because the phonograms and spelling rules are marked in their spelling notebooks, each time students read the words, the spelling rules and phonograms that pertain to each word are reinforced for them. Reading lists of spelling words is neither fun nor glamorous, it's true. But it is useful.

Here's my recommendation: New readers should read their spelling words regularly until they are reading fluently. Students who have difficulties with reading and/or spelling should read their spelling words frequently. But students who are reading fluently and have shown no signs of having difficulties with spelling can probably focus on reading the stories and other books, copywork, and/or our new RSTL workbooks.

Once the list reaches a certain point, the list can be split into parts, and students can read some of the most recent words while reviewing some of the older ones. We separate the spelling book with Post-it® Tabs for the sake of simplicity. **The exact number of words can differ greatly depending on age and ability.** For instance, I had my children (at ages 7-8) read the most recent 100 words and then review 50 older words. But one of my proofreaders said her child would Rather Die than read that many words. She has used O-G programs even longer than I have, and she recommends reading 20 new words and reviewing 10 older words. The important part is to have the child continue practicing by reading the spelling notebook and to meet your child where they are instead of where you think they should be.

Each spelling list has a number which correlates to a story from the *Elson Readers*—for instance, List 9 correlates to Story 9. In the RSTL Primer, some lists have a number plus a letter because some stories have more than one spelling list since children need to learn all of the words in the story before they read it. These lists have the number that correlates to the story plus a letter—for instance, Lists 1A through 1H correlate to Story 1. New readers need to complete all the lessons with that number before reading the story.

# Exceptions, Sight Words, and Lazy Vowels

Imagine this: You are learning Greek. You learn the sounds of each letter of the Greek alphabet, and you're told that now you have all the keys you need to unlock reading the Greek language. Immediately afterwards, you're given ten words with exceptions to those sounds. Take a moment to consider the frustration and, perhaps, the overwhelming desire to stop learning Greek.

Most programs place children into this position with sight words. Children are told to just keep looking at words until they can remember what the words are, with no cues or clues. I'm not merely projecting here. I'm actively remembering the frustration of this experience, forty years later. (My husband says that I can hold a grudge for an exceptionally long time, and after writing the previous sentence, I'm finally starting to see his point.)

Be that as it may, the reality is that some words are exceptions—they don't follow the normal rules. In some cases, a word may break a spelling rule. More commonly, one of its phonograms may simply not make any of its regular sounds.

For older students, when a phonogram does not make one of its regular sounds, we may mark it with an **X** for eXception. Reading experience and a more advanced vocabulary help older students deal with these words as they encounter them. In the spelling lists, the marking is merely a reminder that we have a weird word here.

But this does not solve the problem for new readers because it does nothing to help children remember what sound the phonogram is actually making in the word. We are right back at the beginning of this section—frustrated. So RSTL handles true exceptions by putting a reminder above the phonogram that is not making one of its regular sounds. For instance, when the student encounters the word *of* in spelling list 6A, they will put a small **v** above the *f* to show that it's making an irregular /v/ sound in this particular word, like this:

$$\overset{v}{of}$$

This does not happen often. Many words are quite obvious once they are sounded out according to the regular sounds of the phonograms in the word. Try sounding out a word like *come* or *love* with the regular short /ŏ/ sound. You will find that it is close enough to the way we normally pronounce the word that it doesn't require any special markings to remind children what the word is. This is why most of the time, we teach that children should "think to spell," emphasizing the regular sound of the phonogram within the word.

RSTL has no sight words. I hated sight words when I was six years old. Four decades later, I find my opinion has not changed. It has only become more informed. (Yes, Ernie. Apparently, I do hold a grudge. I'll work on that.)

We do something similar with vowels. In English, the schwa /ə/ is the most common vowel sound. This is the regular sound of a vowel in an unstressed syllable, pronounced similar to a short *u* sound—the /ŭ/ in *bus*.

Since this information is a bit over the head of the average five to six year old, we can explain it by describing these vowels as lazy. In the spelling list, the word *alone* has this notation: "This word has a lazy vowel. When we say it, we usually say /ə-lōn/. We think to spell /ā-lōn/." This way, children learn that when we sound out the word, or "think to spell," we stress the /ā/ sound, but we can point out that it is a lazy vowel, so the child will hear people say /ə-lōn/.

It is important to stress all vowel sounds in the spelling lessons. Otherwise, depending on your accent, *pen* and *pin* might be indistinguishable from one another.

## Adding Suffixes

One of my goals with RSTL is to emphasize the spelling rules and get children thinking about how we change words based on usage, like how to change words by adding affixes. With that in mind, many of the spelling lists have students add suffixes to words that they have just written. In this way, we can teach students to think through the process of adding a suffix and considering what spelling rules apply to each situation. I have attempted to make this process as simple as possible in the instructions. For instance, the instructions will say, "Dictate the word until you get to the suffix." When you get to the suffix, which is indicated by a plus sign (✚, see below), you simply move on to the next step in the instructions.

The actual spelling word that you will call out at the beginning is the one that is underlined in the sample sentence. For instance, consider the examples below. In the first example, the spelling word is *plan*. You will dictate the word *plan* and then follow the instructions for adding the suffix. But in the second example, the spelling word is *bunnies*, so this is the word you call out at the beginning. In either case, the process is the same. Dictate until you get to the suffix, and then move on to the next step in the instructions.

plan ✚ (n) ing          Enjoy the sunshine, but <u>plan</u> for the rain.

bun n✚<u>ies</u>          The <u>bunnies</u> hopped around the forest.

## The Sounds of Phonogram U

This section is for the curious, so if you're new to O-G, keep in mind that understanding this is not necessary to use the program.

RSTL teaches three sounds for the phonogram *u*. Some programs teach that the phonogram *u* has four sounds instead of only three: /ŭ/, /ū/, /ö/, /ü/—bŭs, ūse, true /trö/, püt. Technically, *u* does have four sounds, so if you wonder why I only include three, this section is for you. It is the third sound, the /ö/ in *true*, that I do not include.

Technically, *u* has two long sounds, /ū/ as in *use* and /ö/ as in *true*. The difference is quite subtle, concerning the /y/ sound that you hear at the beginning of the sound in some words (*use*, *amuse*). The /y/ sound is absent in words such as *true* and *blue*. Because it is quite subtle, we can easily explain this slight difference as *u* being a little lazy when it says its name in these cases. This fits with what students are already learning about vowels.

While this simplifies learning this phonogram, that is not my primary purpose. The actual reason to not include /ö/ as one of the sounds concerns the spelling rules. We have spelling rules that govern when vowels say their names; a vowel says its name due to type one silent *e* and also at the end of a syllable. If we instead say that *u* is simply saying its third sound in these cases, then the rules become less useful. But if we say that *u* is lazy in these words, the rule is reinforced.

The alternative would be to teach that *u* has two long sounds. While this is perfectly acceptable with older students, I try to keep things simple for younger students, which is why I actively avoid teaching exceptions to the rules when it can be avoided.

# 30A  Type 1 Silent E, Syllables, and Consonant Blends

As we go through the spelling lists, you will be learning a lot of new information, including many spelling rules. You should listen to these rules, but don't worry if you have trouble remembering all of them or if you don't understand exactly what each new piece of information means at first! You will learn these things slowly as you continue to work through the books. Today, you're going to learn about **type 1 silent e, consonant blends,** and **syllables.**

We have several different reasons for adding a silent **e** to a word. Today, one of your words is a type 1 silent **e**. When a word has a type 1 silent **e**, it makes the vowel say its name, so we draw a bridge from the vowel to the silent **e**.

You have already learned that two letters can join together to make new sounds, like the multi-letter phonograms you are learning. However, sometimes two consonants next to each other in a word both make their normal sounds, and their sounds blend together. We call these **consonant blends**. You don't have to study them like you do new phonograms because they are saying their normal sounds, just blended together!

You know that some words are really short—like **cat, dog,** and **cake**—while other words are really long—like **xylophone, kaleidoscope,** and **hippopotamus.** Short words are much easier to read and spell, but that's okay because we can divide the long words into smaller pieces to make them easier! We call a chunk of a word a **syllable.**

You can find out how many syllables a word has by seeing how many times your jaw goes down when saying the word. Try it a few times. Say each of the following words out loud with your hand under your chin, and count how many times your jaw goes down! [Instructor: Notes to you are written like this. It's good to demonstrate how to do this. You might even do this exercise with your student. It helps to exaggerate each syllable and to make the jaw-drop BIG.]

| | |
|---|---|
| cat | cat |
| kitten | kit ten |
| syllables | syl la bles |
| xylophone | xy lo phone |
| kaleidoscope | ka lei do scope |
| hippopotamus | hip po pot a mus |

One last thing. Today, one of your words is the name of a little girl—**Gustava.** When we write someone's name, we begin the name with a capital letter. If you haven't learned to write capital letters yet, your instructor will show you how to write a capital **G.** Here are some various ways that people write capital **G** and lowercase **g.** Do you see your kind of writing?

Gg    Gg    Gg    Gg    Gg

spring

### Birds build a nest in the spring.

• Spring. How many syllables does this word have? *Wait while student answers each time.* Just one.
• The first phonogram is /s/, /z/. *Wait while student writes each phonogram.*
• The next phonogram is /p/.
• The next phonogram is /r/.
• The next phonogram is /ĭ/, /ī/, /ē /, /y/.
• The last phonogram is /ng/.
•/s/-/p/-/r/-/ĭ/-/ng/. Spring. Now you read the word. Blend /s/, /p/, and /r/ together when you read it, like this—/spr/.

³ ³
Gus ta va

## Gustava is a little girl.
- This word is a **proper name**, so it begins with a capital letter.
- How many syllables does this word have? Three, so this is your first multi-syllable word in this book. The first syllable is **Gus**. The second syllable is **ta**. The third syllable is **va**.
- The first phonogram is /g/, /j/.
- The second phonogram is /ŭ/, /ū/, /ü/.
- The last phonogram of the first syllable is /s/, /z/.
- Leave a little space, about the size of your little finger, between the syllables. The next syllable is **ta**, and the first phonogram is /t/.
- The next phonogram is /ă/, /ā/, /ä/.
- Leave a little space, about the size of your little finger, between the syllables. The next syllable is **va**, and the first phonogram is /v/.
- The last phonogram is /ă/, /ā/, /ä/.
- Put a small 3 above **u** to show that it's saying its third sound.
- Which of its sounds is the first **a** saying? It's saying its third sound, so put a small 3 above it.
- Underline the last **a** because **a** said its third sound at the end of a word. This is a spelling rule.
- /g/-/ü/-/s/—/t/-/ä/—/v/-/ä/. Gus-ta-va. Now you read the word.

**Spelling rule:** At the end of words, vowel *a* says its third sound.

more

## Would you like more spelling words?
- More. How many syllables does this word have? Just one.
- The first phonogram is /m/.
- The next phonogram is /ŏ/, /ō/, /ö/.
- The next phonogram is /r/.
- The last phonogram is **silent e**, so write /ĕ/, /ē/ at the end of the word.
- To show that the **e** is silent, we double underline it. **O** says its name because of the silent **e**, so draw a bridge between the silent **e** and the **o**. This is a spelling rule.
- /m/-/ō/-/r/. More. Now you read the word.

**Spelling rule:** The vowel says its name because of the silent *e*.

met

## We met some kids at the park.
- Met. How many syllables does this word have? Just one.
- The first phonogram is /m/.
- The next phonogram is /ĕ/, /ē/.
- The last phonogram is /t/.
- /m/-/ĕ/-/t/. Met. Now you read the word.

here

## Is everyone here?
- Here. How many syllables does this word have? Just one.
- The first phonogram is /h/.
- The next phonogram is /ĕ/, /ē/.
- The next phonogram is /r/.
- The last phonogram is **silent e**, so write /ĕ/, /ē/ at the end of the word.
- To show that the **e** is silent, we double underline it. **E** says its name because of the silent **e**, so draw a bridge between the silent **e** and the **e**.
- This word is a **homophone**. **Homophone** means **same sound**, and this word has another word that sounds the same but is spelled differently—I can **hear** you speak.
- /h/-/ē/-/r/. Here. Now you read the word.

glad

## We were glad to be home.

- Glad. How many syllables does this word have? Just one.
- The first phonogram is /g/, /j/.
- The next phonogram is /l/.
- The next phonogram is /ă/, /ā/, /ä/.
- The last phonogram is /d/.
- /g/-/l/-/ă/-/d/. Glad. Now you read the word. Blend /g/ and /l/ together when you read it, like this—/gl/.

food

## We're going to the store to buy food.

- Food. How many syllables does this word have? Just one.
- The first phonogram is /f/.
- The next phonogram is /ö/, /ü/, /ō/.
- The last phonogram is /d/.
- Underline the multi-letter phonogram(s).
- /f/-/ö/-/d/. Food. Now you read the word.

soft

## The kitten felt soft.

- Soft. How many syllables does this word have? Just one.
- The first phonogram is /s/, /z/.
- The next phonogram is /ŏ/, /ō/, /ö/.
- The next phonogram is /f/.
- The last phonogram is /t/.
- /s/-/ŏ/-/f/-/t/. Soft. Now you read the word. Blend /f/ and /t/ together when you read it, like this—/ft/.

felt

## The boy felt sad.

- Felt. How many syllables does this word have? Just one.
- The first phonogram is /f/.
- The next phonogram is /ĕ/, /ē/.
- The next phonogram is /l/.
- The last phonogram is /t/.
- /f/-/ĕ/-/l/-/t/. Felt. Now you read the word. Blend /l/ and /t/ together when you read it, like this—/lt/.

bee

## They have a bee hive.

- Bee. How many syllables does this word have? Just one.
- The first phonogram is /b/.
- The last phonogram is /ē/ double /ē/.
- Underline the multi-letter phonogram(s).
- /b/-/ē/. Bee. Now you read the word.

Today, one of your words is a type 2 silent *e*. Type 2 silent *e* is there because English words do not end in *v* or *u*. This is a spelling rule. So if a word would otherwise end in *v* or *u*, it will have a silent *e* on the end.

Now we need to talk about base words and endings. A base word is just a word without endings added to it. We call those endings **suffixes**. We can add *s* to make words plural—more than one—or add *ed* to show that something happened in the past. Listen to these examples:

one **boy** (singular)          two **boys** (plural)

Today, I will **help** mother. Yesterday, I **helped** mother.

These are simple cases where we just add the suffix to the end of the word. But today, you are going to learn two special rules for adding suffixes to words that end in silent *e* or the vowel *y*. Don't worry if you don't understand completely at first. Remember that you will be told what to write down, and you will get plenty of practice with this concept.

A vowel suffix is just a suffix that begins with a vowel—*a, e, i, o,* or *u*—such as *ed* or *ing*.

*want*          *want-ed*          *want-ing*

*Want* is our base word while **wanted** and **wanting** have vowel suffixes added to the base word.

Our first new spelling rule tells us what to do when we add a vowel suffix to a base word that ends with silent *e*—we drop the silent *e* before we add the suffix. Look at these examples, which you will be writing today:

give ⇨ giv + en          giv-en

hide ⇨ hid + ing          hid-ing

like ⇨ lik + ed          liked

The next rule tells us what to do when a word ends in the vowel *y*, when *y* is saying /ĭ/, /ī/, or /ē/. You have probably already noticed that *i* and *y* have a special connection! They make exactly the same sounds. And when a word ends in the vowel *y*, we change it to *i* before vowel suffixes unless the suffix begins with *i*. This is because in English, we cannot have two letters *i* in a row. Look at these examples:

cry ⇨ cry + ing          cry-ing

cry ⇨ cri + ed          cried

Now let's write these words. First, you will write each base word, and then you will write the base word with a suffix.

giv<u>e</u><sub>2</sub>

## Mother will <u>give</u> me a treat.

- Give. How many syllables does this word have? *Wait while student answers each time.* Just one.
- The first phonogram is /g/, /j/.
- The next phonogram is /ĭ/, /ī/, /ē /, /y/.
- The next phonogram is /v/.
- The last phonogram is **silent e**, so write /ĕ/, /ē/ at the end of the word.
- English words do not end in **v**; underline the **v**, and double underline the silent **e**. Put a small 2 next to the silent **e** to show that it is a type 2. This is a spelling rule.
- /g/-/ĭ/-/v/. Give. Now you read the word.

**Spelling rule:** English words do not end in *u* or *v*.

giv ✚en

## Mother has <u>given</u> me a treat.

- Given. How many syllables does this word have? Two. The first syllable is **giv**. The second syllable is **en**. [*Stress the /ĕ/ sound.*]
- The first phonogram is /g/, /j/.
- The next phonogram is /ĭ/, /ī/, /ē /, /y/.
- The next phonogram is /v/.
- ⭕ STOP. We're going to add a suffix. The base word ends in silent **e**, so we drop the silent **e** before adding a vowel suffix. This is a spelling rule.
- Leave a little space, about the size of your little finger, between the syllables. The next syllable is **en**, and the first phonogram is /ĕ/, /ē/.
- The last phonogram is /n/.
- /g/-/ĭ/-/v/—/ĕ/-/n/. Given. Now you read the word.

**Spelling rule:** Drop the final silent *e* when adding a vowel suffix to a base word.

li͡k<u>e</u>

## They <u>like</u> to play games.

- Like. How many syllables does this word have? Just one.
- The first phonogram is /l/.
- The next phonogram is /ĭ/, /ī/, /ē/, /y/.
- The next phonogram is /k/.
- The last phonogram is **silent e**, so write /ĕ/, /ē/ at the end of the word.
- To show that the **e** is silent, we double underline it. *l* says its name because of the silent **e**, so draw a bridge between the silent **e** and the *i*.
- /l/-/ī/-/k/. Like. Now you read the word.

li͡k✚<u>ed</u>³

## We <u>liked</u> dinner last night.

- Like. How many syllables does this word have? Just one.
- The first phonogram is /l/.
- The next phonogram is /ĭ/, /ī/, /ē/, /y/.
- The next phonogram is /k/.
- ⭕ STOP. We're going to add a suffix. The base word ends in silent **e**, so we drop the silent **e** before adding a vowel suffix.
- The last phonogram is /ed/, /d/, /t/.
- Underline the multi-letter phonogram(s).
- *l* says its name because of the silent **e** that we dropped when we added the vowel suffix. Draw a tiny bridge over the *i* as a reminder.
- Which of its sounds is /ed/, /d/, /t/ saying? It's saying its third sound, so put a small 3 above it.
- /l/-/ī/-/k/-/t/. Liked. Now you read the word.

hide

## The children played <u>hide</u> and seek.

- Hide. How many syllables does this word have? Just one.
- The first phonogram is /h/.
- The next phonogram is /ĭ/, /ī/, /ē/, /y/.
- The next phonogram is /d/.
- The last phonogram is **silent e**, so write /ĕ/, /ē/ at the end of the word.
- To show that the **e** is silent, we double underline it. **I** says its name because of the silent **e**, so draw a bridge between the silent **e** and the **i**.
- /h/-/ī/-/d/. Hide. Now you read the word.

hid ✚ing

## He was <u>hiding</u> behind the tree.

- Hiding. How many syllables does this word have? Two. The first syllable is **hid**. The second syllable is **ing**.
- The first phonogram is /h/.
- The next phonogram is /ĭ/, /ī/, /ē/, /y/.
- The next phonogram is /d/.
- ⬡ STOP. We're going to add a suffix. The base word ends in silent **e**, so we drop the silent **e** before adding a vowel suffix.
- Leave a little space, about the size of your little finger, between the syllables. The next syllable is **ing**, and the first phonogram is /ĭ/, /ī/, /ē/, /y/.
- The last phonogram is /ng/.
- Underline the multi-letter phonogram(s).
- **I** says its name because of the silent **e** that we dropped when we added the vowel suffix. Draw a tiny bridge over the **i** as a reminder.
- /h/-/ī/-/d/—/ĭ/-/ng/. Hiding. Now you read the word.

pret ty

## The doll is <u>pretty</u>.

- [Stress the /ĕ/ sound.] Pretty. How many syllables does this word have? Two. The first syllable is **pret**. The second syllable is **ty**.
- The first phonogram is /p/.
- The next phonogram is /r/.
- The next phonogram is /ĕ/, /ē/.
- The next phonogram is /t/.
- Leave a little space, about the size of your little finger, between the syllables. The next syllable is **ty**, and the first phonogram is /t/.
- The last phonogram is /y/, /ĭ/, /ī/, /ē/.
- See "Sounding Out and Lazy Vowels" in the spelling instructions. This word has a lazy vowel, and the /t/ is a little lazy, too! When we're talking, this word can sound like /prĭd-dē/. So think to spell /prĕt-tē/.
- Underline **y** because **y** says /ē/ at the end of a multi-syllable word. This is a spelling rule.
- /p/-/r/-/ĕ/-/t/—/t/-/ē/. Pretty. Now you read the word. Blend /p/ and /r/ together when you read it, like this—/pr/.

**Spelling rule:** Vowel **y** says /ē/ at the end of a multi-syllable base word.

pret t⊕i est  (superscript 3 over t⊕i)

## That flower is the <u>prettiest</u> in the garden.

- [Stress the /ĕ/ sound.] Prettiest. How many syllables does this word have? Three. The first syllable is **pret**. The second syllable is **ti**. The third syllable is **est**.
- The first phonogram is /p/.
- The next phonogram is /r/.
- The next phonogram is /ĕ/, /ē/.
- The next phonogram is /t/.
- Leave a little space, about the size of your little finger, between the syllables. The next syllable is **ti**, and the first phonogram is /t/.
- ◯ STOP. The base word ends in the vowel **y**, so we change the **y** to **i** before adding a suffix.
- The next phonogram is /ĭ/, /ī/, /ē/, /y/.
- Leave a little space, about the size of your little finger, between the syllables. The next syllable is **est**, and the first phonogram is /ĕ/, /ē/.
- The next phonogram is /s/, /z/.
- The last phonogram is /t/.
- Which of its sounds is **i** saying? It's saying its third sound, so put a small 3 above it.
- /p/-/r/-/ĕ/-/t/—/t/-/ē/—/ĕ/-/s/-/t/. Prettiest. Now you read the word. When you read this word, blend /p/ and /r/ together at the beginning, like this—/pr/, and blend /s/ and /t/ together at the end, like this—/st/.

cry  (underlined y)

## The baby will <u>cry</u> when he wakes up.

- Cry. How many syllables does this word have? Just one.
- The first phonogram is /k/, /s/.
- The next phonogram is /r/.
- The last phonogram is /y/, /ĭ/, /ī/, /ē/.
- Underline **y** because **y** says /ī/ at the end of a one-syllable base word. This is a spelling rule.
- /k/-/r/-/ī/. Cry. Now you read the word.

**Spelling rule:** Vowel y says /ī/ at the end of a one-syllable base word.

cr⊕ied  (superscripts 2 2 over ied)

## He's <u>cried</u> many times before.

- Cried. How many syllables does this word have? Just one.
- The first phonogram is /k/, /s/.
- The next phonogram is /r/.
- ◯ STOP. The base word ends in the vowel **y**, so we change the **y** to **i** before adding a suffix. Today, I **cry**. Yesterday, I **cried**.
- The next phonogram is /ĭ/, /ī/, /ē/, /y/.
- The last phonogram is /ed/, /d/, /t/.
- Underline the multi-letter phonogram(s).
- Which of its sounds is **i** saying? It's saying its second sound, so put a small 2 above it.
- Which of its sounds is /ed/, /d/, /t/ saying? It's saying its second sound, so put a small 2 above it.
- /k/-/r/-/ī/-/d/. Cried. Now you read the word.

# New: eau (adv)

**The *vowels* are *a*, *e*, *i*, *o*, *u*, and sometimes *y*.
All other letters are *consonants*.**

[Instructor: If your student(s) doesn't know the vowels, I advise saying them three times at the beginning of each lesson until they're memorized.] Did you know that a vowel's second sound—its long sound—is also the vowel's name? This doesn't work for ***y***, which is a consonant first and only sometimes a vowel! But it does work for the other vowels. Say the sounds of each vowel, and you will hear its name when you get to its second sound.

Today, you have a new phonogram. It's an advanced phonogram. That means that it doesn't appear very often in books for young children, so you won't see it often for a while!

tw<u>ee</u>t

## Those birds <u>tweet</u> in the morning.

- Tweet. How many syllables does this word have? Just one.
- The first phonogram is /t/.
- The next phonogram is /w/.
- The next phonogram is /ē/ double /ē/.
- The last phonogram is /t/.
- Underline the multi-letter phonogram(s).
- /t/-/w/-/ē/-/t/. Tweet. Now you read the word. Blend /t/ and /w/ together when you read it, like this—/tw/.

<u>sh</u>all

## I <u>shall</u> do my work today with a good attitude.

- Shall. How many syllables does this word have? Just one.
- The first phonogram is /sh/.
- The next phonogram is /ă/, /ā/, /ä/.
- The next phonogram is /l/.
- The last phonogram is /l/.
- We often double *l* after a single vowel at the end of a base word. This is a spelling rule.
- Underline the multi-letter phonogram(s).
- /sh/-/ă/-/l/. Shall. Now you read the word.

**Spelling rule:** We often double *l* after a single vowel at the end of a base word.

su<u>ch</u>

## She is <u>such</u> a joker.

- Such. How many syllables does this word have? Just one.
- The first phonogram is /s/, /z/.
- The next phonogram is /ŭ/, /ū/, /ü/.
- The last phonogram is /ch/, /k/, /sh/.
- Underline the multi-letter phonogram(s).
- /s/-/ŭ/-/ch/. Such. Now you read the word.

**beau t✚i ful** ² (with first two letters "ea" underlined)

# No one is more <u>beautiful</u> than mother.

- Beautiful. How many syllables does this word have? Three. The first syllable is **beau**. The second syllable is **ti**. The third syllable is **ful**.
- The first phonogram is /b/.
- The next phonogram is /ō/, /ū/, /ŏ/.
- Leave a little space, about the size of your little finger, between the syllables. The next syllable is **ti**, and the first phonogram is /t/.
- ○ STOP. The base word, **beauty**, ends in the vowel **y**, so we change the **y** to **i** before adding a suffix.
- The next phonogram is /ĭ/, /ī/, /ē/, /y/.
- Leave a little space, about the size of your little finger, between the syllables. The next syllable is **ful**, and the first phonogram is /f/.
- The next phonogram is /ŭ/, /ū/, /ü/.
- The next phonogram is /l/.
- When **full** is a suffix, it loses an **l**. This is a spelling rule.
- Underline the multi-letter phonogram(s).
- Which of its sounds is **eau** saying? It's saying its second sound, so put a small 2 above it.
- /b/-/ū/—/t/-/ĭ/—/f/-/ŭ/-/l/. Beautiful. Now you read the word.
- **Spelling rule:** *Full* loses an *l* when it is a suffix.

**sor ry** (with "ry" underlined)

# I'm <u>sorry</u> I hurt your feelings.

- Sorry. How many syllables does this word have? Two. The first syllable is **sor**. The second syllable is **ry**.
- The first phonogram is /s/, /z/.
- The next phonogram is /ŏ/, /ō/, /ö/.
- The next phonogram is /r/.
- Leave a little space, about the size of your little finger, between the syllables. The next syllable is **ry**, and the first phonogram is /r/.
- The next phonogram is /y/, /ĭ/, /ī/, /ē/.
- Underline **y** because **y** says /ē/ at the end of a multi-syllable word.
- /s/-/ŏ/-/r/-—/r/-/ē/. Sorry. Now you read the word.

**hair** (with "air" underlined)

# River has wild <u>hair</u>. Joshua's <u>hair</u> is wilder.

- Hair. How many syllables does this word have? Just one.
- The first phonogram is /h/.
- The next phonogram is /ā/—2 letter /ā/ we can NOT use at the end of English words.
- The last phonogram is /r/.
- Underline the multi-letter phonogram(s).
- /h/-/ā/-/r/. Hair. Now you read the word.

**ev er** (with "er" underlined)

# Have you <u>ever</u> played that game?

- Ever. How many syllables does this word have? Two. The first syllable is **ev**. The second syllable is **er**.
- The first phonogram is /ĕ/, /ē/.
- The next phonogram is /v/.
- Leave a little space, about the size of your little finger, between the syllables. The next syllable is **er**, and the only phonogram is /er/ as in her.
- Underline the multi-letter phonogram(s).
- /ĕ/-/v/—/er/. Ever. Now you read the word.

**nev er**

<u>Never</u> put things in your nose.
- Never. How many syllables does this word have? Two. The first syllable is *nev*. The second syllable is *er*.
- The first phonogram is /n/.
- The next phonogram is /ĕ/, /ē/.
- The next phonogram is /v/.
- Leave a little space, about the size of your little finger, between the syllables. The next syllable is *er*, and the only phonogram is /er/ as in her.
- Underline the multi-letter phonogram(s).
- /n/-/ĕ/-/v/—/er/. Never. Now you read the word.

**think**

Do you <u>think</u> that's a good idea?
- Think. How many syllables does this word have? Just one.
- The first phonogram is /th/, /TH/.
- The next phonogram is /ĭ/, /ī/, /ē/, /y/.
- The next phonogram is /n/.
- The last phonogram is /k/.
- Underline the multi-letter phonogram(s).
- Which of its sounds is *th* saying? It's saying its first sound, so we don't need to mark it! We only mark phonograms when they're saying a sound other than their first.
- /th/-/ĭ/-/n/-/k/. Think. Now you read the word. Blend /n/ and /k/ together when you read it, like this—/nk/. We don't completely pronounce the *n*. It's like you start to make the *n* sound, but then it gets stuck in your nose. *N* gets stuck in your nose before /g/ and /k/ sounds.
- Remember: Don't put things in your nose.

**hung**

"The stockings were <u>hung</u> by the chimney with care."
(From "A Visit from St. Nicholas" by Clement Clarke Moore)
- Hung. How many syllables does this word have? Just one.
- The first phonogram is /h/.
- The next phonogram is /ŭ/, /ū/, /ü/.
- The last phonogram is /ng/.
- Underline the multi-letter phonogram(s).
- /h/-/ŭ/-/ng/. Hung. Now you read the word.

# The 1+1+1 Rule; Type 3 Silent E

You're going to learn something today that might sound a little confusing at first, but don't worry! Remember, I will be telling you exactly how to spell the word, so all you have to do is listen and write. We will continue to talk about this new rule until you understand it perfectly.

A **verb** is a kind of word. Verbs are what we do, like **hop**, **step**, **get**, and **hum**. You've learned to spell many super short verbs like these that are one-syllable and end with one vowel followed by one consonant. Look at these one-syllable words and notice how each word **ends** in one vowel followed by one consonant. We can add an **s** to these words without any problem. But if we want to add a vowel suffix like **ed**, **er**, or **ing**, we have to double the final consonant before we add the ending.

| hop | step | get | hum |
| hops | steps | gets | hums |
| hopper | stepped | getting | hummed |

This is called the 1+1+1 rule: 1 syllable, 1 vowel, 1 consonant. Remember, I will be telling you exactly how to spell the word, so all you have to do is listen and write. We will continue to talk about this rule until you understand it perfectly.

crick et

## I heard a cricket on a summer night.
- Cricket. How many syllables does this word have? Two. The first syllable is **crick**. The second syllable is **et**.
- The first phonogram is /k/, /s/.
- The next phonogram is /r/.
- The next phonogram is /ĭ/, /ī/, /ē/, /y/.
- The next phonogram is /k/—2 letter /k/.
- Leave a little space, about the size of your little finger, between the syllables. The next syllable is **et**, and the first phonogram is /ĕ/, /ē/.
- The last phonogram is /t/.
- Underline the multi-letter phonogram(s).
- The phonogram **ck** is used only after a single vowel that says its short sound. This is a spelling rule.
- /c/-/r/-/ĭ/-/k/—/ĕ/-/t/. Cricket. Now you read the word. Blend /c/ and /r/ together when you read it, like this—/cr/.

**Spelling rule:** Phonogram *ck* is used only after a single vowel that says its short sound.

high

## The cups are on a high shelf.
- High. How many syllables does this word have? Just one.
- The first phonogram is /h/.
- The last phonogram is /ī—3 letter /ī/.
- Underline the multi-letter phonogram(s).
- /h/-/ī/. High. Now you read the word.

plac e

## Put your things in a safe place.
- Place. How many syllables does this word have? Just one.
- The first phonogram is /p/.
- The next phonogram is /l/.
- The next phonogram is /ă/, /ā/, /ä/.
- The next phonogram is /k/, /s/.
- The last phonogram is **silent e**, so write /ĕ/, /ē/ at the end of the word.
- To show that the **e** is silent, we double underline it. **A** says its name because of the silent **e**, so draw a bridge between the silent **e** and the **a**.
- **C** says /s/ because of the silent **e;** underline the **c**. This is a spelling rule. We do NOT put a small 3 next to the silent **e** to show that it is a type 3, though, because the main job of silent **e** in this word is to make **a** say its name, which makes it a type 1 silent **e**.
- /p/-/l/-/ā/-/s/. Place. Now you read the word. Blend /p/ and /l/ together when you read it, like this—/pl/.

**Spelling rule:** *C* says /s/ before an *e*.

light

## Turn off the light when you leave the room.
- Light. How many syllables does this word have? Just one.
- The first phonogram is /l/.
- The next phonogram is /ī/—3 letter /ī/.
- The last phonogram is /t/.
- Underline the multi-letter phonogram(s).
- /l/-/ī/-/t/. Light. Now you read the word.

try ✚ing

## Always try even if you can't do it perfectly.
- Try. How many syllables does this word have? Two. The first syllable is **try**. The second syllable is **ing**.
- Underline **y** because **y** says /ī/ at the end of a one-syllable base word.
- /t/-/r/-/ ī/. Try. Now you read the word. Blend /t/ and /r/ together when you read it, like this—/tr/.
✚ Now let's add a suffix. The base word ends in the vowel **y**, but we're adding a suffix that begins with an **i**, so we don't change it. English words cannot have two letters **i** in a row.
- Leave a little space, about the size of your little finger, between the syllables. The next syllable is **ing**, and the first phonogram is /ĭ/, /ī/, /ē/, /y/.
- The last phonogram is /ng/.
- Underline the multi-letter phonogram(s).
- Now read the word again.

field

## The farmer worked in the field.
- Field. How many syllables does this word have? Just one.
- The first phonogram is /f/.
- The next phonogram is /ē/—2 letter /ē/.
- The next phonogram is /l/.
- The last phonogram is /d/.
- Underline the multi-letter phonogram(s).
- /f/-/ē/-/l/-/d/. Field. Now you read the word. Blend /l/ and /d/ together when you read it, like this—/ld/.

sun shine

## We long for the sunshine on cloudy days.

- Sunshine. How many syllables does this word have? Two. The first syllable is **sun**. The second syllable is **shine**.
- The first phonogram is /s/.
- The next phonogram is /ŭ/, /ū/, /ü/.
- The next phonogram is /n/.
- Leave a little space, about the size of your little finger, between the syllables. The next syllable is **shine**, and the first phonogram is /sh/.
- The next phonogram is /ĭ/, /ī/, /ē/, /y/.
- The next phonogram is /n/.
- The last phonogram is **silent e**, so write /ĕ/, /ē/ at the end of the word.
- To show that the **e** is silent, we double underline it. **I** says its name because of the silent **e**, so draw a bridge between the silent **e** and the **i**.
- Underline the multi-letter phonogram(s).
- This is a **compound word**. That means that it's two words put together to become one word.
- /s/-/ŭ/-/n/—/sh/-/ī/-/n/. Sunshine. Now you read the word.

plan + (n)ing

## Enjoy the sunshine, but plan for the rain.

- Plan. How many syllables does this word have? Just one.
- The first phonogram is /p/.
- The next phonogram is /l/.
- The next phonogram is /ă/, /ā/, /ä/.
- The last phonogram is /n/.
- /p/-/l/-/ă/-/n/. Plan. Now you read the word. Blend /p/ and /l/ together when you read it, like this—/pl/.
- + Can we add our **ing** suffix to change this word? We can! Listen: I am **planning**. Let's add **ing** to this word as a new syllable.
- The 1+1+1 Rule: This word is one syllable, and it ends with one vowel followed by one consonant, so we double the final consonant before adding a vowel suffix. This is a spelling rule.
- Leave a little space, about the size of your little finger, between the syllables. The next syllable is **ning**, and the first phonogram is /n/.
- The next phonogram is /ĭ/, /ī/, /ē/, /y/.
- The last phonogram is /ng/.
- Underline the multi-letter phonogram(s).
- Circle the extra letter that we added before the suffix.
- Now read the word again.

**Spelling rule:** The 1+1+1 Rule: When adding a vowel suffix to a one-syllable word ending in one vowel followed by one consonant, double the last letter.
We do not double *x*, *w*, or *y*.

squeak

## Mice squeak when they see a cat!

- Squeak. How many syllables does this word have? Just one.
- The first phonogram is /s/, /z/.
- The next phonogram is /kw/.
- The next phonogram is /ē/, /ĕ/, /ā/.
- The last phonogram is /k/.
- Underline the multi-letter phonogram(s).
- /s/-/kw/-/ē/-/k/. Squeak. Now you read the word. Blend /s/ and /kw/ together when you read it, like this—/skw/.

to[3] geth[2] er

Working together makes the work faster.

- Together. How many syllables does this word have? Three. The first syllable is ***to***. The second syllable is ***geth***. The third syllable is ***er***.
- The first phonogram is /t/.
- The next phonogram is /ŏ/, /ō/, /ö/.
- Leave a little space, about the size of your little finger, between the syllables. The next syllable is ***geth***, and the first phonogram is /g/, /j/ .
- The next phonogram is /ĕ/, /ē/.
- The next phonogram is /th/, /TH/.
- Leave a little space, about the size of your little finger, between the syllables. The next syllable is ***er***, and the only phonogram is /er/ as in her.
- Which of its sounds is ***o*** saying? It's saying its third sound, so put a small 3 above it.
- Which of its sounds is ***th*** saying? It's saying its second sound, so put a small 2 above it.
- /t/-/ö/—/g/-/ĕ/-/TH/—/er/. Together. Now you read the word.

The first word in this list is a **contraction**. "Contract" means to make smaller. A **contraction** is formed when we put two words together to make one shorter word. We leave some letters out, and we replace the missing letters with a punctuation mark called an **apostrophe**. Look at these words and see which letters are missing from the contraction. Can you see that that's where the apostrophe is?

| has not | hasn't | | do not | don't |
|---------|--------|---|--------|-------|
| have not | haven't | | does not | doesn't |
| had not | hadn't | | did not | didn't |

This is the way that most contractions work, but the contraction in today's list is **irregular**. That means that it does not follow the regular rules.

will not     won't

**w_o_n't**

## I <u>won't</u> be mean to my sibling.

- This word means **will not**.
- Won't. How many syllables does this word have? Just one.
- The first phonogram is /w/.
- The next phonogram is /ŏ/, /ō/, /ö/.
- The next phonogram is /n/.
- Now you need to add an apostrophe before the last letter! Help them write it if necessary.
- The last phonogram is /t/.
- Underline /ō/ because **o** says its name when followed by two consonants. This is a spelling rule.
- /w/-/ō/-/n/-/t/. Won't. Now you read the word. Blend /n/ and /t/ together when you read it, like this—/nt/.
- Do you remember what we call a word when we make it smaller like this? It's called a **contraction**, and the little mark we use is called an **apostrophe**.

**Spelling rule:** *O* may say /ō/ when followed by two consonants.

**al ways** [3]
<u>(ways underlined)</u>

## They <u>always</u> have dinner at six.

- Always. How many syllables does this word have? Two. The first syllable is *al*. The second syllable is **ways**.
- The next phonogram is /ă/, /ā/, /ä/.
- The next phonogram is /l/.
- Leave a little space, about the size of your little finger, between the syllables. The next syllable is **ways**, and the first phonogram is /w/.
- The next phonogram is /ā/—2 letter /ā/ that we CAN use at the end of English words.
- The last phonogram is /s/, /z/.
- Underline the multi-letter phonogram(s).
- Which of its sounds is *a* saying? It's saying its third sound, so put a small 3 above it.
- When *all* is a prefix, it loses an *l*. This is a spelling rule.
- /ä/-/l/—/w/-/ā/-/z/. Always. Now you read the word.

**Spelling rule:** *All* loses an *l* when it is a prefix.

<sup>3</sup>
gr<u>ea</u>t

## Gr<u>ea</u>t men do gr<u>ea</u>t deeds.
- Great. How many syllables does this word have? Just one.
- The first phonogram is /g/, /j/.
- The next phonogram is /r/.
- The next phonogram is /ē/, /ĕ/, /ā/.
- The last phonogram is /t/.
- Which of its sounds is **ea** saying? It's saying its third sound, so put a small 3 above it.
- /g/-/r/-/ā/-/t/. Great. Now you read the word. Blend /g/ and /r/ together when you read it, like this—/gr/.

ev <u>er</u> y̲

## Do <u>every</u> task with a good attitude.
- Every. How many syllables does this word have? Three. The first syllable is **ev**. The second syllable is **er**. The third syllable is **y**
- The first phonogram is /ĕ/, /ē/.
- The next phonogram is /v/.
- Leave a little space, about the size of your little finger, between the syllables. The next syllable is **er**, and the only phonogram is /er/ as in her.
- Leave a little space, about the size of your little finger, between the syllables. The next syllable is **y**, and the only phonogram is /y/, /ĭ/, /ī/, /ē/.
- Underline the multi-letter phonogram(s).
- Underline **y** because **y** says /ē/ at the end of a multi-syllable word.
- /ĕ/-/v/—/er/—/ē/. Every. Now you read the word.

w<u>ai</u>t ✚<u>ing</u>

## You must w<u>ai</u>t until tonight.
- Wait. How many syllables does this word have? Just one.
- The first phonogram is /w/.
- The next phonogram is /ā/—2 letter /ā/ that may NOT be used at the end of English words.
- The last phonogram is /t/.
- Underline the multi-letter phonogram(s).
- /w/-ā/-/t/. Wait. Now you read the word.
- ✚ Can we add our **ing** suffix to change this word? We can! Listen: I am **waiting**. Let's add **ing** to this word as a new syllable.
- Leave a little space, about the size of your little finger, between the syllables. The next syllable is **ing**, and the first phonogram is /ĭ/, /ī/, /ē/, /y/.
- The last phonogram is /ng/.
- Now read the word again.

<sup>3</sup>
f<u>a</u>ll

## In the f<u>a</u>ll, the leaves will change colors.
- Fall. How many syllables does this word have? Just one.
- The first phonogram is /f/.
- The next phonogram is /ă/, /ā/, /ä/.
- The next phonogram is /l/.
- The last phonogram is /l/.
- Which of its sounds is **a** saying? It's saying its third sound, so put a small 3 above it.
- We often double **l** after a single vowel at the end of a base word. This is a spelling rule.
- /f/-/ä/-/l/. Fall. Now you read the word.

laugh➕ed
_(with small 2 above "augh" and small 3 above "ed")_

## They didn't <u>laugh</u> at my joke.
- Laugh. How many syllables does this word have? Just one.
- The first phonogram is /l/.
- The last phonogram is /ă/, /ăf/.
- Underline the multi-letter phonogram(s).
- Which of its sounds is **augh** saying? It's saying its second sound, so put a small 2 above it.
- /l/-/ăf/. Laugh. Now you read the word.
- ➕ Can we add the ending **ed** as a suffix to change this word? We can! Listen: Today, I *laugh*. Yesterday, I *laughed*. Let's add **ed** to this word as a suffix.
- The last phonogram is /ed/, /d/, /t/.
- Underline the multi-letter phonogram(s).
- Which of its sounds is **ed** saying? It's saying its third sound, so put a small 3 above it.
- Now read the word again.

own ➕<u>er</u>

## This toy is my <u>own</u>.
- Own. How many syllables does this word have? Just one.
- The first phonogram is /ow/, /ō/.
- The last phonogram is /n/.
- Underline the multi-letter phonogram(s).
- /ō/-/n/. Own. Now you read the word.
- ➕ Can we add the ending **er** as a suffix to change this word? We can! Listen: The boy was the **owner** of the toy. Let's add **er** to this word as a new syllable.
- Leave a small space between syllables.
- The last phonogram is /er/ as in her.
- Underline the multi-letter phonogram(s).
- Now read the word again.

pr<u>ou</u>d

## Will mother be <u>proud</u> of my behavior?
- Proud. How many syllables does this word have? Just one.
- The first phonogram is /p/.
- The next phonogram is /r/.
- The next phonogram is /ow/, /ō/, /ö/, /ŭ/, /ü/.
- The last phonogram is /d/.
- Underline the multi-letter phonogram(s).
- /p/-/r/-/ow/-/d/. Proud. Now you read the word. Blend /p/ and /r/ together when you read it, like this—/pr/.

sum m<u>er</u>

## Do you have plans for <u>summer</u>?
- Summer. How many syllables does this word have? Two. The first syllable is **sum**. The second syllable is **mer**. .
- The first phonogram is /s/, /z/.
- The next phonogram is /ŭ/, /ū/, /ü/.
- The next phonogram is /m/.
- Leave a little space, about the size of your little finger, between the syllables. The next syllable is **mer**, and the first phonogram is /m/.
- The last phonogram is /er/ as in her.
- Underline the multi-letter phonogram(s).
- /s/-/ŭ/-/m/—/m/-/er/. Summer. Now you read the word.

[Instructor: Now that you have had some practice in dictating spelling lists, the instructions start to simplify. They no longer include the sounds for each phonogram—I recommend keeping the one page phonogram list nearby as a handy reference when dictating spelling words. Continue to follow the pattern that you have been following thus far: Say the word—the one in the example sentence—at the beginning before you ask the student how many syllables the word has. After you have dictated the word, say the sounds and then the word before having the student do the same.]

Today, one of your words is the name of a little girl—**Penny.** When we write someone's name, we begin the name with a capital letter. If you haven't learned to write capital letters yet, your instructor will show you how to write a capital *P*. Here are some various ways that people write capital *P* and lowercase *p*. Do you see your kind of writing?

Pp     Pp     Pp     Pp     Pp

Pen ny

## My friend has a dog named Penny.

- This word is a ***proper name***, so it begins with a capital letter.
- Stress the /ĕ/ sound. How many syllables does this word have? Dictate the first syllable.
- Leave a small space between syllables. Dictate the other syllable(s).
- Underline *y* because *y* says /ē/ at the end of a multi-syllable word.
- Read the word. Now you read the word.

first

## Be the first to offer help.

- How many syllables does this word have? Dictate the word.
- Underline the multi-letter phonogram(s).
- Read the word. Now you read the word. Blend /s/ and /t/ together when you read it, like this—/st/.

ba by

## Spring brings the arrival of baby animals.

- How many syllables does this word have? Dictate the first syllable.
- Leave a small space between syllables. Dictate the other syllable(s).
- Underline /ā/ because *a* says its name at the end of a syllable.
- Underline *y* because *y* says /ē/ at the end of a multi-syllable word.
- Read the word. Now you read the word.

dog gie

## Her doggie is cute.

- How many syllables does this word have? Dictate the first syllable.
- Leave a small space between syllables. Dictate the other syllable(s).
- Underline the multi-letter phonogram(s).
- Read the word. Now you read the word.

cun ning

## He had a cunning plan.

- How many syllables does this word have? Dictate the first syllable.
- Leave a small space between syllables. Dictate the other syllable(s).
- Underline the multi-letter phonogram(s).
- Read the word. Now you read the word.

creep ✚ing

## Insects <u>creep</u> across the branches.

- How many syllables does this word have? Dictate the word until you get to the suffix.
- Underline the multi-letter phonogram(s).
- Read the word. Now you read the word. Blend /c/ and /r/ together when you read it, like this—/cr/.

✚ Can we add our *ing* suffix to change this word? We can! Listen: I am ***creeping.*** Let's add *ing* to this word as a new syllable.

- Leave a small space between syllables. Dictate the next syllable—*ing*. Underline *ng*.
- Now read the word again.

bun ny

## River wants a pet <u>bunny</u>.

- How many syllables does this word have? Dictate the first syllable.
- Leave a small space between syllables. Dictate the other syllable(s).
- Underline *y* because *y* says /ē/ at the end of a multi-syllable word.
- Read the word. Now you read the word.

bun n✚ies

## The <u>bunnies</u> hopped around the forest.

- How many syllables does this word have? Dictate the first syllable.
- Leave a small space between syllables. Dictate the word until you get to the suffix.

O STOP. We're going to add a suffix. The base word ends in the vowel *y*, so we change the *y* to *i* before adding a suffix. To make this word plural, we change the *y* to *i* and add ***e-s.***

- Dictate the other phonograms—***ie-s.***
- Underline the multi-letter phonogram(s). When we changed the *y* to *i* and added ***e-s,*** it formed the phonogram /ē/—2 letter /ē/.
- Read the word. Now you read the word.

geese₅

## A flock of <u>geese</u> flew south for the winter.

- How many syllables does this word have? Dictate the word.
- Double underline the silent *e.* Put a small 5 next to the silent *e* to show that it is a type 5—the miscellaneous silent *e.*
- Underline the multi-letter phonogram(s).
- Read the word. Now you read the word.

down y

## The <u>downy</u> chicks huddled together for warmth.

- How many syllables does this word have? Dictate the first syllable.
- Leave a small space between syllables. Dictate the other syllable(s).
- Underline the multi-letter phonogram(s).
- Underline *y* because *y* says /ē/ at the end of a multi-syllable word.
- Read the word. Now you read the word.

In today's spelling list, some of the words **rhyme**. That means that they have the same vowel sound and the same ending sound. The rhyming words in this list are also spelled the same way except for the first letter. Let's look at these words.

| well | fell | bell | sell |

Do you notice what else they all have in common? They all end with a double *l* instead of just one. We often double *l* after a single vowel at the end of a base word. This is a spelling rule.

**well**

They dug a new <u>well</u>.
- How many syllables does this word have? Dictate the word. Emphasize the /ĕ/ sound.
- We often double *l* after a single vowel at the end of a base word.
- Read the word. Now you read the word.

**fell**

The tree <u>fell</u> in the woods.
- How many syllables does this word have? Dictate the word. Emphasize the /ĕ/ sound.
- We often double *l* after a single vowel at the end of a base word.
- This word rhymes with **well**.
- Read the word. Now you read the word.

**bell**

The sleigh <u>bell</u> makes a jingling noise.
- How many syllables does this word have? Dictate the word. Emphasize the /ĕ/ sound.
- We often double *l* after a single vowel at the end of a base word.
- This word rhymes with **well** and **fell**.
- Read the word. Now you read the word.

**sell**

They <u>sell</u> the blankets we want.
- How many syllables does this word have? Dictate the word. Emphasize the /ĕ/ sound.
- We often double *l* after a single vowel at the end of a base word.
- This word rhymes with **well**, **fell**, and **bell**.
- Read the word. Now you read the word.

**lam<u>b</u>✚s** [2]

A <u>lamb</u> is a baby sheep.
- How many syllables does this word have? Dictate the word until you get to the suffix.
- Underline the multi-letter phonogram(s).
- Read the word. Now you read the word.
✚ Now let's make it plural! Add /s/, /z/ and read the word again. Put a small 2 above the **s** to show that it's saying its second sound.

lul la̱ by

## Mother sang a lullaby to the baby.

- How many syllables does this word have? Dictate the first syllable.
- Leave a small space between syllables. Dictate the other syllable(s).
- This word has a lazy vowel. When we say it, we usually say /lul-lə-bī/. We think to spell /lul-lā-bī/.
- Underline *a* because *a* said its third sound at the end of a word. This is a spelling rule.
- This is a compound word. The word "lullaby" is a blend of the words "lull," which means to calm or soothe, and "by," as in good-bye. A lullaby is a song used to sing a baby to sleep. So remember that even though *by* is at the end of this multi-syllable word, *by* is actually a one-syllable word, so we need to...
- Underline *y* because *y* says /ī/ at the end of a one-syllable base word.
- Read the word. Now you read the word.

clos⊕ed

## The store was closed.

- How many syllables does this word have? Dictate the word until you get to the suffix.
- ⃝ STOP. We're going to add a suffix. The base word ends in silent *e*, so we drop the silent *e* before adding a vowel suffix.
- Dictate the last phonogram—*ed*.
- Underline the multi-letter phonogram(s).
- *O* says its name because of the silent *e* that we dropped when we added the vowel suffix. Draw a tiny bridge over the *o* as a reminder.
- Which of its sounds is *s* saying? It's saying its second sound, so put a small 2 above it.
- Which of its sounds is *ed* saying? It's saying its second sound, so put a small 2 above it.
- Read the word. Now you read the word. Blend /c/ and /l/ together when you read it, like this—/cl/.

mo͟o͟n

## The full moon lit up the night.

- How many syllables does this word have? Dictate the word.
- Underline the multi-letter phonogram(s).
- Read the word. Now you read the word.

sta͟r⊕s

## The sun is a star.

- How many syllables does this word have? Dictate the word until you get to the suffix.
- Underline the multi-letter phonogram(s).
- Read the word. Now you read the word. Blend /s/ and /t/ together when you read it, like this—/st/.
- ✚ Now let's make it plural! Add /s/, /z/ and read the word again. Put a small 2 above the *s* to show that it's saying its second sound.

pe͟e͟p ⊕ing

## The girl will peep around the corner at the baby.

- How many syllables does this word have? Dictate the word until you get to the suffix.
- Underline the multi-letter phonogram(s).
- Read the word. Now you read the word.
- ✚ Can we add our *ing* suffix to change this word? We can! Listen: I am *peeping*. Let's add *ing* to this word as a new syllable.
- Leave a small space between syllables. Dictate the next syllable—*ing*.
- Underline the multi-letter phonogram(s).
- Now read the word again.

*Singular* means one, like *single*. *Plural* means more than one.
We can make most words plural just by adding *s* to the end of the word, like this:

### cat        cats

Now listen to the end sounds of these words: kiss, fish, inch, fox, quiz. We say that the end phonograms in these words *hiss*. When a word ends in a phonogram that hisses, we add *es* instead of just *s* to make the word plural, and this adds another syllable. Today, you have a word in your spelling list that we'll make plural in this way.

Some other words are *irregular*. That means that they do not follow the regular way of making plurals. Today, you will learn a word that has an irregular plural.

### child        children

You are one **child** (singular), but many **children** (plural) were at the park.

catch ✚es

## Who can catch the ball?

- How many syllables does this word have? Dictate the word until you get to the suffix.
- Underline the multi-letter phonogram(s).
- Phonogram *tch* is used only after a single vowel that does not say its long sound. This is a spelling rule.
- Read the word. Now you read the word.
- ✚ Can we add the ending *es* as a suffix to change this word? We can! Listen: I *catch*. He *catches*. Let's add *es* to this word as a new syllable.
- Leave a small space between syllables. Dictate the next syllable.
- Now read the word again.

**Spelling rule:** Phonogram *tch* is used only after a single vowel that does not say its long sound.

ch i ld

## Be a polite child.

- How many syllables does this word have? Dictate the word.
- Underline the multi-letter phonogram(s).
- Underline /ī/ because *i* says its name when followed by two consonants.
- Read the word. Now you read the word. Blend /l/ and /d/ together when you read it, like this—/ld/.

child ren

## Play in the park with the other children.

- How many syllables does this word have? Dictate the first syllable.
- Leave a small space between syllables. Dictate the other syllable(s).
- Underline the multi-letter phonogram(s).
- Read the word. Now you read the word. Blend /l/ and /d/ together when you read it, like this—/ld/.

leaf

## The leaf turned yellow in the fall.

- How many syllables does this word have? Dictate the word.
- Underline the multi-letter phonogram(s).
- Which of its sounds is *ea* saying? It's saying its first sound, so we don't need to mark it! We only mark phonograms when they're saying a sound other than their first.
- Read the word. Now you read the word.

**blew**

The wind bl<u>ew</u> the leaves away.
- How many syllables does this word have? Dictate the word.
- Underline the multi-letter phonogram(s).
- Read the word. Now you read the word. Blend /b/ and /l/ together when you read it, like this—/bl/.

**som<u>e</u>₅ tim<u>e</u>s** ²

<u>Sometimes</u>, mother lets us have treats.
- How many syllables does this word have? Dictate the first syllable. Emphasize the ŏ sound.
- Double underline the silent *e*. Put a small 5 next to the silent *e* to show that it is a type 5—the miscellaneous silent *e*.
- Leave a small space between syllables. Dictate the other syllable(s).
- *I* says its name because of the silent *e*; underline the silent *e* twice, and draw a bridge between the silent *e* and the *i*.
- Which of its sounds is *s* saying? It's saying its second sound, so put a small 2 above it.
- This is a **compound word**. That means that it's two words put together to become one word.
- Read the word. Now you read the word.

**kept**

The dog <u>kept</u> the stick I threw.
- How many syllables does this word have? Dictate the word.
- Read the word. Now you read the word. Blend /p/ and /t/ together when you read it, like this—/pt/.

**near**

Don't go n<u>ea</u>r the street.
- How many syllables does this word have? Dictate the word.
- Which of its sounds is *ea* saying? It's saying its first sound, so we don't need to mark it! We only mark phonograms when they're saying a sound other than their first.
- Read the word. Now you read the word.

**saf<u>e</u>**

Stay in the yard where it is <u>safe</u>.
- How many syllables does this word have? Dictate the word.
- *A* says its name because of the silent *e*; underline the silent *e* twice, and draw a bridge between the silent *e* and the *a*.
- Read the word. Now you read the word.

**ant**

The <u>ant</u> followed the others to the picnic.
- How many syllables does this word have? Dictate the word.
- Read the word. Now you read the word. Blend /n/ and /t/ together when you read it, like this—/nt/.

We have five different types of silent *e* words. Today, you will have a type 3 silent *e* in your spelling list.

Type 1 silent *e* makes a vowel say its name, like the words *hide* and *safe*.

hide       safe

Type 2 silent *e* is there because English words do not end in **v** or **u**. So if a word would otherwise end in **v** or **u**, it will have a silent *e* on the end, like the words *give* and *blue*.

giv e₂      blu e₂

Type 3 silent *e* is there to make **g** say /j/ or **c** say /s/, like the words *bulge* and *voice*.

bulg e₃      voi c e₃

Type 4 silent *e* is there because every syllable must have a written vowel, like the words *little* and *apple*. Without the silent *e*, the second syllable would not have a vowel.

lit-tle₄      ap-ple₄

And type 5 silent *e* is our *miscellaneous* type. This means that there can be other reasons for a silent *e*, reasons that are not as common, like the words *were* and *please*. Type 5 silent *e* can prevent a word that would otherwise end in **s** from looking plural. Other times, it is there to make a word look bigger or to make homophones look different! And sometimes, it makes **th** say its second sound, /TH/.

wer e₅  please₅  or e₅  brea th e₅

---

cool ✚er

## In the fall, the days are often cool.

- How many syllables does this word have? Dictate the word until you get to the suffix.
- Underline the multi-letter phonogram(s).
- Which of its sounds is **oo** saying? It's saying its second sound, so put a small 2 above it.
- Read the word. Now you read the word.

✚ Can we add the ending **er** as a suffix to change this word? We can! Listen: The weather was *cooler* today. Let's add **er** to this word as a new syllable.

- Leave a small space between syllables. Dictate the next syllable—**er**. Underline **er**.
- Now read the word again.

---

voi c e₃

## She has a beautiful singing voice.

- How many syllables does this word have? Dictate the word.
- Underline the multi-letter phonogram(s).
- **C** says /s/ because of the silent *e*; underline the **c**, and double underline the silent *e*. Put a small 3 next to the silent *e* to show that it is a type 3. This is a spelling rule.
- Read the word. Now you read the word.

**Spelling rule:** *C* says /s/ before *e*, *i*, and *y*.

shād ✚ed

## The yard is shaded under the tree.

- How many syllables does this word have? Dictate the word until you get to the suffix.
- ⭕ STOP. We're going to add a suffix. The base word ends in silent *e*, so we drop the silent *e* before adding a vowel suffix.
- Phonogram *ed* forms a new syllable when the base word ends in /d/ or /t/.
- Leave a small space between syllables. Dictate the next syllable—*ed*.
- Underline the multi-letter phonogram(s).
- *A* says its name because of the silent *e* that we dropped when we added the vowel suffix. Draw a tiny bridge over the *a* as a reminder.
- Read the word. Now you read the word.

swing ✚ing

## The park only has one swing.

- How many syllables does this word have? Dictate the word until you get to the suffix.
- Underline the multi-letter phonogram(s).
- Read the word. Now you read the word. Blend /s/ and /w/ together when you read it, like this—/sw/.
- ✚ Can we add our *ing* suffix to change this word? We can! Listen: I am *swinging*. Let's add *ing* to this word as a new syllable.
- Leave a small space between syllables. Dictate the next syllable—*ing*. Underline *ng*.
- Now read the word again.

sing✚s
²

## Do you like to sing?

- How many syllables does this word have? Dictate the word until you get to the suffix.
- Underline the multi-letter phonogram(s).
- Read the word. Now you read the word.
- ✚ Can we add the ending *s* as a suffix to change this word? We can! Listen: I *sing*. He *sings*. Let's add *s* to this word.
- Add /s/, /z/ and read the word again. Put a small 2 above the *s* to show that it's saying its second sound.

through
³

## We can play when we're through with the work.

- How many syllables does this word have? Dictate the word.
- Underline the multi-letter phonogram(s).
- Which of its sounds is *ough* saying? It's saying its third sound, so put a small 3 above it.
- Read the word. Now you read the word. Blend /th/ and /r/ together when you read it, like this—/thr/.

be low
²

## The cat lay below the window.

- How many syllables does this word have? Dictate the first syllable.
- Leave a small space between syllables. Dictate the other syllable(s).
- Underline the multi-letter phonogram(s).
- Underline /ē/ because *e* says its name at the end of a syllable. This is a spelling rule.
- Which of its sounds is *ow* saying? It's saying its second sound, so put a small 2 above it.
- Read the word. Now you read the word.

**Spelling rule:** Vowels *a, e, o, u* usually say /ā, ē, ō, ū/ at the end of a syllable.

roots

## Carrots are a <u>root</u> vegetable.
- How many syllables does this word have? Dictate the word until you get to the suffix.
- Underline the multi-letter phonogram(s).
- Read the word. Now you read the word.
- ✚ Now let's make it plural! Does **root** end in a hiss? No, it doesn't! So we will make it plural in the regular way.
- Add /s/, /z/ and read the word again.

d i <u>e</u>

## Leaves <u>die</u> in the fall.
- How many syllables does this word have? Dictate the word.
- *I* says its name because of the silent *e*; underline the silent *e* twice, and draw a bridge between the silent *e* and the *i*.
- Read the word. Now you read the word.

clos<u>e</u>

## They sat <u>close</u> together while they played their game.
- How many syllables does this word have? Dictate the word.
- *O* says its name because of the silent *e*; underline the silent *e* twice, and draw a bridge between the silent *e* and the *o*.
- This word is a *homograph. Homograph* means *same writing*, and this word has two meanings. It can be a verb, like he will *close* the door—can you hear *s* making its second sound? But it can also mean that something is nearby, and when we use *close* in this way, *s* says its first sound. They sound different, but they are spelled the same.
- Read the word. Now you read the word. Blend /c/ and /l/ together when you read it, like this—/cl/.

# 38

# New: dge; Irregular Verbs

A **verb** is what we do. We can walk, laugh, jump, love, and sniff. These are all verbs.
The **ed** ending—the /ed/, /d/, /t/ phonogram that you have learned—shows that something happened in the past. Listen to these sentences:

> Today, it will **rain**. Yesterday, it **rained**.

But some verbs are irregular. That means that these words don't follow the regular pattern. You have two irregular verbs in your spelling list today. Listen to these sentences:

> I will **tell** you a story. Yesterday, I **told** you a story.
> I **think** I know the answer. Yesterday, I **thought** I knew the answer.

t<u>o</u>ld

## Father <u>told</u> the children to clean the yard.
- How many syllables does this word have? Dictate the word.
- Underline /ō/ because **o** says its name when followed by two consonants.
- Read the word. Now you read the word. Blend /l/ and /d/ together when you read it, like this—/ld/.

shad <u>ow</u>✚s

## They sat in the <u>shadow</u> of the tree.
- How many syllables does this word have? Dictate the first syllable.
- Leave a small space between syllables. Dictate the word until you get to the suffix.
- Underline the multi-letter phonogram(s).
- Which of its sounds is **ow** saying? It's saying its second sound, so put a small 2 above it.
- Read the word. Now you read the word.
✚ Now let's make it plural! Does **shadow** end in a hiss? No, it doesn't! So we will make it plural in the regular way.
- Add /s/, /z/ and read the word again. Put a small 2 above the **s** to show that it's saying its second sound.

<u>a</u> cross

## The dog ran <u>across</u> the yard.
- How many syllables does this word have? Dictate the first syllable.
- Leave a small space between syllables. Dictate the other syllable(s).
- This word has a lazy vowel. When we say it, we usually say /ə-cross/. We think to spell /ā-cross/.
- Underline /ā/ because **a** says its name at the end of a syllable.
- We often double **s** after a single vowel at the end of a base word. This is a spelling rule.
- Read the word. Now you read the word. Blend /c/ and /r/ together when you read it, like this—/cr/.

**Spelling rule:** We often double s after a single vowel at the end of a base word.

<u>o</u>ld

## Calling your mother <u>old</u> is a bad idea.
- How many syllables does this word have? Dictate the word.
- Underline /ō/ because **o** says its name when followed by two consonants.
- Read the word. Now you read the word. Blend /l/ and /d/ together when you read it, like this—/ld/.

g**o**ld

## Goldilocks has hair of g**o**ld.

- How many syllables does this word have? Dictate the word.
- Underline /ō/ because **o** says its name when followed by two consonants.
- This word rhymes with **old**.
- Read the word. Now you read the word. Blend /l/ and /d/ together when you read it, like this—/ld/.

br**idge**

## The river had a br**idge** so we could cross.

- How many syllables does this word have? Dictate the word.
- Underline the multi-letter phonogram(s).
- The phonogram **dge** is used only after a single vowel that says its short sound. This is a spelling rule.
- Read the word. Now you read the word. Blend /b/ and /r/ together when you read it, like this—/br/.

**Spelling rule:** Phonogram *dge* is used only after a single vowel that says its short sound.

th **ough** t ✚ful

## The boy th**ough**t about his answer.

- How many syllables does this word have? Dictate the word until you get to the suffix.
- Underline the multi-letter phonogram(s).
- Read the word. Now you read the word.

✚ Can we add the suffix **full** to change this word? We can! Listen: That was a *thoughtful* gift. It means a gift that someone put a lot of thought into. Let's add **full** to this word as a new syllable.

- Leave a small space between syllables. Dictate the next syllable—*ful*.
- When **full** is a suffix, it loses an *l*. This is a spelling rule.
- Now read the word again.

an **o**²**th** er

## Let's play an**oth**er time.

- How many syllables does this word have? Dictate the first syllable.
- Leave a small space between syllables. Dictate the other syllable(s).
- Underline the multi-letter phonogram(s).
- Put a small 2 above /TH/ to show that it's saying its second sound.
- This word has a lazy vowel. When we say it, we usually say /ăn-əth-er/. We think to spell /ăn-ŏth-er/.
- Read the word. Now you read the word.

s**ee**n

## Have you s**ee**n that movie?

- How many syllables does this word have? Dictate the word.
- Underline the multi-letter phonogram(s).
- Read the word. Now you read the word.

b**o**n**e**

## I broke my wrist b**o**n**e** while building a house.

- How many syllables does this word have? Dictate the word.
- **O** says its name because of the silent **e**; underline the silent **e** twice, and draw a bridge between the silent **e** and the **o**.
- Read the word. Now you read the word.

Reading & Spelling Through Literature Book 1

Let's review some of what you've learned! [Instructor: Give the student a chance to answer, but simply read the answer if they do not know it.]

Can you name the vowels? [Instructor: Say the vowels three times each lesson if the student cannot say them without help.] The vowels are *a*, *e*, *i*, *o*, *u*, and sometimes *y*. What are the other letters called? The other letters, and *y* when it is not making a vowel sound, are called **consonants**.

What does singular mean? Singular means only one.

What does plural mean? Plural means more than one.

How do you make most words plural? You just add an *s*! What if the last sound in the word hisses by saying /s/, /z/, /ks/, /sh/, or /ch/? Then you add *e-s* to make the word plural!

What is a multi-syllable word? A multi-syllable word has more than one syllable.

---

but t<u>er</u> f<u>ly</u>

## The caterpillar became a <u>butterfly</u>.
- How many syllables does this word have? Dictate the first syllable.
- Leave a small space between syllables. Dictate the other syllable(s).
- Underline the multi-letter phonogram(s).
- This is a **compound word**. That means that it's two words put together to become one word. So remember that even though *fly* is at the end of this multi-syllable word, *fly* is actually a one-syllable base word, so we need to...
- Underline *y* because *y* says /ī/ at the end of a one-syllable base word.
- Read the word. Now you read the word. Blend /f/ and /l/ together when you read it, like this—/fl/.

---

cl<u>oud</u>✚s²

## The day was bright and clear with no <u>cloud</u> in the sky.
- How many syllables does this word have? Dictate the word until you get to the suffix.
- Underline the multi-letter phonogram(s).
- Read the word. Now you read the word. Blend /c/ and /l/ together when you read it, like this—/cl/.
- ✚ Now let's make it plural! Does **cloud** end in a hiss? No, it doesn't! So we will make it plural in the regular way.
- Add /s/, /z/ and read the word again. Put a small 2 above the *s* to show that it's saying its second sound.

---

may b<u>e</u>

## M<u>ay</u>b<u>e</u> they can come over later.
- How many syllables does this word have? Dictate the first syllable.
- Leave a small space between syllables. Dictate the other syllable(s).
- Underline the multi-letter phonogram(s).
- Underline /ē/ because *e* says its name at the end of a syllable.
- This is a **compound word**. That means that it's two words put together to become one word.
- Read the word. Now you read the word.

---

b<u>e</u> gan

## We b<u>e</u>gan a new book.
- How many syllables does this word have? Dictate the first syllable.
- Leave a small space between syllables. Dictate the other syllable(s).
- Underline /ē/ because *e* says its name at the end of a syllable.
- Read the word. Now you read the word.

---

ti✛ed

He tied his shoes.
- How many syllables does this word have? Dictate the word until you get to the suffix.
- ⬡ STOP. We're going to add a suffix. The base word ends in silent *e*, so we drop the silent *e* before adding a vowel suffix.
- Dictate the last phonogram—*ed*.
- Underline the multi-letter phonogram(s).
- *I* says its name because of the silent *e* that we dropped when we added the vowel suffix. Draw a tiny bridge over the *i* as a reminder.
- Which of its sounds is *ed* saying? It's saying its second sound, so put a small 2 above it.
- Read the word. Now you read the word.

string

The ballon had a string to hold it.
- How many syllables does this word have? Dictate the word.
- Underline the multi-letter phonogram(s).
- Read the word. Now you read the word. Blend /s/, /t/, and /r/ together when you read it, like this—/str/.

cross ✛es

They will cross the river over the bridge.
- How many syllables does this word have? Dictate the word until you get to the suffix.
- We often double *s* after a single vowel at the end of a base word.
- Read the word. Now you read the word. Blend /c/ and /r/ together when you read it, like this—/cr/.
- ✛ Can we add the ending *s* or *e-s* as a suffix to change this word? We can! Listen: I *cross* the river. He *crosses* the river. Let's add the proper suffix to this word.
- Does *cross* end in a hiss? Yes, it does! We will add *e-s* as a new syllable.
- Leave a small space between syllables. Dictate the next syllable—*es*.
- This word is a *homograph*. *Homograph* means *same writing*, and this word has three meanings. It can be a verb, what we do, like *cross* the river. But it can also be a noun, the name of a thing, like the Christian *cross*. And to be *cross* about something means to be angry or upset.
- Now read the word again.

its

The dog chased its tail.
- How many syllables does this word have? Dictate the word.
- This word is a *homophone*. *Homophone* means *same sound*, and this word has another word that sounds the same but is spelled differently—the contraction *it's* that means *it is*.
- Read the word. Now you read the word.

side

The children played on the shady side of the house.
- How many syllables does this word have? Dictate the word.
- *I* says its name because of the silent *e*; underline the silent *e* twice, and draw a bridge between the silent *e* and the *i*.
- Read the word. Now you read the word.

long

How long until dinner?
- How many syllables does this word have? Dictate the word.
- Underline the multi-letter phonogram(s).
- Read the word. Now you read the word.

# 40 Suffix -ish; Review: 1+1+1 Rule

We're going to talk about the 1+1+1 rule again today. Remember that the 1+1+1 rule concerns words that have 1 syllable and end with 1 vowel and 1 consonant.

Verbs are what we do, like *hop*, *step*, *get*, and *hum*. You've learned to spell many super short verbs like these that are one-syllable and end with one vowel followed by one consonant. Look at these one-syllable words and notice how each word ends in one vowel followed by one consonant. We can add an *s* to these words without any problem. But if we want to add a vowel suffix like *ed*, *er*, or *ing*, we have to double the final consonant before we add the ending. This is called the 1+1+1 rule because it has 1 syllable, 1 vowel, and 1 consonant at the end.

| hop | step | get | hum |
|---|---|---|---|
| hops | steps | gets | hums |
| hopping | stepped | getting | hummed |

We're going to add a NEW suffix to a word today. We add the suffix *ish* to nouns to show that something has the characteristic of that noun. Listen: The man has a *boyish* face. This tells us that his face has the characteristic of being like a boy's even though he's a man. So something that is *foolish* has the characteristic of being like a fool. We might say that someone has made a *foolish* decision, like spending all the grocery money on a single, expensive meal!

fool ✚ish

A <u>fool</u> and his money are soon parted. This is a proverb, a wise saying.
- How many syllables does this word have? Dictate the word until you get to the suffix.
- Underline the multi-letter phonogram(s).
- Which of its sounds is *oo* saying? It's saying its second sound, so put a small 2 above it.
- Read the word. Now you read the word.
✚ Let's add *ish* to this word as a new syllable.
- The 1+1+1 rule does not apply because this word is one syllable, and it ends in one consonant, but it has two vowels! We add the suffix as usual.
- Leave a small space between syllables. Dictate the next syllable—*ish*. Underline *sh*.
- Now read the word again.

right

Mother decided who was <u>right</u> in the argument.
- How many syllables does this word have? Dictate the word.
- Underline the multi-letter phonogram(s).
- This word is a *homophone*. *Homophone* means *same sound*, and this word has two other words that sound the same and are also spelled the same. *Right* means *correct*. It can also mean the opposite direction of *left*. And it can also refer to our *rights* as human beings to life, liberty, and the pursuit of happiness.
- Read the word. Now you read the word.

tr{ck}

The old dog learned a new <u>tr</u>ick.
- How many syllables does this word have? Dictate the word.
- Underline the multi-letter phonogram(s).
- Read the word. Now you read the word. Blend /t/ and /r/ together when you read it, like this—/tr/.

h<u>a</u>

The naughty boy said, "<u>Ha</u>, ha," as he ran off.
- How many syllables does this word have? Dictate the word.
- Underline *a* because *a* said its third sound at the end of a word. This is a spelling rule.
- Read the word. Now you read the word.

bet t<u>er</u>

She can sing <u>better</u> than I.
- How many syllables does this word have? Dictate the first syllable.
- Leave a small space between syllables. Dictate the other syllable(s).
- Underline the multi-letter phonogram(s).
- Read the word. Now you read the word.

<u>th</u>an

I would rather sing <u>than</u> dance.
- How many syllables does this word have? Dictate the word.
- Underline the multi-letter phonogram(s).
- Which of its sounds is *th* saying? It's saying its second sound, so put a small 2 above it.
- Read the word. Now you read the word.

n<u>oi</u><u>=</u>e

<u>Noise</u> came from the children's room.
- How many syllables does this word have? Dictate the word.
- Underline the multi-letter phonogram(s).
- Which of its sounds is *s* saying? It's saying its second sound, so put a small 2 above it.
- Double underline the silent *e*. Put a small 5 next to the silent *e* to show that it is a type 5—the miscellaneous silent *e*. This type 5 silent *e* is there to keep the word *noise* from looking like it's a plural word. Without silent *e*, *noise* would end in an *s*.
- Read the word. Now you read the word.

hunt ✚er

They <u>hunt</u> for the car keys.
- How many syllables does this word have? Dictate the word until you get to the suffix.
- Read the word. Now you read the word. Blend /n/ and /t/ together when you read it, like this—/nt/.
- ✚ Can we add the ending *er* as a suffix to change this word? We can! Listen: A person who hunts is a *hunter*. Let's add *er* to this word as a new syllable.
- Leave a small space between syllables. Dictate the next syllable—*er*. Underline *er*.
- Now read the word again.

run ✛(n)<u>ing</u>

## Some people <u>run</u> for exercise. I do not.

- How many syllables does this word have? Dictate the word until you get to the suffix.
- Read the word. Now you read the word.
- ✛ Can we add our *ing* suffix to change this word? We can! Listen: I am *running* only because something is chasing me. Let's add *ing* to this word as a new syllable.
- The 1+1+1 Rule: This word is one syllable, and it ends with one vowel followed by one consonant, so we double the final consonant before adding a vowel suffix.
- Leave a small space between syllables. Dictate the next syllable—*ning*.
- Underline the multi-letter phonogram(s).
- Circle the extra letter that we added before the suffix.
- Now read the word again.

b<u>ar</u>k ✛<u>ing</u>

## The puppy likes to b<u>ar</u>k.

- How many syllables does this word have? Dictate the word until you get to the suffix.
- Underline the multi-letter phonogram(s).
- Read the word. Now you read the word.
- ✛ Can we add our *ing* suffix to change this word? We can! Listen: The dog is *barking*. Let's add *ing* to this word as a new syllable.
- The 1+1+1 rule does not apply because this word is one syllable, and it has one vowel, but it ends in two consonants! We add the suffix as usual.
- Leave a small space between syllables. Dictate the next syllable—*ing*. Underline *ng*.
- Now read the word again.

# 41 New: wor, wr; Suffix -ly; Irregular Verbs

Today, we have a new suffix. We add the suffix *ly* to words to change their meanings. The new word that we make describes how things are done. Listen to these examples:

The boy *sadly* told the story.
They buy the paper *weekly*.
The banana was *extremely* ripe.
The doctor gave the girl a *fatherly* smile.

Remember that a **verb** is what we do. We can hope, dream, and scratch our armpits. These are all verbs.

The **ed** ending—the /ed/, /d/, /t/ phonogram that you have learned—shows that something happened in the past. Listen to these sentences:

Today, I will **scratch** my armpit. Yesterday, I **scratched** my armpit.

But some verbs are **irregular**. That means that these words don't follow the regular pattern. You have an irregular verb in your spelling list today. Listen to these sentences:

Today, I will **write** my spelling words. Yesterday, I **wrote** my spelling words.

This will make your instructor much happier than scratching your armpits will!

---

sh<u>or</u>t ✚ly  **He writes short stories.**
- How many syllables does this word have? Dictate the word until you get to the suffix.
- Underline the multi-letter phonogram(s).
- Read the word. Now you read the word.
- ✚ We're going to add our NEW suffix to this word. Listen: Mother said she'll be with us *shortly*. This means in a short amount of time. Let's add *ly* to this word as a new syllable.
- Leave a small space between syllables. Dictate the next syllable—*ly*.
- Underline *y* because *y* says /ē/ at the end of a multi-syllable word.
- Now read the word again.

sl<u>ow</u> ✚ly  **Slow and steady wins the race. ~Aesop**
- How many syllables does this word have? Dictate the word until you get to the suffix.
- Underline the multi-letter phonogram(s).
- Which of its sounds is **ow** saying? It's saying its second sound, so put a small 2 above it.
- Read the word. Now you read the word. Blend /s/ and /l/ together when you read it, like this—/sl/.
- ✚ Can we add the ending *ly* as a suffix to change this word? We can! Listen: The snail moved *slowly*. Let's add *ly* to this word as a new syllable.
- Leave a small space between syllables. Dictate the next syllable—*ly*.
- Underline *y* because *y* says /ē/ at the end of a multi-syllable word.
- Now read the word again.

*Reading & Spelling Through Literature Book 1*

³ ³
wa|lk✛ed

## Walk, don't run.
- How many syllables does this word have? Dictate the word until you get to the suffix.
- Double underline the silent *l*.
- Which of its sounds is *a* saying? It's saying its third sound, so put a small 3 above it.
- Read the word. Now you read the word.

✛ Can we add the ending *ed* as a suffix to change this word? We can! Listen: Today, I *walk*. Yesterday, I *walked*.
- Let's add *ed* to this word as a suffix. Dictate the phonogram—*ed*.
- Underline the multi-letter phonogram(s).
- Which of its sounds is *ed* saying? It's saying its third sound, so put a small 3 above it.
- Now read the word again.

worm

## The worm inched towards the apple.
- How many syllables does this word have? Dictate the word.
- Underline the multi-letter phonogram(s).
- Read the word. Now you read the word.

sh ⌒
sure

## Are you sure about the answer?
- How many syllables does this word have? Dictate the word.
- This word has an exception. The *s* is not making its regular sound. Instead, it sounds like /sh/, so put a small *sh* over it to remind you what sound it is making.
- *U* says its name because of the silent *e*; underline the silent *e* twice, and draw a bridge between the silent *e* and the *u*.
- Sometimes, *u* is a little lazy. It drops the /y/ sound at the beginning of its name and only says /ö/ instead of /ū/.
- Read the word. Now you read the word.

tree  top

## The bird made its nest in the treetop.
- How many syllables does this word have? Dictate the first syllable.
- Leave a small space between syllables. Dictate the other syllable(s).
- Underline the multi-letter phonogram(s).
- This is a *compound word*. That means that it's two words put together to become one word.
- Read the word. Now you read the word. Blend /t/ and /r/ together when you read it, like this—/tr/.

⌒
shake✛s

## The dog will shake after its bath.
- How many syllables does this word have? Dictate the word until you get to the suffix.
- Underline the multi-letter phonogram(s).
- *A* says its name because of the silent *e*; underline the silent *e* twice, and draw a bridge between the silent *e* and the *a*.
- This word is a *homophone*. *Homophone* means *same sound*, and this word has another word that sounds the same and is spelled the same—the frozen *shake* that you drink.
- Read the word. Now you read the word.

✛ Can we add the ending *s* or *e-s* as a suffix to change this word? We can! Listen: I *shake*. He *shakes*. Let's add the proper suffix to this word.
- Does *shake* end in a hiss? No, it doesn't! Just add /s/, /z/ and read the word again.

h<u>aw</u>k

The h<u>aw</u>k soared through the sky.
- How many syllables does this word have? Dictate the word.
- Underline the multi-letter phonogram(s).
- Read the word. Now you read the word.

wr<u>i</u>t<u>e</u>

Can you wr<u>i</u>t<u>e</u> the alphabet?
- How many syllables does this word have? Dictate the word.
- Underline the multi-letter phonogram(s).
- *I* says its name because of the silent *e*; underline the silent *e* twice, and draw a bridge between the silent *e* and the *i*.
- Read the word. Now you read the word.

wr<u>o</u>t<u>e</u>

Who wr<u>o</u>t<u>e</u> this book?
- This is an irregular verb. Listen: Today, I **write**. Yesterday, I **wrote**.
- How many syllables does this word have? Dictate the word.
- Underline the multi-letter phonogram(s).
- *O* says its name because of the silent *e*; underline the silent *e* twice, and draw a bridge between the silent *e* and the *o*.
- Read the word. Now you read the word.

Today, one of your words is the name of a little girl—*Molly*. When we write someone's name, we begin the name with a capital letter. If you haven't learned to write capital letters yet, your instructor will show you how to write a capital **M**. Here are some various ways that people write capital **M** and lowercase **m**. Do you see your kind of writing?

*Mm    Mm    Mm    Mm    Mm*

Mol ly

## Does Molly have chickens?
- This word is a **proper name**, so it begins with a capital letter.
- How many syllables does this word have? Dictate the first syllable.
- Leave a small space between syllables. Dictate the other syllable(s).
- Underline **y** because **y** says /ē/ at the end of a multi-syllable word.
- Read the word. Now you read the word.

pail

## The pail tipped and spilled.
- How many syllables does this word have? Dictate the word.
- Underline the multi-letter phonogram(s).
- Read the word. Now you read the word.

mon ey²

## Mother has the grocery money.
- How many syllables does this word have? Dictate the first syllable.
- Leave a small space between syllables. Dictate the other syllable(s).
- Underline the multi-letter phonogram(s).
- Which of its sounds is **ey** saying? It's saying its second sound, so put a small 2 above it.
- This word has a lazy vowel. When we say it, we usually say /mən-ē/. We think to spell /mŏn-ē/.
- Read the word. Now you read the word.

bu y

## We will buy baking supplies at the store.
- How many syllables does this word have? Dictate the word.
- Underline the multi-letter phonogram(s).
- Underline **y** because **y** says /ī/ at the end of a one-syllable base word.
- Read the word. Now you read the word.

grow² ✛ing

## The chick will grow into a hen.
- How many syllables does this word have? Dictate the word until you get to the suffix.
- Underline the multi-letter phonogram(s).
- Read the word. Now you read the word. Blend /g/ and /r/ together when you read it, like this—/gr/.
- ✛ Can we add our *ing* suffix to change this word? We can! Listen: You are **growing**. Let's add *ing* to this word as a new syllable.
- Leave a small space between syllables. Dictate the next syllable—*ing*.
- Underline the multi-letter phonogram(s).
- Now read the word again.

**hatch✚ed** [3]

## The egg will <u>hatch</u> a baby chick.

- How many syllables does this word have? Dictate the word until you get to the suffix.
- Underline the multi-letter phonogram(s).
- Phonogram *tch* is used only after a single vowel that does not say its long sound.
- Read the word. Now you read the word.
- ✚ Can we add the ending *ed* as a suffix to change this word? We can! Listen: Today, they *hatch*. Yesterday, they *hatched*.
- *Ed* does not form a new syllable in this word, so we just add it to the word without leaving a space. Dictate the next phonogram—*ed*. Underline *ed*.
- Which of its sounds is *ed* saying? It's saying its third sound, so put a small 3 above it.
- Now read the word again.

**p<u>oo</u>r** [3] **✚ly**

## His handwriting is <u>poor</u>, so he needs to practice.

- How many syllables does this word have? Dictate the word until you get to the suffix.
- Which of its sounds is *oo* saying? It's saying its third sound, so put a small 3 above it.
- Read the word. Now you read the word.
- ✚ Can we add the ending *ly* as a suffix to change this word? We can! Listen: They played the game *poorly*, but they still had fun! Let's add *ly* to this word as a new syllable.
- Leave a small space between syllables. Dictate the next syllable—*ly*.
- Underline *y* because *y* says /ē/ at the end of a multi-syllable word.
- Now read the word again.

**b<u>ui</u>ld ✚er**

## We will <u>build</u> a dog house.

- How many syllables does this word have? Dictate the word until you get to the suffix.
- Underline the multi-letter phonogram(s).
- Read the word. Now you read the word.
- ✚ Can we add the ending *er* as a suffix to change this word? We can! Listen: The *builders* build the building. Let's add *er* to this word as a new syllable.
- Leave a small space between syllables. Dictate the next syllable—*er*. Underline *er*.
- Now read the word again.

**b<u>ui</u>lt**

## The children <u>built</u> a birdhouse.

- This is an irregular verb. Listen: Today, I *build*. Yesterday, I *built*.
- How many syllables does this word have? Dictate the word.
- Underline the multi-letter phonogram(s).
- Read the word. Now you read the word. Blend /l/ and /t/ together when you read it, like this—/lt/.

**c<u>ou</u>nt ✚ing**

## Can you <u>count</u> to twenty?

- How many syllables does this word have? Dictate the word until you get to the suffix.
- Underline the multi-letter phonogram(s).
- Read the word. Now you read the word. Blend /n/ and /t/ together when you read it, like this—/nt/.
- ✚ Can we add our *ing* suffix to change this word? We can! Listen: I am *counting*. Let's add *ing* to this word as a new syllable.
- Leave a small space between syllables. Dictate the next syllable—*ing*. Underline *ng*.
- Now read the word again.

Let's review the 1+1+1 rule. It's an important rule in spelling, so we'll keep talking about it until you understand it perfectly!

Verbs are what we do, like *run, stop, pat,* and **hum**. You've learned to spell many super short verbs like these that are one-syllable and end with one vowel followed by one consonant. Look at these one-syllable words and notice how each word ends in one vowel followed by one consonant. We can add an *s* to these words without any problem. But if we want to add a vowel suffix like *ed , er,* or *ing,* we have to double the final consonant before we add the ending. This is called the 1+1+1 rule because it has 1 syllable, 1 vowel, and 1 consonant at the end.

| run | stop | pat | hum |
|---|---|---|---|
| runs | stops | pats | hums |
| running | stopper | patting | hummed |

pat ✚(t)er

## She pat the crying baby.
- How many syllables does this word have? Dictate the word until you get to the suffix.
- Read the word. Now you read the word.
- ✚ Can we add our *er* suffix to change this word? We can! Listen: We heard the **patter** of little feet. Let's add *er* to this word as a new syllable.
- The 1+1+1 Rule: This word is one syllable, and it ends with one vowel followed by one consonant, so we double the final consonant before adding a vowel suffix.
- Leave a small space between syllables. Dictate the next syllable—*ter.*
- Underline the multi-letter phonogram(s).
- Circle the extra letter that we added before the suffix.
- Now read the word again.

caught

## The dog caught the frisbee.
- This is an irregular verb. Listen: Today, I **catch.** Yesterday, I *caught.*
- How many syllables does this word have? Dictate the word.
- Underline the multi-letter phonogram(s).
- Read the word. Now you read the word.

a fraid

## Some people are afraid of the dark.
- How many syllables does this word have? Dictate the first syllable.
- Leave a small space between syllables. Dictate the other syllable(s).
- Underline the multi-letter phonogram(s).
- This word has a lazy vowel. When we say it, we usually say /ə-frād/. We think to spell /ā-frād/.
- Underline /ā/ because *a* says its name at the end of a syllable.
- Read the word. Now you read the word. Blend /f/ and /r/ together when you read it, like this—/fr/.

**neck**

## She wore a scarf around her neck.
- How many syllables does this word have? Dictate the word.
- Underline the multi-letter phonogram(s).
- The phonogram **ck** is used only after a single vowel that says its short sound.
- Read the word. Now you read the word.

**hang**

## Hang your coat up.
- How many syllables does this word have? Dictate the word.
- Underline the multi-letter phonogram(s).
- Read the word. Now you read the word.

**joy ✚ful**

## His praise filled her with joy.
- How many syllables does this word have? Dictate the word until you get to the suffix.
- Underline the multi-letter phonogram(s).
- Read the word. Now you read the word.
✚ Can we add the ending **full** as a suffix to change this word? We can! Listen: The **joyful** people sang songs. Let's add **full** to this word as a new syllable.
- Leave a small space between syllables. Dictate the next syllable—**ful**.
- When **full** is a suffix, it loses an **l**. This is a spelling rule.
- Now read the word again.

**wise ✚ly**

## A wise teacher is priceless.
- How many syllables does this word have? Dictate the word until you get to the suffix.
- **I** says its name because of the silent **e**; underline the silent **e** twice, and draw a bridge between the silent **e** and the **i**.
- Which of its sounds is **s** saying? It's saying its second sound, so put a small 2 above it.
- Read the word. Now you read the word.
✚ Can we add the ending **ly** as a suffix to change this word? We can! Listen: They behaved **wisely**. Let's add **ly** to this word as a new syllable.
- Leave a small space between syllables. Dictate the next syllable—**ly**.
- Underline **y** because **y** says /ē/ at the end of a multi-syllable word.
- Now read the word again.

**some₅ ōⁿe₅**

## Someone left the door open!
- How many syllables does this word have? Dictate the first syllable.
- This is a **compound word**. That means that it's two words put together to become one word. Let's look at each part of this word.
- **Some** has a lazy vowel. When we say it, we usually say /səm/. We think to spell /sŏm/.
- Double underline the silent **e**. Put a small 5 next to the silent **e** to show that it is a type 5—the miscellaneous silent **e**.
- Now let's look at **one**.
- Double underline the silent **e**. Put a small 5 next to the silent **e** to show that it is a type 5—the miscellaneous silent **e**. This silent **e** used to make **o** say its name when it rhymed with **lone**.
- This word is an exception. **One** begins with the /w/ sound, but that phonogram is not in the word! Put a small **w** over the **o** to remind you of the beginning sound.
- Read the word. Now you read the word.

Reading & Spelling Through Literature Book 1

way

She knows the <u>way</u> home.
- How many syllables does this word have? Dictate the word.
- Underline the multi-letter phonogram(s).
- Read the word. Now you read the word.

fine

It was a <u>fine</u> day.
- How many syllables does this word have? Dictate the word.
- *I* says its name because of the silent *e*; underline the silent *e* twice, and draw a bridge between the silent *e* and the *i*.
- Read the word. Now you read the word.

# Review: Irregular Verbs

Verbs are what we do. We can write, buy, build. But yesterday, we wrote, bought, and built!

Do you remember what we call verbs who break the rules? Irregular! They do not follow the regular pattern.

The *ed* ending—the /ed/, /d/, /t/ phonogram that you have learned—shows that something happened in the past. You have another irregular verb in today's spelling list. Listen to these sentences:

Tonight, I will *sleep*. Last night, I *slept*.

Most verbs do follow the rules. But as you can see, many common verbs do not, so we have to learn to spell these words individually instead of just adding an ending.

hare

## A rabbit and a <u>hare</u> are similar but different kinds of animals.
- How many syllables does this word have? Dictate the word.
- *A* says its name because of the silent *e*; underline the silent *e* twice, and draw a bridge between the silent *e* and the *a*.
- Read the word. Now you read the word.

tor toise

## A <u>tortoise</u> lives on the land, but a turtle prefers the water.
- How many syllables does this word have? Dictate the first syllable.
- Leave a small space between syllables. Dictate the other syllable(s).
- Underline the multi-letter phonogram(s).
- This word has an exception. *Oi* is not making its regular sound. Instead, it sounds like /ŭ/, so put a small *u* over it to remind you what sound it is making.
- Double underline the silent *e*. Put a small 5 next to the silent *e* to show that it is a type 5—the miscellaneous silent *e*.
- This type 5 silent *e* is there to keep the word *tortoise* from looking like it's a plural word. Without silent *e*, *tortoise* would end in an *s*.
- Read the word. Now you read the word.

near ✚ly

## The grocery store is <u>near</u> the park.
- How many syllables does this word have? Dictate the word until you get to the suffix.
- Underline the multi-letter phonogram(s).
- Read the word. Now you read the word.
- ✚ Can we add the ending *ly* as a suffix to change this word? We can! Listen: The day was *nearly* over. Let's add *ly* to this word as a new syllable.
- Leave a small space between syllables. Dictate the next syllable—*ly*.
- Underline *y* because *y* says /ē/ at the end of a multi-syllable word.
- Now read the word again.

slept

## The hare <u>slept</u> under a tree.
- This is an irregular verb. Listen: Today, I *sleep*. Yesterday, I *slept*.
- How many syllables does this word have? Dictate the word.
- Read the word. Now you read the word. Blend /s/ and /l/ together at the beginning when you read it, like this—/sl/. Blend /p/ and /t/ together at the end when you read it, like this—/pt/.

**rest** ✚**ed**

## We will rest when we get home.
- How many syllables does this word have? Dictate the word until you get to the suffix.
- Read the word. Now you read the word. Blend /s/ and /t/ together when you read it, like this—/st/.
✚ Can we add the ending **ed** as a suffix to change this word? We can! Listen: Today, I **rest**. Yesterday, I **rested**. Let's add **ed** to this word as a suffix.
- Phonogram **ed** forms a new syllable when the base word ends in /d/ or /t/.
- Leave a small space between syllables. Dictate the next syllable—**ed**. Underline **ed**.
- Now read the word again.

**be fore**

## We should work before we play.
- How many syllables does this word have? Dictate the first syllable.
- Leave a small space between syllables. Dictate the other syllable(s).
- Underline /ē/ because **e** says its name at the end of a syllable.
- **O** says its name because of the silent **e**; underline the silent **e** twice, and draw a bridge between the silent **e** and the **o**.
- Read the word. Now you read the word.

**hop**✚**(p)ed**³

## The bunnies hop through the yard.
- How many syllables does this word have? Dictate the word until you get to the suffix.
- Read the word. Now you read the word.
✚ Can we add our **ed** suffix to change this word? We can! Listen: Today, I **hop**. Yesterday, I **hopped**. Let's add **ed** to this word as a suffix.
- The 1+1+1 Rule: This word is one syllable, and it ends with one vowel followed by one consonant, so we double the final consonant before adding a vowel suffix.
- **Ed** does not form a new syllable in this word, so we just add it to the word without leaving a space. Dictate the next phonograms—**p-ed**. Underline **ed**.
- Which of its sounds is **ed** saying? It's saying its third sound, so put a small 3 above it.
- Circle the extra letter that we added before the suffix.
- Now read the word again.

**beat** ✚**en**

## They beat the other team at sports ball.
- How many syllables does this word have? Dictate the word until you get to the suffix.
- Underline the multi-letter phonogram(s).
- Read the word. Now you read the word.
✚ Can we add the ending **en** as a suffix to change this word? We can! Listen: They had **beaten** this team last year. Let's add **en** to this word as a new syllable.
- Leave a small space between syllables. Dictate the next syllable—**en**.
- Now read the word again.

**rac e**

## I do not race because I am slow.
- How many syllables does this word have? Dictate the word.
- **A** says its name because of the silent **e**; underline the silent **e** twice, and draw a bridge between the silent **e** and the **a**.
- **C** says /s/ because of the silent **e**; underline the **c**. We do NOT put a small 3 next to the silent **e** to show that it is a type 3, though, because the main job of silent **e** in this word is to make **a** say its name, which makes it a type 1 silent **e**.
- Read the word. Now you read the word.

swim ✚Ⓜ ing

I love to s̲w̲i̲m̲ in the ocean.

- How many syllables does this word have? Dictate the word until you get to the suffix.
- Read the word. Now you read the word. Blend /s/ and /w/ together when you read it, like this—/sw/.

✚ Can we add our *ing* suffix to change this word? We can! Listen: I am ***swimming***. Let's add *ing* to this word as a new syllable.

- The 1+1+1 Rule: This word is one syllable, and it ends with one vowel followed by one consonant, so we double the final consonant before adding a vowel suffix.
- Leave a small space between syllables. Dictate the next syllable—***ming***.
- Underline the multi-letter phonogram(s).
- Circle the extra letter that we added before the suffix.
- Now read the word again.

# 45

In today's spelling list, you will learn the word *friend*. This word has a phonogram that does not make its normal sound. It's an exception. So we have a memory tip to help us remember how to spell it. Let's look at this sentence.

## A fri<u>end</u> is a fri<u>end</u> till the <u>end</u>.

The word *friend* ends with the word *end*. So this memory tip reminds us how to spell the word while remembering something about friendship as well.

We have memory tricks for a number of words. Let's look at two more:

## des-ert des-sert

These two words are spelled almost exactly alike! But one has two *s*'s while the other only has one. The first word is *desert*, a place that gets very little rain. The other is *dessert*, the sweet treat that comes at the end of a meal. So how do you remember? Ask yourself: Would you rather have one or two? Most of us would rather have one desert and two desserts, so we remember that desert has one *s* and dessert has two!

flap✚ⓟ<u>ed</u>³

## Birds <u>flap</u> their wings to fly.

- How many syllables does this word have? Dictate the word until you get to the suffix.
- Read the word. Now you read the word. Blend /f/ and /l/ together when you read it, like this—/fl/.
- ✚ Can we add our *ed* suffix to change this word? We can! Listen: Today, they *flap*. Yesterday, they *flapped*. Let's add *ed* to this word as a suffix.
- The 1+1+1 Rule: This word is one syllable, and it ends with one vowel followed by one consonant, so we double the final consonant before adding a vowel suffix.
- *Ed* does not form a new syllable in this word, so we just add it to the word without leaving a space. Dictate the next phonograms—*p-ed*. Underline *ed*.
- Which of its sounds is *ed* saying? It's saying its third sound, so put a small 3 above it.
- Circle the extra letter that we added before the suffix.
- Now read the word again.

call³✚<u>ed</u>²

## He will <u>call</u> before he comes home.

- How many syllables does this word have? Dictate the word until you get to the suffix.
- Which of its sounds is *a* saying? It's saying its third sound, so put a small 3 above it.
- We often double *l* after a single vowel at the end of a base word.
- Read the word. Now you read the word.
- ✚ Can we add the ending *ed* as a suffix to change this word? We can! Listen: Today, I *call*. Yesterday, I *called*.
- *Ed* does not form a new syllable in this word, so we just add it to the word without leaving a space. Dictate the next phonogram—*ed*. Underline *ed*.
- Which of its sounds is *ed* saying? It's saying its second sound, so put a small 2 above it.
- Now read the word again.

**rea ch✚ed** [2]

## The baby will <u>reach</u> for the toy.
- How many syllables does this word have? Dictate the word until you get to the suffix.
- Underline the multi-letter phonogram(s).
- Read the word. Now you read the word.
- ✚ Can we add the ending *ed* as a suffix to change this word? We can! Listen: Today, I *reach*. Yesterday, I *reached*.
- The 1+1+1 rule does not apply because this word is one syllable, but it has two vowels and ends in two consonants! We add the suffix as usual.
- *Ed* does not form a new syllable in this word, so we just add it to the word without leaving a space. Dictate the next phonogram—*ed*. Underline *ed*.
- Which of its sounds is *ed* saying? It's saying its second sound, so put a small 2 above it.
- Now read the word again.

**fr<u>i</u> end**

## She made a new <u>friend</u> at the library.
- How many syllables does this word have? Dictate the word.
- We're going to mark this word a little differently to remind us of the memory tip.
- Double underline the silent *i*.
- Memory tip: A fri<u>end</u> is a fri<u>end</u> till the <u>end</u>. Underline <u>end</u>.
- Read the word. Now you read the word. Blend /f/ and /r/ together when you read it, like this—/fr/.

**b<u>ea</u>st✚s**

## The word <u>beast</u> is another word for animal.
- How many syllables does this word have? Dictate the word until you get to the suffix.
- Underline the multi-letter phonogram(s).
- Read the word. Now you read the word. Blend /s/ and /t/ together when you read it, like this—/st/.
- ✚ Now let's make it plural! Does *beast* end in a hiss? If necessary, point out that the final sound is actually the /t/ sound, not the /s/ sound. No, it doesn't! So we will make it plural in the regular way.
- Add /s/, /z/ and read the word again.

**h<u>ur</u>t**

## She <u>hurt</u> her arm when she fell.
- How many syllables does this word have? Dictate the word.
- Underline the multi-letter phonogram(s).
- Read the word. Now you read the word.

**an y mor<u>e</u>**

## We don't go there <u>anymore</u>.
- How many syllables does this word have? Dictate the first syllable.
- Leave a small space between syllables. Dictate the other syllable(s).
- This is a *compound word*. That means that it's two words put together to become one word. So remember that even though *any* is not at the end of this multi-syllable word, *any* is actually a multi-syllable word all by itself, so we need to...
- Underline *y* because *y* says /ē/ at the end of a multi-syllable word.
- *O* says its name because of the silent *e*; underline the silent *e* twice, and draw a bridge between the silent *e* and the *o*.
- Read the word. Now you read the word.

**stay✚ed**²

## Today we will <u>stay</u> home.

- How many syllables does this word have? Dictate the word until you get to the suffix.
- Underline the multi-letter phonogram(s).
- Read the word. Now you read the word. Blend /s/ and /t/ together when you read it, like this—/st/.
✚ Can we add the ending *ed* as a suffix to change this word? We can! Listen: Today, I *stay*. Yesterday, I *stayed*.
- *Ed* does not form a new syllable in this word, so we just add it to the word without leaving a space. Dictate the next phonogram—*ed*. Underline *ed*.
- Which of its sounds is *ed* saying? It's saying its second sound, so put a small 2 above it.
- Now read the word again.

**ask ✚ing**

## <u>Ask</u> before getting a cookie.

- How many syllables does this word have? Dictate the word until you get to the suffix.
- Read the word. Now you read the word. Blend /s/ and /k/ together when you read it, like this—/sk/.
✚ Can we add our *ing* suffix to change this word? We can! Listen: I am *asking*. Let's add *ing* to this word as a new syllable.
- Leave a small space between syllables. Dictate the next syllable—*ing*.
- Underline the multi-letter phonogram(s).
- Now read the word again.

**hast<u>e</u>**

## We returned home in <u>haste</u>. That means we hurried.

- How many syllables does this word have? Dictate the word.
- *A* says its name because of the silent *e*; underline the silent *e* twice, and draw a bridge between the silent *e* and the *a*.
- Read the word. Now you read the word. Blend /s/ and /t/ together when you read it, like this—/st/.

# 46

Today, one of your words is the name of a little girl—*Holly*. When we write someone's name, we begin the name with a capital letter. If you haven't learned to write capital letters yet, your instructor will show you how to write a capital *H*. Here are some various ways that people write capital *H* and lowercase *h*. Do you see your kind of writing?

Hh     Hh     Hh     H h     Hh

Another one of your words is the name of a holiday—*Thanksgiving*. Names of holidays also begin with a capital letter. Here are some various ways that people write capital *T* and lowercase *t*.

Tt     Tt     Tt     It     Tt

**Thanks giv ing**

Many people have turkey on Thanksgiving.
- This word is a **proper name**, so it begins with a capital letter.
- How many syllables does this word have? Dictate the first syllable.
- Leave a small space between syllables. Dictate the other syllable(s).
- Underline the multi-letter phonogram(s).
- Read the word. Now you read the word. Blend /n/ and /k/ together when you read it, like this—/nk/. We don't completely pronounce the *n*. It's like you start to make the *n* sound, but then it gets stuck in your nose. *N* gets stuck in your nose before /g/ and /k/ sounds.
- Remember: Don't put things in your nose.

**in deed**

He is a friend indeed.
- How many syllables does this word have? Dictate the first syllable.
- Leave a small space between syllables. Dictate the other syllable(s).
- Underline the multi-letter phonogram(s).
- Read the word. Now you read the word.

**hun gry**

The hungry toddler needed a snack.
- How many syllables does this word have? Dictate the first syllable.
- Leave a small space between syllables. Dictate the other syllable(s).
- Underline *y* because *y* says /ē/ at the end of a multi-syllable word.
- Read the word. Now you read the word. Blend /g/ and /r/ together when you read it, like this—/gr/.

**out side**

We can go outside when the weather is nice.
- How many syllables does this word have? Dictate the first syllable.
- Leave a small space between syllables. Dictate the other syllable(s).
- Underline the multi-letter phonogram(s).
- *I* says its name because of the silent *e*; underline the silent *e* twice, and draw a bridge between the silent *e* and the *i*.
- This is a **compound word**. That means that it's two words put together to become one word.
- Read the word. Now you read the word.

ye͟ar ✚ly

## Thanksgiving comes once a ye͟ar.

- How many syllables does this word have? Dictate the word until you get to the suffix.
- Underline the multi-letter phonogram(s).
- Read the word. Now you read the word.
- ✚ Can we add the ending *ly* as a suffix to change this word? We can! Listen: This holiday happens **yearly**. Let's add *ly* to this word as a new syllable.
- Leave a small space between syllables. Dictate the next syllable — *ly*.
- Underline *y* because *y* says /ē/ at the end of a multi-syllable word.
- Now read the word again.

so͟ng

## That so͟ng gets stuck in my head.

- How many syllables does this word have? Dictate the word.
- Underline the multi-letter phonogram(s).
- Read the word. Now you read the word.

lo͟ud ✚ly

## How lo͟ud can you yell? No, don't demonstrate!

- How many syllables does this word have? Dictate the word until you get to the suffix.
- Underline the multi-letter phonogram(s).
- Read the word. Now you read the word.
- ✚ Can we add the ending *ly* as a suffix to change this word? We can! Listen: The children entered the room **loudly**. Let's add *ly* to this word as a new syllable.
- Leave a small space between syllables. Dictate the next syllable — *ly*.
- Underline *y* because *y* says /ē/ at the end of a multi-syllable word.
- Now read the word again.

wh ea͟t

## Most bread is made from wh ea͟t.

- How many syllables does this word have? Dictate the word.
- Underline the multi-letter phonogram(s).
- Read the word. Now you read the word.

Hol ly͟

## Hol͟ly likes sharing a name with a plant.

- This word is a **proper name**, so it begins with a capital letter.
- How many syllables does this word have? Dictate the first syllable.
- Leave a small space between syllables. Dictate the other syllable(s).
- Underline *y* because *y* says /ē/ at the end of a multi-syllable word.
- Read the word. Now you read the word.

 eve ning

## We'll go outside this eve͟ning when it's cooler.

- How many syllables does this word have? Dictate the first syllable.
- Leave a small space between syllables. Dictate the other syllable(s).
- Underline the multi-letter phonogram(s).
- *E* says its name because of the silent *e*; underline the silent *e* twice, and draw a bridge between the silent *e* and the initial *e*.
- Read the word. Now you read the word.

Verbs are what we do. We have names for other kinds of words, too. Today we're going to talk about nouns.

*Nouns* are naming words. Nouns name people, places, things, and ideas. If something has a name, that name is a noun. Dog, cat, brother, sister, store, and toy are all nouns. We also have names for ideas, like freedom.

Many nouns can be singular (only one) or plural (more than one). So when we make words plural by adding **s** or **es**, those words are nouns.

fair y

## A fairy is so small that it only has room for one feeling at a time.
(Adapted from Peter Pan by J. M. Barrie)
• How many syllables does this word have? Dictate the first syllable.
• Leave a small space between syllables. Dictate the other syllable(s).
• Underline the multi-letter phonogram(s).
• Underline **y** because **y** says /ē/ at the end of a multi-syllable word.
• Read the word. Now you read the word.

noth ing

## There was nothing in the cookie jar, not even crumbs.
• How many syllables does this word have? Dictate the first syllable.
• Leave a small space between syllables. Dictate the other syllable(s).
• Underline the multi-letter phonogram(s).
• This word has a lazy vowel. When we say it, we usually say /nəth-ing/. We think to spell /nŏth-ing/.
• Read the word. Now you read the word.

tir+ed

## The baby is tired and grumpy.
• How many syllables does this word have? Dictate the word until you get to the suffix.
◯ STOP. We're going to add a suffix. The base word ends in silent **e**, so we drop the silent **e** before adding a vowel suffix.
• **Ed** does not form a new syllable in this word, so we just add it to the word without leaving a space. Dictate the next phonogram—**ed**. Underline **ed**.
• **I** says its name because of the silent **e** that we dropped when we added the vowel suffix. Draw a tiny bridge over the **i** as a reminder.
• Which of its sounds is **ed** saying? It's saying its second sound, so put a small 2 above it.
• Read the word. Now you read the word.

car +ing

## She was caring for the sick child.
• How many syllables does this word have? Dictate the word until you get to the suffix.
◯ STOP. We're going to add a suffix. The base word ends in silent **e**, so we drop the silent **e** before adding a vowel suffix.
• Leave a small space between syllables. Dictate the last syllable—**ing**.
• Underline the multi-letter phonogram(s).
• **A** says its name because of the silent **e** that we dropped when we added the vowel suffix. Draw a tiny bridge over the **a** as a reminder.
• Read the word. Now you read the word.

sh oo̱k
(2 above oo)

## The dishes <u>shook</u> when he ran into the table.

- This is an irregular verb. Listen: Today, I **shake**. Yesterday, I **shook**.
- How many syllables does this word have? Dictate the word.
- Underline the multi-letter phonogram(s).
- Which of its sounds is **oo** saying? It's saying its second sound, so put a small 2 above it.
- Read the word. Now you read the word.

<u>bright</u> ✚ly

## The <u>bright</u> sun came out after the rain.

- How many syllables does this word have? Dictate the word until you get to the suffix.
- Underline the multi-letter phonogram(s).
- Read the word. Now you read the word. Blend /b/ and /r/ together when you read it, like this—/br/.
- ✚ Can we add the ending **ly** as a suffix to change this word? We can! Listen: The sun was shining **brightly**. Let's add **ly** to this word as a new syllable.
- Leave a small space between syllables. Dictate the next syllable—**ly**.
- Underline **y** because **y** says /ē/ at the end of a multi-syllable word.
- Now read the word again.

sh<u>i</u>n ✚ing

## How brightly the sun is <u>shining</u>!

- How many syllables does this word have? Dictate the word until you get to the suffix.
- ◯ STOP. We're going to add a suffix. The base word ends in silent **e**, so we drop the silent **e** before adding a vowel suffix.
- Leave a small space between syllables. Dictate the last syllable—**ing**.
- Underline the multi-letter phonogram(s).
- **i** says its name because of the silent **e** that we dropped when we added the vowel suffix. Draw a tiny bridge over the **i** as a reminder.
- Read the word. Now you read the word.

won d<u>e</u>r ✚ful

## The child's eyes shone with <u>wonder</u>.

- How many syllables does this word have? Dictate the word until you get to the suffix.
- This word has a lazy vowel. When we say it, we usually say /wən-der/. We think to spell /wŏn-der/.
- Read the word. Now you read the word.
- ✚ Can we add the suffix **full** to change this word? We can! Listen: We had a **wonderful** day. Let's add **full** to this word as a new syllable.
- Leave a small space between syllables. Dictate the next syllable—**ful**.
- When **full** is a suffix, it loses an **l**. This is a spelling rule.
- Now read the word again.

<u>light</u> ✚<u>ed</u>

## Turn off the <u>light</u>!

- How many syllables does this word have? Dictate the word until you get to the suffix.
- Underline the multi-letter phonogram(s).
- Read the word. Now you read the word.
- ✚ Can we add the ending **ed** as a suffix to change this word? We can! Listen: Today, I light the lamp. Yesterday, I **lighted** the lamp. Let's add **ed** to this word as a suffix.
- Phonogram **ed** forms a new syllable when the base word ends in /d/ or /t/.
- Leave a small space between syllables. Dictate the next syllable—**ed**. Underline **ed**.
- Now read the word again.

cone+s

## They found a pine <u>cone</u> in the forest.

- How many syllables does this word have? Dictate the word until you get to the suffix.
- *O* says its name because of the silent *e*; underline the silent *e* twice, and draw a bridge between the silent *e* and the *o*.
- Read the word. Now you read the word.
- ✚ Now let's make it plural! Does **cone** end in a hiss? No, it doesn't! So we will make it plural in the regular way.
- Add /s/, /z/ and read the word again. Put a small 2 above the *s* to show that it's saying its second sound.
- Now read the word again.

# 48

You have probably already noticed that *i* and *y* have a special connection! They make exactly the same sounds. When *y* is saying /ĭ/, /ī/, or /ē/, it is acting as a vowel. And when a word ends in the vowel *y*, we change it to *i* before any vowel suffix—unless the suffix begins with *i*. This is because in English, we cannot have two letters *i* in a row. This is a spelling rule. Look at these examples:

cry ⇨ crȳ + ing crȳ-ing

cry ⇨ crī + es crīes

Remember that nouns are naming words. When a noun ends in the vowel *y*, we cannot just add an *s* to make it plural! Instead, we change the *y* to *i* and add *e-s*. In this spelling list, you will be writing a word that ends in the vowel *y* as a plural. So let's look at that word before we write it as a plural noun.

good-ȳ ⇨ good-īes

Today, one of your words is a name from a Christmas story you'll be reading—*Santa*. When we write someone's name, we begin the name with a capital letter. If you haven't learned to write capital letters yet, your instructor will show you how to write a capital *S*. Here are some various ways that people write capital *S* and lowercase *s*. Do you see your kind of writing?

Ss     Ss     Ss     Ss     Ss

stock ing

She hung the stocking on the mantle.
- How many syllables does this word have? Dictate the first syllable.
- Leave a small space between syllables. Dictate the other syllable(s).
- Underline the multi-letter phonogram(s).
- The phonogram *ck* is used only after a single vowel that says its short sound.
- Read the word. Now you read the word. Blend /s/ and /t/ together when you read it, like this—/st/.

dar ling

The baby wore a darling bow.
- How many syllables does this word have? Dictate the first syllable.
- Leave a small space between syllables. Dictate the other syllable(s).
- Underline the multi-letter phonogram(s).
- Read the word. Now you read the word.

hang ✚ing

Hang the clothes in the closet.
- How many syllables does this word have? Dictate the word until you get to the suffix.
- Underline the multi-letter phonogram(s).
- Read the word. Now you read the word.
✚ Can we add our *ing* suffix to change this word? We can! Listen: The clothes are *hanging* in the closet. Let's add *ing* to this word as a new syllable.
- Leave a small space between syllables. Dictate the next syllable—*ing*.
- Underline the multi-letter phonogram(s).
- Now read the word again.

c**o**rn **er**

### They put the Christmas tree in the corner of the room.
- How many syllables does this word have? Dictate the first syllable.
- Leave a small space between syllables. Dictate the other syllable(s).
- Underline the multi-letter phonogram(s).
- Read the word. Now you read the word.

San t**a**

### Christmas cards often have a picture of Santa.
- This word is a **proper name**, so it begins with a capital letter.
- How many syllables does this word have? Dictate the first syllable.
- Leave a small space between syllables. Dictate the other syllable(s).
- This word has a lazy vowel. When we say it, we usually say /San-tə/. We think to spell /San-tä/.
- Underline **a** because **a** said its third sound at the end of a word. This is a spelling rule.
- Read the word. Now you read the word.

g**o͞o**d ✚**ies**

### They gave out goodies at the party.
- How many syllables does this word have? Dictate the first syllable.
- Leave a small space between syllables. Dictate the word until you get to the suffix.
- ⃝ STOP. We're going to add a suffix. The base word ends in the vowel **y**, so we change the **y** to **i** before adding a suffix. To make this word plural, we change the **y** to **i** and add **e-s**.
- Dictate the other phonogram(s)—**ie-s**.
- Underline the multi-letter phonogram(s). When we changed the **y** to **i** and added **e-s**, it formed the phonogram /ē/—2 letter /ē/.
- Which of its sounds is **oo** saying? It's saying its second sound, so put a small 2 above it.
- Read the word. Now you read the word.

t**oe**

### He stubbed his toe.
- This could technically be a silent **e** word, as similar words like **tie** are taught. However, since we have the phonogram, we emphasize the phonogram.
- How many syllables does this word have? Dictate the word.
- Underline the multi-letter phonogram(s).
- Which of its sounds is **oe** saying? It's saying its first sound, so we don't need to mark it! We only mark phonograms when they're saying a sound other than their first.
- This word is a **homophone. Homophone** means **same sound**, and this word has another word that sounds the same but is spelled differently—to **tow** a car.
- Read the word. Now you read the word.

sh **o͞e**✚s

### Did you find your shoe?
- How many syllables does this word have? Dictate the word until you get to the suffix.
- Underline the multi-letter phonogram(s).
- Which of its sounds is **oe** saying? It's saying its second sound, so put a small 2 above it.
- Read the word. Now you read the word.
- ✚ Now let's make it plural! Does **shoe** end in a hiss? If necessary, point out that this word BEGINS with a hiss, but it does not END with a hiss. No, it doesn't! So we will make it plural in the regular way.
- Add /s/, /z/ and read the word again. Put a small 2 above the **s** to show that it's saying its second sound.

phone

She carries her <u>phone</u> in her purse.
- How many syllables does this word have? Dictate the word.
- Underline the multi-letter phonogram(s).
- *O* says its name because of the silent *e*; underline the silent *e* twice, and draw a bridge between the silent *e* and the *o*.
- Read the word. Now you read the word.

plant ✚ing

The rabbit ate the green leaves of the <u>plant</u>.
- How many syllables does this word have? Dictate the word until you get to the suffix.
- Read the word. Now you read the word. When you read this word, blend /p/ and /l/ together at the beginning, like this—/pl/, and blend /n/ and /t/ together at the end, like this—/nt/.
✚ Can we add our *ing* suffix to change this word? We can! Listen: I am *planting* a garden. Let's add *ing* to this word as a new syllable.
- Leave a small space between syllables. Dictate the next syllable—*ing*.
- Underline the multi-letter phonogram(s).
- Now read the word again.

# 49

# Silent Letters

In this lesson, you have a word with a silent letter, and it's not an *e*! Silent *e* is the most common silent letter, but many other letters can be silent in words. You can think to spell these words by saying the sound of the silent letter, but this isn't always easy to say. However, as you read the words and get more familiar with them, they will become easier to remember.

Today, two of your words are the name of a president—*Abraham Lincoln*, and you'll also learn to write the name of our country—*America*. When we write proper names, we begin the name with a capital letter. If you haven't learned to write capital letters yet, your instructor will show you how to write a capitals *A* and *L*. Here are some various ways that people write capitals *A* and *L* and lowercase *a* and *l*. Do you see your kind of writing?

| | | | | |
|---|---|---|---|---|
| Aa | Aa | Aa | Aa | Aa |
| Ll | Ll | Cl | Ll | Ll |

coun⁴ try

## Our <u>country</u> is called the United States of America.

- How many syllables does this word have? Dictate the first syllable.
- Leave a small space between syllables. Dictate the other syllable(s).
- Underline the multi-letter phonogram(s).
- Which of its sounds is *ou* saying? It's saying its fourth sound, so put a small 4 above it.
- Underline *y* because *y* says /ē/ at the end of a multi-syllable word.
- Read the word. Now you read the word. Blend /t/ and /r/ together when you read it, like this—/tr/.

try ✚ing

## He will <u>try</u> to hit the ball.

- How many syllables does this word have? Dictate the word until you get to the suffix.
- Read the word. Now you read the word. Blend /t/ and /r/ together when you read it, like this—/tr/.
- ✚ Can we add our *ing* suffix to change this word? We can! Listen: I am *trying*. Let's add *ing* to this word as a new syllable.
- Leave a small space between syllables. Dictate the next syllable—*ing*. Underline *ng*.
- Now read the word again.

nām✚ed²

## She <u>named</u> the puppy.

- How many syllables does this word have? Dictate the word until you get to the suffix.
- ○ STOP. We're going to add a suffix. The base word ends in silent *e*, so we drop the silent *e* before adding a vowel suffix.
- *Ed* does not form a new syllable in this word, so we just add it to the word without leaving a space. Dictate the next phonogram—*ed*. Underline *ed*.
- *A* says its name because of the silent *e* that we dropped when we added the vowel suffix. Draw a tiny bridge over the *a* as a reminder.
- Which of its sounds is *ed* saying? It's saying its second sound, so put a small 2 above it.
- Read the word. Now you read the word.

Reading & Spelling Through Literature Book 1

A̲ bra³ ham

## Abraham wore a big hat.
- This word is a **proper name**, so it begins with a capital letter.
- How many syllables does this word have? Dictate the first syllable.
- Leave a small space between syllables. Dictate the other syllable(s).
- In the first syllable, underline /ā/ because **a** says its name at the end of a syllable.
- This word has a lazy vowel. When we say it, we usually say /Ā-brə-ham/. We think to spell /Ā-brä-ham/.
- In the second syllable, which of its sounds is **a** saying? It's saying its third sound, so put a small 3 above it.
- Read the word. Now you read the word. Blend /b/ and /r/ together when you read it, like this—/br/.

Lin co̲ln

## Abraham Lincoln was the President.
- This word is a **proper name**, so it begins with a capital letter.
- How many syllables does this word have? Dictate the first syllable.
- Leave a small space between syllables. Dictate the other syllable(s).
- Double underline the silent **l**.
- Read the word. Now you read the word.

men

## The men worked hard.
- This is an irregular noun. Listen: One **man**, two **men**.
- How many syllables does this word have? Dictate the word.
- The vowel in this word is not lazy, but some people might say /mĭn/ instead of /mĕn/. However you say it, we think to spell /mĕn/.
- Read the word. Emphasize the /ĕ/ sound. Now you read the word.

bre̲a³k ✚ing

## Did you break the toy?
- How many syllables does this word have? Dictate the word until you get to the suffix.
- Which of its sounds is **ea** saying? It's saying its third sound, so put a small 3 above it.
- Read the word. Now you read the word. Blend /b/ and /r/ together when you read it, like this—/br/.
- ✚ Can we add our **ing** suffix to change this word? We can! Listen: The toy is **breaking**. Let's add **ing** to this word as a new syllable.
- Leave a small space between syllables. Dictate the next syllable—**ing**. Underline **ng**.
- This word is a **homophone**. **Homophone** means **same sound**, and this word has another word that sounds the same but is spelled differently—Mother slammed on the **brakes** while driving.
- Now read the word again.

tro̲ ph̲y

## He won a trophy at the fair.
- How many syllables does this word have? Dictate the first syllable.
- Leave a small space between syllables. Dictate the other syllable(s).
- Underline the multi-letter phonogram(s).
- Underline /ō/ because **o** says its name at the end of a syllable.
- Underline **y** because **y** says /ē/ at the end of a multi-syllable word.
- Read the word. Now you read the word. Blend /t/ and /r/ together when you read it, like this—/tr/.

neigh ✚ing

## Did you hear the horse <u>neigh</u>?

- How many syllables does this word have? Dictate the word until you get to the suffix.
- Read the word. Now you read the word.
- ✚ Can we add our *ing* suffix to change this word? We can! Listen: The horse is *neighing*. Let's add *ing* to this word as a new syllable.
- The 1+1+1 rule does not apply because this word is one syllable, but it has two vowels and ends in two consonants! We add the suffix as usual.
- Leave a small space between syllables. Dictate the next syllable—*ing*. Underline *ng*.
- Now read the word again.

A-mer-i-c<u>a</u>³

## The name of our country is the United States of <u>America</u>.

- How many syllables does this word have? Dictate the first syllable.
- Leave a small space between syllables. Dictate the other syllable(s).
- This word has a lazy vowel. When we say it, we usually say /ə-mer-ĭ-cä/. We think to spell /ā-mer-ĭ-cä/.
- Underline the first *a* because *a* says its name at the end of a syllable.
- Underline the last *a* because *a* said its third sound at the end of a word.
- Read the word. Now you read the word.

I have some news to break to you. Your mother may not have spoken to you about this sensitive subject before, but it involves spelling, so I have to tell you.

Poets are weird. I know! It's a shocking statement to make.

Listen to the first two lines of this poem:

## Twin-kle, twin-kle, lit-tle star,
## How I won-der what you are.

If you count, you'll notice that each line has the same number of syllables. Poets love that! They love it so much that sometimes, they make new contractions in order to remove a syllable or two from a line.

Remember that we make a contraction when we put two words together to form one new word. When this happens, we remove some of the letters. We add an apostrophe where the missing letters would have been.

### I am     I'm          they are        they're

We use many contractions in ordinary speech. But poets use contractions that most people do not use regularly. In your story for this list, you will be reading a patriotic song (that means a song about loving one's country), and it has an unusual contraction in it. It is another contraction for *it is*, and since the missing letter is the first one, the contraction starts with an apostrophe. Notice that the two words have two syllables, but the new contraction is only one syllable.

### it is      'tis

The same poem also has the word *thee*, which is an old form of the word *you*. The word *you* used to have forms for both singular—only one—and plural—more than one. That means thou would have had to use different words depending on how many people thou were talking to! We still do that with some other words.

### I love *thee*, Mother.          I love *you*, Mother and Father.
### I love *her*.                    I love *them*.

hue

### The light has a greenish hue.
- How many syllables does this word have? Dictate the word.
- *U* says its name because of the silent *e*; underline the silent *e* twice, and draw a bridge between the silent *e* and the *u*.
- English words do not end in *u*; underline the *u*. This is a spelling rule. We do NOT put a small 2 next to the silent *e* to show that it is a type 2, though, because the main job of silent *e* in this word is to make *u* say its name, which makes it a type 1 silent *e*.
- Read the word. Now you read the word.

stripe✚s

### She added a stripe to her picture.
- How many syllables does this word have? Dictate the word until you get to the suffix.
- *I* says its name because of the silent *e*; underline the silent *e* twice, and draw a bridge between the silent *e* and the *i*.
- Read the word. Now you read the word. Blend /s/, /t/, and /r/ together when you read it, like this—/str/.
- ✚ Now let's make it plural! Add /s/, /z/ and read the word again.

'tis²

## 'Tis a fine day.
- This word is a contraction for *it is*. It begins with the apostrophe, so write that first.
- How many syllables does this word have? Dictate the word.
- Which of its sounds is *s* saying? It's saying its second sound, so put a small 2 above it.
- Read the word. Now you read the word.

th²ee

## I will pass thee the salt.
- How many syllables does this word have? Dictate the word.
- Underline the multi-letter phonogram(s).
- Which of its sounds is *th* saying? It's saying its second sound, so put a small 2 above it.
- Read the word. Now you read the word.

sweet ✛ly

## The baby gave a sweet smile.
- How many syllables does this word have? Dictate the word until you get to the suffix.
- Underline the multi-letter phonogram(s).
- Read the word. Now you read the word. Blend /s/ and /w/ together when you read it, like this—/sw/.
- ✛ Can we add the ending *ly* as a suffix to change this word? We can! Listen: The baby smiled *sweetly*. Let's add *ly* to this word as a new syllable.
- Leave a small space between syllables. Dictate the next syllable—*ly*.
- Underline *y* because *y* says /ē/ at the end of a multi-syllable word.
- Now read the word again.

lib er ty

## Liberty means freedom.
- How many syllables does this word have? Dictate the first syllable.
- Leave a small space between syllables. Dictate the other syllable(s).
- Underline the multi-letter phonogram(s).
- Underline *y* because *y* says /ē/ at the end of a multi-syllable word.
- Read the word. Now you read the word.

pil grim

## The pilgrim journeyed to the Holy Land.
- How many syllables does this word have? Dictate the first syllable.
- Leave a small space between syllables. Dictate the other syllable(s).
- Read the word. Now you read the word. Blend /g/ and /r/ together when you read it, like this—/gr/.

pride

## The pride of lions lounged on the savana.
- How many syllables does this word have? Dictate the word.
- *I* says its name because of the silent *e*; underline the silent *e* twice, and draw a bridge between the silent *e* and the *i*.
- Read the word. Now you read the word. Blend /p/ and /r/ together when you read it, like this—/pr/.

moun tain

## We saw snow on the mountain top.
- How many syllables does this word have? Dictate the first syllable.
- Leave a small space between syllables. Dictate the other syllable(s).
- This word has a lazy vowel. When we say it, we usually say /moun-tən/. We think to spell /moun-tān/.
- Read the word. Now you read the word.

fr<u>ee</u> dom

Let fr<u>ee</u>dom ring.

- How many syllables does this word have? Dictate the first syllable.
- Leave a small space between syllables. Dictate the other syllable(s).
- This word has a lazy vowel. When we say it, we usually say /frē-dəm/. We think to spell /frē-dŏm/.
- Read the word. Now you read the word. Blend /f/ and /r/ together when you read it, like this—/fr/.

# 51

# Practice the Sounds; Proper Nouns

Remember to say the sounds of each phonogram as you write them! This will help you remember the phonograms, and you are also training your ears to hear the sounds in the words. This will help you to spell words properly because the first part of spelling properly is hearing properly. When you can separate all the sounds that you hear in a word, you are well on your way to spelling them correctly!

Today, two of your words are the name of a president—*George Washington*. Nouns are naming words. A person's name is a **proper noun**. When we write someone's name, we begin the name with a capital letter—both names! If you haven't learned to write capital letters yet, your instructor will show you how to write a capitals *G* and *W*. Here are some various ways that people write capitals *G* and *W* and lowercase *g* and *w*. Do you see your kind of writing?

Gg    Gg    Gg    *Gg*    *Gg*
Ww   Ww   Ww   *Ww*   *Ww*

par ade

### The parade will start after lunch.
- How many syllables does this word have? Dictate the first syllable.
- Leave a small space between syllables. Dictate the other syllable(s).
- Underline the multi-letter phonogram(s).
- *A* says its name because of the silent *e*; underline the silent *e* twice, and draw a bridge between the silent *e* and the *a*.
- Read the word. Now you read the word.

Wash ing ton

### The capital of the United States is Washington, D.C.
- This word is a **proper noun**, so it begins with a capital letter.
- How many syllables does this word have? Dictate the first syllable.
- Leave a small space between syllables. Dictate the other syllable(s).
- Underline the multi-letter phonogram(s).
- Which of its sounds is *a* saying? It's saying its third sound, so put a small 3 above it.
- This word has a lazy vowel. When we say it, we usually say /Wäsh-ing-tən/. We think to spell /Wäsh-ing-tŏn/.
- Read the word. Now you read the word.

birth day

### Today is River's eleventh birthday .
- How many syllables does this word have? Dictate the first syllable.
- Leave a small space between syllables. Dictate the other syllable(s).
- Underline the multi-letter phonogram(s).
- Which of its sounds is *th* saying? It's saying its first sound, so we don't need to mark it! We only mark phonograms when they're saying a sound other than their first.
- This is a **compound word**. That means that it's two words put together to become one word.
- Read the word. Now you read the word.

**grand fa t͟h er** (with small 3 above second *a*, small 2 above *th*)

## My grandfather always wore jumpsuits.

- How many syllables does this word have? Dictate the first syllable.
- Leave a small space between syllables. Dictate the other syllable(s).
- Underline the multi-letter phonogram(s).
- Which of its sounds is the second *a* saying? It's saying its third sound, so put a small 3 above it.
- Which of its sounds is *th* saying? It's saying its second sound, so put a small 2 above it.
- This is a **compound word**. That means that it's two words put together to become one word.
- Read the word. Now you read the word. When you read this word, blend /g/ and /r/ together at the beginning, like this—/gr/, and blend /n/ and /d/ together at the end, like this—/nd/.

**lov✚ed** (with small 2 above *ed*)

## She loved her present.

- How many syllables does this word have? Dictate the word until you get to the suffix.
- ⭘ STOP. We're going to add a suffix. The base word ends in silent *e*, so we drop the silent *e* before adding a vowel suffix.
- *Ed* does not form a new syllable in this word, so we just add it to the word without leaving a space. Dictate the next phonogram—*ed*. Underline *ed*.
- Which of its sounds is *ed* saying? It's saying its second sound, so put a small 2 above it.
- This word has a lazy vowel. When we say it, we usually say /ləv/. We think to spell /lŏv/.
- Read the word. Now you read the word.

**win dow** (with small 2 above *ow*)

## He opened the window.

- How many syllables does this word have? Dictate the first syllable.
- Leave a small space between syllables. Dictate the other syllable(s).
- Underline the multi-letter phonogram(s).
- Which of its sounds is *ow* saying? It's saying its second sound, so put a small 2 above it.
- Read the word. Now you read the word.

**George** (with small 3 at end)

## George Washington was our first president.

- This word is a **proper noun**, so it begins with a capital letter.
- How many syllables does this word have? Dictate the word.
- Underline the multi-letter phonogram(s).
- Double underline the first silent *e*. This is not any of our normal types of silent *e* because those occur at the end of words. Some words just have silent letters.
- Underline the first *g* because *g may* say /j/ before *e*, *i*, and *y*. This is a spelling rule. Without the first silent *e*, this name would be *Gorge* with a hard /g/ sound.
- For the silent *e* on the end: *G* says /g/ because of the silent *e*; underline the *g*, and double underline the silent *e*. Put a small 3 next to the silent *e* to show that it is a type 3.
- Read the word. Now you read the word.

**Spelling Rule:** *G* may say /j/ before *e*, *i*, and *y*. Otherwise, *g* says /g/.

**ripe** (with bridge mark over *i*, silent *e* double underlined)

## They picked the ripe peaches from the tree.

- How many syllables does this word have? Dictate the word.
- *I* says its name because of the silent *e*; underline the silent *e* twice, and draw a bridge between the silent *e* and the *i*.
- Read the word. Now you read the word.

rip ✚en

## They had to wait for the fruit to ripen.

- Did you notice that this word is almost exactly the same as the previous word? *Ripen* has a vowel suffix—*en.*
- How many syllables does this word have? Dictate the word until you get to the suffix.
- ⭕ STOP. We're going to add a suffix. The base word ends in silent *e*, so we drop the silent *e* before adding a vowel suffix.
- Leave a small space between syllables. Dictate the other syllable(s).
- *I* says its name because of the silent *e* that we dropped when we added the vowel suffix. Draw a tiny bridge over the *i* as a reminder.
- Read the word. Now you read the word.

street✚s

## What street do you live on?

- How many syllables does this word have? Dictate the word until you get to the suffix.
- Underline the multi-letter phonogram(s).
- Read the word. Now you read the word. Blend /s/,/t/ , and /r/ together when you read it, like this—/str/.
- ✚ Now let's make it plural! Does **street** end in a hiss? If necessary, point out that this word BEGINS with a hiss, but it does not END with a hiss. No, it doesn't! So we will make it plural in the regular way.
- Add /s/, /z/ and read the word again.

Reading & Spelling Through Literature Book 1

# 52

# Plurals With Words Ending in F

Today, you have a word in the spelling list that makes its plural in a different way. First, listen to these two phrases: one *loaf*, two *loaves*. Did you hear the difference in the sounds at the end of the words?

The phonograms *f* and *v* make very similar sounds, but *f* is soft while *v* is hard. Sometimes when a word ends in *f*, the sound changes from /f/ to /v/, and the spelling changes, too. We change the *f* to *v* and add *e-s* to make words like *loaf* plural.

**grain**

## They ground the grain into flour.
- How many syllables does this word have? *Dictate the word.*
- Underline the multi-letter phonogram(s).
- Read the word. Now you read the word. Blend /g/ and /r/ together when you read it, like this—/gr/.

**flour**

## They used the flour to bake bread.
- How many syllables does this word have? *Dictate the word.*
- Underline the multi-letter phonogram(s).
- Which of its sounds is *ou* saying? It's saying its first sound, so we don't need to mark it! We only mark phonograms when they're saying a sound other than their first.
- This word is a **homophone**. *Homophone* means *same sound*, and this word has another word that sounds the same but is spelled differently—the *flower* in the garden.
- Read the word. Now you read the word. Blend /f/ and /l/ together when you read it, like this—/fl/.

**dough** (²)

## Bread dough is sticky.
- How many syllables does this word have? *Dictate the word.*
- Underline the multi-letter phonogram(s).
- Which of its sounds is *ough* saying? It's saying its second sound, so put a small 2 above it.
- Read the word. Now you read the word.

**reap ✛ing**

## Reap is another word for harvest.
- How many syllables does this word have? *Dictate the word until you get to the suffix.*
- Underline the multi-letter phonogram(s).
- Read the word. Now you read the word.
- ✛ Can we add our *ing* suffix to change this word? We can! Listen: They were *reaping* the grain. Let's add *ing* to this word as a new syllable.
- The 1+1+1 rule does not apply because this word is one syllable, and it ends in one consonant, but it has two vowels! We add the suffix as usual.
- Leave a small space between syllables. *Dictate the next syllable—ing.* Underline *ng*.
- Now read the word again.

**loaf**

## She baked a loaf of bread.
- How many syllables does this word have? *Dictate the word.*
- Underline the multi-letter phonogram(s).
- Read the word. Now you read the word.

loa✛ve s (with superscript 2, and small 5 under ve)

## They baked five <u>loaves</u> of bread.
- How many syllables does this word have? Dictate the word until you get to the suffix.
- ⭘ STOP. The base word ends in *f*, so we change the *f* to *v* and add *e-s* to make this word plural.
  - Dictate the next phonograms—*v-e-s*.
  - Underline the multi-letter phonogram(s).
  - Double underline the silent *e*. Put a small 5 next to the silent *e* to show that it is a type 5—the miscellaneous silent *e*.
  - Which of its sounds is *s* saying? It's saying its second sound, so put a small 2 above it.
  - Read the word. Now you read the word.

thre<u>sh</u> ✛es

## After harvesting, they will <u>thresh</u> the grain.
- How many syllables does this word have? Dictate the word until you get to the suffix.
- Underline the multi-letter phonogram(s).
- Read the word. Now you read the word. Blend /th/ and /r/ together when you read it, like this—/thr/.
- ✛ Can we add the ending *s* or *e-s* as a suffix to change this word? We can! Listen: I *thresh*. He *threshes*. Let's add the proper suffix to this word.
- Does *thresh* end in a hiss? Yes, it does! To make it plural, we will add *e-s* as a new syllable.
- Leave a small space between syllables. Dictate the next syllable—*es*.
- Now read the word again.

thre<u>sh</u>✛ed (with superscript 2)

## They <u>threshed</u> the grain.
- How many syllables does this word have? Dictate the word until you get to the suffix.
- ⭘ STOP. Before we add the suffix, let's talk about this word. This is a one syllable word, and we're adding a suffix. The 1+1+1 rule does not apply because this word is one syllable, and it has one vowel, but it ends in two consonants! We add the suffix as usual.
- *Ed* does not form a new syllable in this word, so we just add it to the word without leaving a space. Dictate the next phonogram—*ed*.
- Underline the multi-letter phonogram(s).
- Which of its sounds is *ed* saying? It's saying its second sound, so put a small 2 above it.
- Read the word. Now you read the word. Blend /th/ and /r/ together when you read it, like this—/thr/.

bak<u>e</u>

## Will they <u>bake</u> a cake?
- How many syllables does this word have? Dictate the word.
- *A* says its name because of the silent *e*; underline the silent *e* twice, and draw a bridge between the silent *e* and the *a*.
- Read the word. Now you read the word.

bâk <u>er</u> <u>y</u>

## They bake many cakes at the <u>bakery</u>.
- How many syllables does this word have? Dictate the first syllable.
- Leave a small space between syllables. Dictate the other syllable(s).
- Underline the multi-letter phonogram(s).
- The base word ends in silent *e*. *A* says its name because of the silent *e* that we dropped when we added the vowel suffix. Draw a tiny bridge over the *a* as a reminder.
- Underline *y* because *y* says /ē/ at the end of a multi-syllable word.
- Read the word. Now you read the word.

# 53

# Spelling by Tens

Can you count by ten? Well, today you will learn to spell by ten, from thirty to one-hundred. The sound *ty* at the end of each word—thir*ty*, for*ty*, fif*ty*—means ten, so these words mean three tens, four tens, and five tens.

Today, one of your words is a name—***Brownie***. Nouns are naming words. A person's name is a ***proper noun***. When we write someone's name, we begin the name with a capital letter. If you haven't learned to write capital letters yet, your instructor will show you how to write a capital ***B***. Here are some various ways that people write capital ***B*** and lowercase ***b***. Do you see your kind of writing?

Bb     Bb     Bb     Bb     Bb

**Brow nie**

## Brownie is a hen.
- This word is a ***proper noun***, so it begins with a capital letter.
- How many syllables does this word have? Dictate the first syllable.
- Leave a small space between syllables. Dictate the other syllable(s).
- Underline the multi-letter phonogram(s).
- Read the word. Now you read the word. Blend /b/ and /r/ together when you read it, like this—/br/.

**hark**

## Hark! Who goes there?
- How many syllables does this word have? Dictate the word.
- Underline the multi-letter phonogram(s).
- Read the word. Now you read the word.

**thir ty**

## The number thirty is between 29 and 31. (29, 30, 31)
- How many syllables does this word have? Dictate the first syllable.
- Leave a small space between syllables. Dictate the other syllable(s).
- Underline the multi-letter phonogram(s).
- Underline *y* because *y* says /ē/ at the end of a multi-syllable word.
- Read the word. Now you read the word.

**for ty**

## The number forty is between 39 and 41. (39, 40, 41)
- How many syllables does this word have? Dictate the first syllable.
- Leave a small space between syllables. Dictate the other syllable(s).
- Underline the multi-letter phonogram(s).
- Underline *y* because *y* says /ē/ at the end of a multi-syllable word.
- Read the word. Now you read the word.

**fif ty**

## The number fifty is between 49 and 51. (49, 50, 51)
- How many syllables does this word have? Dictate the first syllable.
- Leave a small space between syllables. Dictate the other syllable(s).
- Underline *y* because *y* says /ē/ at the end of a multi-syllable word.
- Read the word. Now you read the word.

six ty

The number <u>sixty</u> is between 59 and 61. (59, 60, 61)
- How many syllables does this word have? Dictate the first syllable.
- Leave a small space between syllables. Dictate the other syllable(s).
- Underline *y* because *y* says /ē/ at the end of a multi-syllable word.
- Read the word. Now you read the word.

sev en ty

The number <u>seventy</u> is between 69 and 71. (69, 70, 71)
- How many syllables does this word have? Dictate the first syllable.
- Leave a small space between syllables. Dictate the other syllable(s).
- Underline *y* because *y* says /ē/ at the end of a multi-syllable word.
- Read the word. Now you read the word.

<u>eight</u> y

The number <u>eighty</u> is between 79 and 81. (79, 80, 81)
- How many syllables does this word have? Dictate the first syllable.
- Leave a small space between syllables. Dictate the other syllable(s).
- Underline the multi-letter phonogram(s).
- Underline *y* because *y* says /ē/ at the end of a multi-syllable word.
- Read the word. Now you read the word.

nine ty

The number <u>ninety</u> is between 89 and 91. (89, 90, 91)
- How many syllables does this word have? Dictate the first syllable.
- Leave a small space between syllables. Dictate the other syllable(s).
- *I* says its name because of the silent *e*; underline the silent *e* twice, and draw a bridge between the silent *e* and the *i*.
- Underline *y* because *y* says /ē/ at the end of a multi-syllable word.
- Read the word. Now you read the word.

one - hun dred

The number <u>one-hundred</u> is between 99 and 101. (99, 100, 101)
- How many syllables does this word have? Dictate the first syllable.
- We put a small line, called a hyphen or dash (-), between *one* and *hundred*.
- Leave a small space between syllables. Dictate the other syllable(s).
- Now let's look at *one*.
- Double underline the silent *e*. Put a small 5 next to the silent *e* to show that it is a type 5—the miscellaneous silent *e*. This silent *e* used to make *o* say its name when it rhymed with *lone*.
- This word is an exception. *One* begins with the /w/ sound, but that phonogram is not in the word! Put a small *w* over *o* to remind you of the beginning sound.
- Read the word. Now you read the word. Blend /d/ and /r/ together when you read it, like this—/dr/.

Reading & Spelling Through Literature Book 1

# 54 New: au; Five Ways to Spell /er/; Plurals With F

We have five different ways to spell the sound /er/, and we have two sentences that we can use to remember these ways.

## Oyst<u>er</u>s t<u>ur</u>n d<u>ir</u>t into p<u>ear</u>ls.

## M<u>er</u>maids t<u>ur</u>n and tw<u>ir</u>l with p<u>ear</u>ls.

Most of the time, we use the first way, /er/ as in *her*. This is the most common spelling of the sound. But today, you'll get to use one of the less common ways to spell /er/.

Today, you also have a word in the spelling list that makes its plural in a different way. First, listen to these two phrases: one *wolf*, two *wolves*. Did you hear the difference in the sounds at the end of the words?

The phonograms *f* and *v* make very similar sounds, but *f* is soft while *v* is hard. Sometimes, when a word ends in *f*, the sound changes from /f/ to /v/, and the spelling changes, too. We change the *f* to *v* and add *e-s* to make words like *wolf* and *loaf* plural.

---

**tur nip**

### She harvested a <u>turnip</u> from the garden.
- How many syllables does this word have? Dictate the first syllable.
- Leave a small space between syllables. Dictate the other syllable(s).
- Underline the multi-letter phonogram(s).
- Read the word. Now you read the word.

**grass ✚es**

### Dad mowed the <u>grass</u>.
- How many syllables does this word have? Dictate the word until you get to the suffix.
- We often double *s* after a single vowel at the end of a base word.
- Read the word. Now you read the word. Blend /g/ and /r/ together when you read it, like this—/gr/.
- ✚ Now let's make it plural! Does *grass* end in a hiss? Yes, it does! To make it plural, we will add *e-s* as a new syllable.
- Leave a small space between syllables. Dictate the next syllable—*es*.
- Now read the word again.

**be cause₅²**

### They lit a fire <u>because</u> it was cold.
- How many syllables does this word have? Dictate the first syllable.
- Leave a small space between syllables. Dictate the other syllable(s).
- Underline the multi-letter phonogram(s).
- Underline /ē/ because *e* says its name at the end of a syllable.
- Which of its sounds is *s* saying? It's saying its second sound, so put a small 2 above it.
- Double underline the silent *e*. Put a small 5 next to the silent *e* to show that it is a type 5—the miscellaneous silent *e*.
- Read the word. Now you read the word.

cr✚ie s

# The baby <u>cries</u> because she is hungry.

- How many syllables does this word have? Dictate the word until you get to the suffix.
- ⬡ STOP. We're going to add a suffix. The base word ends in the vowel *y*, so we change the *y* to *i* before adding a suffix. Listen: I *cry*. She *cries*.
- Dictate the other phonogram(s).
- *I* says its name because of the silent *e*; underline the silent *e* twice, and draw a bridge between the silent *e* and the *i*.
- Which of its sounds is *s* saying? It's saying its second sound, so put a small 2 above it.
- Read the word. Now you read the word. Blend /c/ and /r/ together when you read it, like this—/cr/.

wolf

# The <u>wolf</u> howled.

- How many syllables does this word have? Dictate the word.
- Read the word. Now you read the word. Blend /l/ and /f/ together when you read it, like this—/lf/.

wol✚ve s

# The other <u>wolves</u> howled back.

- How many syllables does this word have? Dictate the word until you get to the suffix.
- ⬡ STOP. The base word ends in *f*, so we change the *f* to *v* and add *e-s* to make this word plural.
- Dictate the next phonograms—*v-e-s*.
- Double underline the silent *e*. Put a small 5 next to the silent *e* to show that it is a type 5—the miscellaneous silent *e*.
- Which of its sounds is *s* saying? It's saying its second sound, so put a small 2 above it.
- Read the word. Now you read the word. Blend /l/ and /v/ together when you read it, like this—/lv/.

dodge

# They like to play <u>dodge</u> ball.

- How many syllables does this word have? Dictate the word.
- Underline the multi-letter phonogram(s).
- The phonogram *dge* is used only after a single vowel that says its short sound. This is a spelling rule.
- Read the word. Now you read the word.

dodg ✚ing

# The goal is to keep <u>dodging</u> the balls that are thrown.

- How many syllables does this word have? Dictate the word until you get to the suffix.
- ⬡ STOP. We're going to add a suffix. The base word ends in silent *e*, so we drop the silent *e* before adding a vowel suffix.
- Leave a small space between syllables. Dictate the other syllable(s).
- Underline the multi-letter phonogram(s).
- The phonogram *dge* is used only after a single vowel that says its short sound. This is a spelling rule.
- When we dropped the silent *e* to add our suffix, we took it away from *dge*, 3 letter /j/. Let's underline *dg* as a reminder that these letters work together as a phonogram.
- Read the word. Now you read the word.

*Reading & Spelling Through Literature Book 1*

knit ✚(t)ing

## I like to knit socks and hats.

- How many syllables does this word have? Dictate the word until you get to the suffix.
- Underline the multi-letter phonogram(s).
- Read the word. Now you read the word.

✚ Can we add our *ing* suffix to change this word? We can! Listen: I am *knitting*. Let's add *ing* to this word as a new syllable.

- The 1+1+1 Rule: This word is one syllable, and it ends with one vowel followed by one consonant, so we double the final consonant before adding a vowel suffix.
- Leave a small space between syllables. Dictate the next syllable — *ting*.
- Underline the multi-letter phonogram(s).
- Circle the extra letter that we added before the suffix.
- Now read the word again.

knot ✚(t)ed

## He tied a knot in his shoelaces.

- How many syllables does this word have? Dictate the word until you get to the suffix.
- Underline the multi-letter phonogram(s).
- Read the word. Now you read the word.

✚ Can we add our *ed* suffix to change this word? We can! Listen: He *knotted* his laces. Let's add *ed* to this word as a new syllable.

- The 1+1+1 Rule: This word is one syllable, and it ends with one vowel followed by one consonant, so we double the final consonant before adding a vowel suffix.
- Leave a small space between syllables. Dictate the next syllable — *ted*.
- Underline the multi-letter phonogram(s).
- Circle the extra letter that we added before the suffix.
- Now read the word again.

# 55

Review

Let's review some of what you've learned! [Instructor: Give the student a chance to answer, but simply read the answer if they do not know it.]

Can you name the vowels? [Instructor: Say the vowels three times each lesson if the student cannot say them without help.] The vowels are *a, e, i, o, u*, and sometimes *y*. What are the other letters called? The other letters, and *y* when it is not making a vowel sound, are called *consonants*.

What does singular mean? Singular means only one.

What does plural mean? Plural means more than one.

How do you make most words plural? You just add an *s*! What if the last sound in the word hisses by saying /s/, /z/, /ks/, /sh/, or /ch/? Then you add *es* to make the word plural!

What is a multi-syllable word? A multi-syllable word has more than one syllable.

## The crane flew over the sea.
- How many syllables does this word have? *Dictate the word until you get to the suffix.*
- *A* says its name because of the silent *e*; underline the silent *e* twice, and draw a bridge between the silent *e* and the *a*.
- Read the word. *Now you read the word. Blend /c/ and /r/ together when you read it, like this—/cr/.*
- ✚ Now let's make it plural! Does *crane* end in a hiss? No, it doesn't! So we will make it plural in the regular way.
- Add *s* and read the word again. Put a small 2 above the *s* to show that it's saying its second sound.

sea

## I like to swim in the sea.
- How many syllables does this word have? *Dictate the word.*
- Underline the multi-letter phonogram(s).
- Which of its sounds is *ea* saying? It's saying its first sound, so we don't need to mark it! We only mark phonograms when they're saying a sound other than their first.
- This word is a *homophone. Homophone* means *same sound*, and this word has another word that sounds the same but is spelled differently—the verb, *to see*, that means to look at something.
- Read the word. *Now you read the word.*

swam

## Last year, I swam in the sea.
- This is an irregular verb. Listen: Today, I *swim*. Yesterday, I *swam*.
- How many syllables does this word have? *Dictate the word.*
- Read the word. *Now you read the word. Blend /s/ and /w/ together when you read it, like this—/sw/.*

strong

## When you're strong, you can lift heavy things.
- How many syllables does this word have? *Dictate the word.*
- Underline the multi-letter phonogram(s).
- Read the word. *Now you read the word. Blend /s/, /t/, and /r/ together when you read it, like this—/str/*

*Reading & Spelling Through Literature Book 1*

**b<u>ea</u>k**

## The hen pecked the ground with her <u>beak</u>.

- How many syllables does this word have? *Dictate the word.*
- Underline the multi-letter phonogram(s).
- Read the word. Now you read the word.

**<u>claw</u>✛s** [2]

## The bird wrapped each <u>claw</u> around the branch.

- How many syllables does this word have? *Dictate the word until you get to the suffix.*
- Underline the multi-letter phonogram(s).
- Read the word. Now you read the word. Blend /c/ and /l/ together when you read it, like this—/cl/.
✛ Now let's make it plural! Does *claw* end in a hiss? No, it doesn't! So we will make it plural in the regular way.
- Add *s* and read the word again. Put a small 2 above the *s* to show that it's saying its second sound.

**fat ✛(t)er**

## The <u>fat</u> chicken waddled across the yard.

- How many syllables does this word have? *Dictate the word until you get to the suffix.*
- Read the word. Now you read the word.
✛ Can we add our *er* suffix to change this word? We can! Listen: The other chicken is *fatter*. Let's add *er* to this word as a new syllable.
- The 1+1+1 Rule: This word is one syllable, and it ends with one vowel followed by one consonant, so we double the final consonant before adding a vowel suffix.
- Leave a small space between syllables. *Dictate the next syllable—ter.*
- Underline the multi-letter phonogram(s).
- Circle the extra letter that we added before the suffix.
- Now read the word again.

**w<u>ide</u>**

## The path is <u>wide</u>.

- How many syllables does this word have? *Dictate the word.*
- *I* says its name because of the silent *e*; underline the silent *e* twice, and draw a bridge between the silent *e* and the *i*.
- Read the word. Now you read the word.

**on to** [3]

## He got <u>onto</u> the horse.

- How many syllables does this word have? *Dictate the first syllable.*
- Leave a small space between syllables. *Dictate the other syllable(s).*
- Which of its sounds is *o* saying? It's saying its third sound, so put a small 3 above it.
- This is a **compound word**. That means that it's two words put together to become one word.
- Read the word. Now you read the word.

**held**

## She <u>held</u> her doll.

- This is an irregular verb. Listen: Today, I *hold*. Yesterday, I *held*.
- How many syllables does this word have? *Dictate the word.*
- Read the word. Now you read the word. Blend /l/ and /d/ together when you read it, like this—/ld/.

Today, one of your words is a name—*Jenny.* When we write someone's name, we begin the name with a capital letter. If you haven't learned to write capital letters yet, your instructor will show you how to write a capital *J.* Here are some various ways that people write capital *J* and lowercase *j.* Do you see your kind of writing?

Jj    Jj    Jj    Jj    Jj

**rob in**

## The robin found a worm.
- How many syllables does this word have? Dictate the first syllable.
- Leave a small space between syllables. Dictate the other syllable(s).
- Read the word. Now you read the word.

**rea son** (2)

## What is the reason the robin flies away?
- How many syllables does this word have? Dictate the first syllable.
- Leave a small space between syllables. Dictate the other syllable(s).
- Underline the multi-letter phonogram(s).
- Which of its sounds is **s** saying? It's saying its second sound, so put a small 2 above it.
- This word has a lazy vowel. When we say it, we usually say /rē-zən/. We think to spell /rē-zŏn/.
- Read the word. Now you read the word.

**lark**

## The lark built a nest.
- How many syllables does this word have? Dictate the word.
- Underline the multi-letter phonogram(s).
- Read the word. Now you read the word.

**Jen ny**

## Jenny Wren flies away in the winter.
- This word is a **proper noun**, so it begins with a capital letter.
- How many syllables does this word have? Dictate the first syllable.
- Leave a small space between syllables. Dictate the other syllable(s).
- Underline **y** because **y** says /ē/ at the end of a multi-syllable word.
- Read the word. Now you read the word.

**wren**

## The wren hatched her eggs.
- How many syllables does this word have? Dictate the word.
- Underline the multi-letter phonogram(s).
- Read the word. Now you read the word.

car di n[3]al      One kind of <u>car</u>dinal is bright red.

- How many syllables does this word have? Dictate the first syllable.
- Leave a small space between syllables. Dictate the other syllable(s).
- Underline the multi-letter phonogram(s).
- Which of its sounds is **a** saying? It's saying its third sound, so put a small 3 above it.
- This word has a lazy **syllable!** When we say it, we usually say /cärd-näl/. We think to spell all three syllables /cär-dĭ-näl/.
- Read the word. Now you read the word.

fin<u>ch</u> ✚es      The saffron <u>fin</u>ch is a small yellow bird.

- How many syllables does this word have? Dictate the word until you get to the suffix.
- Underline the multi-letter phonogram(s).
- Read the word. Now you read the word. Blend /n/ and /ch/ together when you read it, like this—/nch/.

✚ Now let's make it plural! Does **finch** end in a hiss? Yes, it does! To make it plural, we will add **e-s** as a new syllable.

- Leave a small space between syllables. Dictate the next syllable—**es**.
- Now read the word again.

<u>chick</u> <u>a</u> d<u>ee</u>      The <u>chick</u>adee stays to see the snow

- How many syllables does this word have? Dictate the first syllable.
- Leave a small space between syllables. Dictate the other syllable(s).
- Underline the multi-letter phonogram(s).
- This word has a lazy vowel. When we say it, we usually say /chick-ə-dee/. We think to spell /chick-ā-dee/.
- Underline /ā/ because **a** says its name at the end of a syllable.
- Read the word. Now you read the word.

pen g[2]<u>u</u>in      The <u>pen</u>guin likes the cold.

- How many syllables does this word have? Dictate the first syllable.
- Leave a small space between syllables. Dictate the other syllable(s).
- Which of its sounds is **gu** saying? It's saying its second sound, so put a small 2 above it.
- This word has a lazy vowel. When we say it, we usually say /pĭn-gwĭn/. We think to spell /pĕn-gwĭn/. Emphasize the /ĕ/ sound.
- Underline the multi-letter phonogram(s).
- Read the word. Now you read the word.

s<u>tay</u>✚s[2]      Will you s<u>tay</u> for lunch?

- How many syllables does this word have? Dictate the word until you get to the suffix.
- Underline the multi-letter phonogram(s).
- Read the word. Now you read the word. Blend /s/ and /t/ together when you read it, like this—/st/.

✚ Can we add the ending **s** as a suffix to change this word? We can! Listen: I **stay**. He **stays**. Let's add **s** to this word.

- Add **s** and read the word again. Put a small 2 above the **s** to show that it's saying its second sound.

# Review: Suffixes, 1+1+1 Rule

Let's review suffixes and the 1+1+1 rule. It's an important rule in spelling, so we'll keep talking about it until you understand it perfectly!

Verbs are what we do, like *run*, *strap*, and *hum*. We can add suffixes to verbs to show different things about what we do. We can add *ed* to show that something happened in the past, and we can add *ing* to show that something is continuing to happen. We can even add *er* sometimes to turn a verb into a noun!

Today, I **help**. Yesterday, I **helped**. I am **helping**. I am a **helper**.

We can also add suffixes to nouns. We add *s* or *e-s* to make plurals. And we can even add suffixes to describing words, like *fat*!

My cat is *fat*. My dog is *fatter*.

You've learned to spell many super short words that are one-syllable and end with one vowel followed by one consonant. Look at these one-syllable words and notice how each word ends in one vowel followed by one consonant. We can add an *s* to these words without any problem. But if we want to add a vowel suffix like *ed* , *er*, or *ing*, we have to double the final consonant before we add the ending. This is called the 1+1+1 rule because it has 1 syllable, 1 vowel, and 1 consonant at the end.

| | | | |
|---|---|---|---|
| run | strap | fat | hum |
| runⓢ | strapⓢ | fatⓢ | humⓢ |
| runⓝer | strapⓟing | fatⓣer | humⓜed |

does
ᵘ 2

## Who does the cooking?
- How many syllables does this word have? Dictate the word.
- Underline the multi-letter phonogram(s).
- This word has an exception. The *oe* is not making its regular sound. Instead, it sounds like /ŭ/, so put a small *u* over it to remind you what sound it is making.
- Which of its sounds is *s* saying? It's saying its second sound, so put a small 2 above it.
- This word is a *homograph*. *Homograph* means *same writing*, and this word has two meanings. It can be a verb, like he *does* his chores. But it can also be a noun, the plural of *doe*, a female deer. They sound different, but they are spelled the same.
- Read the word. Now you read the word.

bir die

## What does little birdie say?
- How many syllables does this word have? Dictate the first syllable.
- Leave a small space between syllables. Dictate the other syllable(s).
- Underline the multi-letter phonogram(s).
- Read the word. Now you read the word.

**long ☩er**

## That book is long.

- How many syllables does this word have? Dictate the word until you get to the suffix.
- Underline the multi-letter phonogram(s).
- Read the word. Now you read the word.
- ☩ Can we add the ending **er** as a suffix to change this word? We can! Listen: This book is *longer.* Let's add **er** to this word as a new syllable.
- The 1+1+1 rule does not apply because this word is one syllable, and it has one vowel, but it ends in two consonants! We add the suffix as usual.
- Leave a small space between syllables. Dictate the next syllable—**er**. Underline **er.**
- Now read the word again.

**strong er**

## They exercise to get stronger.

- How many syllables does this word have? Dictate the first syllable.
- Leave a small space between syllables. Dictate the other syllable(s).
- Underline the multi-letter phonogram(s).
- This word rhymes with *longer.*
- Read the word. Now you read the word. Blend /s/, /t/, and /r/ together when you read it, like this—/str/.

**till**

## Little birdie rests till its wings are stronger.

- How many syllables does this word have? Dictate the word.
- Underline the multi-letter phonogram(s).
- We often double *l* after a single vowel at the end of a base word.
- This word has a **synonym**, a word that means the same thing—*until.* Poets like *till* because it only has one syllable. Remember, poets are weird.
- This word is a **homograph. Homograph** means **same writing**, and this word has two meanings. It can also be a verb, like they *till* the garden. They are spelled the same and even sound the same, but they have different meanings.
- Read the word. Now you read the word.

**rest ☩s**

## Get plenty of rest when you're sick.

- How many syllables does this word have? Dictate the word until you get to the suffix.
- Read the word. Now you read the word. Blend /s/ and /t/ together when you read it, like this—/st/.
- ☩ Can we add the ending **s** as a suffix to change this word? We can! Listen: I *rest.* He *rests.* Let's add **s** to this word.
- Add **s** and read the word again.

**limb☩s**²

## A limb is one of your arms or legs.

- How many syllables does this word have? Dictate the word until you get to the suffix.
- Underline the multi-letter phonogram(s).
- This word is a **homograph. Homograph** means **same writing**, and this word has two meanings. It can mean your arms and legs, but it can also mean a tree *limb.* They are spelled the same and even sound the same, but they have different meanings.
- Read the word. Now you read the word.
- ☩ Now let's make it plural! Does *limb* end in a hiss? No, it doesn't! So we will make it plural in the regular way.
- Add **s** and read the word again. Put a small 2 above the **s** to show that it's saying its second sound.

fl✛i<u>e</u>s

# When little birdie is stronger, it <u>flies</u>.
- How many syllables does this word have? Dictate the word until you get to the suffix.
- ⬡ STOP. We're going to add a suffix. The base word ends in the vowel *y*, so we change the *y* to *i* before adding a suffix. To add this suffix, we change the *y* to *i* and add *e-s*. Listen: Many birds *fly*. One bird *flies*.
- Dictate the other phonograms—*i-e-s*.
- *I* says its name because of the silent *e*; underline the silent *e* twice, and draw a bridge between the silent *e* and the *i*.
- Which of its sounds is *s* saying? It's saying its second sound, so put a small 2 above it.
- This word is a *homograph*. *Homograph* means *same writing*, and this word has two meanings. It can be a verb, like the bird *flies*. But it can also be a noun, the small bugs called *flies*. They are spelled the same and even sound the same, but they have different meanings.
- Read the word. Now you read the word. Blend /f/ and /l/ together when you read it, like this—/fl/.

ris<u>e</u>

# <u>Rise</u> and shine, sunshine.
- How many syllables does this word have? Dictate the word.
- *I* says its name because of the silent *e*; underline the silent *e* twice, and draw a bridge between the silent *e* and the *i*.
- Which of its sounds is *s* saying? It's saying its second sound, so put a small 2 above it.
- Read the word. Now you read the word.

ris ✛ing

# The sun is <u>rising</u>.
- How many syllables does this word have? Dictate the word until you get to the suffix.
- ⬡ STOP. We're going to add a suffix. The base word ends in silent *e*, so we drop the silent *e* before adding a vowel suffix.
- Leave a small space between syllables. Dictate the other syllable(s).
- Underline the multi-letter phonogram(s).
- *I* says its name because of the silent *e* that we dropped when we added the vowel suffix. Draw a tiny bridge over the *i* as a reminder.
- Which of its sounds is *s* saying? It's saying its second sound, so put a small 2 above it.
- Read the word. Now you read the word.

# 58   Plurals: Irregular Nouns

Nouns are naming words. Nouns name people, places, things, and ideas. If something has a name, that name is a noun. Dog, cat, brother, sister, store, and toy are all nouns. We also have names for ideas, like freedom.

*Singular* means one, like *single*. *Plural* means more than one.

We can make most nouns plural just by adding **s** or **es** to the end of the word, like this:

## cat        cats        fox        fox-es

Some other words are *irregular*. That means that they do not follow the regular way of making plurals. Today, you will learn a word that has an irregular plural.

## wo-man        wo-men

Your mother is one **woman** (singular), but many **women** (plural) were at the park with their children.

tr⊕ied

## The hen tried to get an acorn, but she needed help.
• How many syllables does this word have? Dictate the word until you get to the suffix.
O STOP. We're going to add a suffix. The base word ends in the vowel **y**, so we change the **y** to **i** before adding a suffix. Today, I *try*. Yesterday, I *tried*.
• Dictate the other phonogram(s).
• Underline the multi-letter phonogram(s).
• Which of its sounds is **i** saying? It's saying its second sound, so put a small 2 above it.
• Which of its sounds is **ed** saying? It's saying its second sound, so put a small 2 above it.
• Read the word. Now you read the word.

tie

## Can you tie your shoes?
• How many syllables does this word have? Dictate the word.
• **I** says its name because of the silent **e**; underline the silent **e** twice, and draw a bridge between the silent **e** and the **i**.
• Read the word. Now you read the word.

wo man

## That woman has five children.
• How many syllables does this word have? Dictate the first syllable.
• Leave a small space between syllables. Dictate the other syllable(s).
• This word has a lazy vowel. When we say it, we usually say /wə-man/. We think to spell /wō-man/.
• Underline /ō/ because **o** says its name at the end of a syllable.
• Read the word. Now you read the word.

wo men

## The women talked while the children played.
• This is an irregular noun. Listen: One **woman**, two **women**.
• How many syllables does this word have? Dictate the first syllable.
• Leave a small space between syllables. Dictate the other syllable(s).
• This word has a lazy vowel. When we say it, we usually say /wə-men/. We think to spell /wō-men/.
• Underline /ō/ because **o** says its name at the end of a syllable.
• Read the word. Now you read the word.

cl**o**<u>th</u>

### She bought <u>cloth</u> to make a dress.
- How many syllables does this word have? Dictate the word.
- Underline the multi-letter phonogram(s).
- Read the word. Now you read the word. Blend /c/ and /l/ together when you read it, like this—/cl/.

<u>a</u> c<u>or</u>n

### The tiny <u>acorn</u> grew into a mighty oak tree.
- How many syllables does this word have? Dictate the first syllable.
- Leave a small space between syllables. Dictate the other syllable(s).
- Underline /ā/ because **a** says its name at the end of a syllable.
- Underline the multi-letter phonogram(s).
- Read the word. Now you read the word. Blend /or/ and /n/ together when you read it, like this—/orn/.

<u>oa</u>k

### The <u>oak</u> tree provided acorns for the squirrel.
- How many syllables does this word have? Dictate the word.
- Underline the multi-letter phonogram(s).
- Read the word. Now you read the word.

w<u>oo</u>d ✚en

### They collected <u>wood</u> for a fire.
- How many syllables does this word have? Dictate the word until you get to the suffix.
- Underline the multi-letter phonogram(s).
- Which of its sounds is **oo** saying? It's saying its second sound, so put a small 2 above it.
- Read the word. Now you read the word.
- ✚ Can we add our **en** suffix to change this word? We can! Listen: The girl sat on the **wooden** bench. Let's add **en** to this word as a new syllable.
- The 1+1+1 rule does not apply because this word is one syllable, and it ends in one consonant, but it has two vowels! We add the suffix as usual.
- Leave a small space between syllables. Dictate the next syllable—**en**.
- Now read the word again.

f<u>or</u> est✚s

### I live in a <u>forest</u>.
- How many syllables does this word have? Dictate the first syllable.
- Leave a small space between syllables. Dictate the word until you get to the suffix.
- Underline the multi-letter phonogram(s).
- Read the word. Now you read the word. Blend /s/ and /t/ together when you read it, like this—/st/.
- ✚ Now let's make it plural! Does **forest** end in a hiss? If necessary, point out that the final sound is actually the /t/ sound, not the /s/ sound. No, it doesn't! So we will make it plural in the regular way.
- Add **s** and read the word again.

jun gl<u>e</u>₄

### I used to live in a <u>jungle</u>.
- How many syllables does this word have? Dictate the first syllable.
- Leave a small space between syllables. Dictate the other syllable(s).
- Every syllable must have a written vowel; double underline the silent **e**. Put a small 4 next to the silent **e** to show that it is a type 4.
- Read the word. Now you read the word. Blend /g/ and /l/ together when you read it, like this—/gl/.

Let's review the different ways we use silent *e*. We have five different types of silent *e* words. Today, you will have a type 4 silent *e* in your spelling list.

Type 1 silent *e* makes a vowel say its name, like the words *hide* and *safe*.

hide           safe

Type 2 silent *e* is there because English words do not end in *v* or *u*. So if a word would otherwise end in *v* or *u*, it will have a silent *e* on the end, like the words *give* and *blue*.

giv e₂          blu e₂

Type 3 silent *e* is there to make *g* say /j/ or *c* say /s/, like the words *bulge* and *voice*.

bulg e₃          voi c e₃

Type 4 silent *e* is there because every syllable must have a written vowel, like the words *little* and *apple*. Without the silent *e*, the second syllable would not have a vowel.

lit-tle₄          ap-ple₄

And type 5 silent *e* is our *miscellaneous* type. This means that there can be other reasons for a silent *e*, reasons that are not as common, like the words *were* and *please*. Type 5 silent *e* can prevent a word that would otherwise end in *s* from looking plural. Other times, it is there to make a word look bigger or to make homophones look different! And sometimes, it makes *th* say its second sound, /TH/.

wer e₅          please₅          or e₅          brea the e₅

pine

The forest was full of young pine trees.
- How many syllables does this word have? Dictate the word.
- *I* says its name because of the silent *e*; underline the silent *e* twice, and draw a bridge between the silent *e* and the *i*.
- Read the word. Now you read the word.

 nee dle₄ ✚s

She found a pine needle on the ground.
- How many syllables does this word have? Dictate the first syllable.
- Leave a small space between syllables. Dictate the word until you get to the suffix.
- Underline the multi-letter phonogram(s).
- Every syllable must have a written vowel; double underline the silent *e*. Put a small 4 next to the silent *e* to show that it is a type 4.
- Read the word. Now you read the word. Blend /d/ and /l/ together when you read it, like this—/dl/.
- ✚ Now let's make it plural! Does *needle* end in a hiss? No, it doesn't! So we will make it plural in the regular way.
- Add *s* and read the word again. Put a small 2 above the *s* to show that it's saying its second sound.

glass ✚es

## The cookies are in the glass jar.
- How many syllables does this word have? Dictate the word until you get to the suffix.
- We often double *s* after a single vowel at the end of a base word.
- Read the word. Now you read the word. Blend /g/ and /l/ together when you read it, like this—/gl/.
- ✚ Now let's make it plural! Does **glass** end in a hiss? Yes, it does! To make it plural, we will add **e-s** as a new syllable.
- Leave a small space between syllables. Dictate the next syllable—**es**.
- Now read the word again.

broke

## The glass broke when it was dropped.
- This is an irregular verb. Listen: Today, I **break** things. Yesterday, I **broke** things.
- How many syllables does this word have? Dictate the word.
- **O** says its name because of the silent **e**; underline the silent **e** twice, and draw a bridge between the silent **e** and the **o**.
- Read the word. Now you read the word. Blend /b/ and /r/ together when you read it, like this—/br/.

brok ✚en

## The broken glass has sharp edges.
- How many syllables does this word have? Dictate the word until you get to the suffix.
- ◯ STOP. We're going to add the vowel suffix **en**. The base word ends in silent **e**, so we drop the silent **e** before adding a vowel suffix.
- Leave a small space between syllables. Dictate the next syllable—**en**.
- **O** says its name because of the silent **e** that we dropped when we added the vowel suffix. Draw a tiny bridge over the **o** as a reminder.
- Read the word. Now you read the word. Blend /b/ and /r/ together when you read it, like this—/br/.

s i gn

## The sign said not to walk on the grass.
- How many syllables does this word have? Dictate the word.
- Underline the multi-letter phonogram(s).
- Underline /ī/ because *i* says its name when followed by two consonants. This is a spelling rule.
- This two letter /n/ can be used at either the beginning or the end of a word.
- Read the word. Now you read the word.

**Spelling rule:** *I* may say its name when followed by two consonants.

gnome

## The garden gnome wore a red hat.
- How many syllables does this word have? Dictate the word.
- Underline the multi-letter phonogram(s).
- **O** says its name because of the silent **e**; underline the silent **e** twice, and draw a bridge between the silent **e** and the **o**.
- This two letter /n/ can be used at either the beginning or the end of a word.
- Read the word. Now you read the word.

*Reading & Spelling Through Literature Book 1*

**drought**[4]

A <u>drought</u> is a long period of time with no rain.
- How many syllables does this word have? Dictate the word.
- Underline the multi-letter phonogram(s).
- Which of its sounds is **ough** saying? It's saying its fourth sound, so put a small 4 above it.
- Read the word. Now you read the word. Blend /d/ and /r/ together when you read it, like this—/dr/.

**cough** ✚**ing**[6]

He's still sick, but his <u>cough</u> is better.
- How many syllables does this word have? Dictate the word until you get to the suffix.
- Underline the multi-letter phonogram(s).
- Which of its sounds is **ough** saying? It's saying its sixth sound, so put a small 6 above it.
- Read the word. Now you read the word.
- ✚ Can we add our **ing** suffix to change this word? We can! Listen: The boy is **coughing**. Let's add **ing** to this word as a new syllable.
- The 1+1+1 rule does not apply because this word is one syllable, but it has two vowels and ends in two consonants! We add the suffix as usual.
- Leave a small space between syllables. Dictate the next syllable—**ing**. Underline **ng**.
- Now read the word again.

**ph<u>o</u> t<u>o</u>**

He took a <u>photo</u> of the garden gnome.
- How many syllables does this word have? Dictate the first syllable.
- Leave a small space between syllables. Dictate the other syllable(s).
- Underline the multi-letter phonogram(s).
- Both of the letters **o** say their names at the end of a syllable in this word! For each **o**: Underline /ō/ because **o** says its name at the end of a syllable.
- Read the word. Now you read the word.

Today, you have a word in the spelling list that makes its plural in a different way. First, listen to these two phrases: one *calf*, two *calves*. Did you hear the difference in the sounds at the end of the words?

The phonograms *f* and *v* make very similar sounds, but *f* is soft while *v* is hard. Sometimes, when a word ends in *f*, the sound changes from /f/ to /v/, and the spelling changes, too. We change the *f* to *v* and add *e-s* to make words like *calf* and *loaf* plural.

We're going to add a NEW suffix to two words today. Remember that nouns are naming words and verbs are what we do. We can add the suffix *tion* to some verbs to make them nouns! Listen: The man will *act*. He will take *action*. Your new phonogram *ti* is used for this suffix.

learn ✚ing

## Did you <u>learn</u> the new phonogram?

- How many syllables does this word have? Dictate the word until you get to the suffix.
- Underline the multi-letter phonogram(s).
- Read the word. Now you read the word. Blend /ear/ and /n/ together when you read it, like this—/earn/.

✚ Can we add our *ing* suffix to change this word? We can! Listen: You are *learning* all the phonograms. Let's add *ing* to this word as a new syllable.

- The 1+1+1 rule does not apply because this word is one syllable, but it has two vowels and ends in two consonants! We add the suffix as usual.
- Leave a small space between syllables. Dictate the next syllable—*ing*. Underline *ng*.
- Now read the word again.

gos² ling

## A <u>gosling</u> is a baby goose.

- How many syllables does this word have? Dictate the first syllable.
- Leave a small space between syllables. Dictate the other syllable(s).
- Underline the multi-letter phonogram(s).
- *S* is saying its second sound, so put a small 2 above it.
- Read the word. Now you read the word.

duck ling

## And a <u>duckling</u> is a baby duck.

- How many syllables does this word have? Dictate the first syllable.
- Leave a small space between syllables. Dictate the other syllable(s).
- Underline the multi-letter phonogram(s).
- The phonogram *ck* is used only after a single vowel that says its short sound.
- Read the word. Now you read the word.

colt

## The <u>colt</u> followed his mother around the pasture.

- How many syllables does this word have? Dictate the word.
- Underline /ō/ because *o* says its name when followed by two consonants.
- Read the word. Now you read the word. Blend /l/ and /t/ together when you read it, like this—/lt/.

calf

## The newborn <u>calf</u> wobbled as it stood for the first time.

- How many syllables does this word have? Dictate the word.
- Double underline the silent *l*.
- Read the word. Now you read the word.

ca<u>l</u>✚ve<u>s</u><sup>2</sup><sub>5</sub>

## There are many <u>calves</u> in the pasture during the summer.

- How many syllables does this word have? Dictate the word until you get to the suffix.
- ⭕ STOP. The base word ends in *f*, so we change the *f* to *v* and add *e-s* to make this word plural.
- Dictate the next phonograms—*v-e-s*.
- Double underline the silent *l*.
- Double underline the silent *e*. Put a small 5 next to the silent *e* to show that it is a type 5—the miscellaneous silent *e*.
- Which of its sounds is *s* saying? It's saying its second sound, so put a small 2 above it.
- Read the word. Now you read the word.

<u>peep</u>✚<u>ed</u><sup>3</sup>

## The boy wants to <u>peep</u> into the box.

- How many syllables does this word have? Dictate the word until you get to the suffix.
- Underline the multi-letter phonogram(s).
- Read the word. Now you read the word.
- ✚ Can we add our *ed* suffix to change this word? We can! Listen: Today, I **peep**. Yesterday, I **peeped**. Let's add *ed* to this word as a suffix.
- The 1+1+1 rule does not apply because this word is one syllable, and it ends in one consonant, but it has two vowels! We add the suffix as usual.
- *Ed* does not form a new syllable in this word, so we just add it to the word without leaving a space. Dictate the next phonogram—*ed*. Underline *ed*.
- Which of its sounds is *ed* saying? It's saying its third sound, so put a small 3 above it.
- Now read the word again.

<sup>2</sup>  <sup>3</sup>
<u>leaped</u>

## They <u>leaped</u> for joy when they hear the news.

- This word is usually pronounced /lĕpt/, but in your story, it's pronounced /lēpt/ to rhyme with **peeped**. These stories are old, and pronunciation can change over time.
- How many syllables does this word have? Dictate the word.
- Underline the multi-letter phonogram(s).
- Which of its sounds is *ea* saying? It's saying its second sound, so put a small 2 above it.
- Which of its sounds is *ed* saying? It's saying its third sound, so put a small 3 above it.
- Read the word. Now you read the word.

ac <u>t</u>ion

## The director called, "<u>Action</u>," when they were ready to begin.

- How many syllables does this word have? Dictate the first syllable.
- Leave a small space between syllables. Dictate the other syllable(s).
- Underline the multi-letter phonogram(s).
- This word has a lazy vowel. When we say it, we usually say /ak-shən/. We think to spell /ak-shŏn/.
- Read the word. Now you read the word.

m<u>o</u> <u>t</u>ion

## The <u>motion</u> of the car made them carsick.

- How many syllables does this word have? Dictate the first syllable.
- Leave a small space between syllables. Dictate the other syllable(s).
- Underline the multi-letter phonogram(s).
- Underline /ō/ because *o* says its name at the end of a syllable.
- This word has a lazy vowel. When we say it, we usually say /mō-shən/. We think to spell /mō-shŏn/.
- Read the word. Now you read the word.

# Vowels at the End of a Syllable

The vowels *a, e, o, u* usually say their names at the end of a syllable.

## a-c<u>o</u>rn   b<u>e</u>-l<u>ow</u>   tr<u>o</u>-phy   bl<u>u</u> <u>e</u>

Because this is a spelling rule, we don't put a 2 above the vowel to show that it's making its second sound! Instead, we underline the vowel to show that its following a spelling rule.

**st<u>ay</u> ✚ing**

She will <u>stay</u> at home.
- How many syllables does this word have? Dictate the word until you get to the suffix.
- Underline the multi-letter phonogram(s).
- Read the word. Now you read the word. Blend /s/ and /t/ together when you read it, like this—/st/.
- ✚ Can we add our *ing* suffix to change this word? We can! Listen: I am *staying*. Let's add *ing* to this word as a new syllable.
- The 1+1+1 rule does not apply to this word because we do not double *x, w,* or *y* before adding a suffix. This is a spelling rule. We add the suffix as usual.
- Leave a small space between syllables. Dictate the next syllable—*ing*. Underline *ng*.
- Now read the word again.

**Spelling Rule:** Do not double *x, w,* or *y* before adding a suffix.

**m<u>u</u>l<u>e</u>**

The <u>mule</u> was in the barn with the horses.
- How many syllables does this word have? Dictate the word.
- *U* says its name because of the silent *e*; underline the silent *e* twice, and draw a bridge between the silent *e* and the *u*.
- Read the word. Now you read the word.

**w<u>or</u>ld ✚l<u>y</u>**

She wants to travel the <u>world</u>.
- How many syllables does this word have? Dictate the word until you get to the suffix.
- Underline the multi-letter phonogram(s).
- Read the word. Now you read the word. Blend /l/ and /d/ together when you read it, like this—/ld/.
- ✚ Can we add the ending *ly* as a suffix to change this word? We can! Listen: They focus on *worldly* things instead of spiritual things. Let's add *ly* to this word as a new syllable.
- Leave a small space between syllables. Dictate the next syllable—*ly*.
- Underline *y* because *y* says /ē/ at the end of a multi-syllable word.
- Now read the word again.

**pul ✚l<u>ing</u>**

He was <u>pulling</u> the rope to ring the bell.
- How many syllables does this word have? Dictate the word until you get to the suffix.
- ⭕ STOP. We're going to add a suffix. We often double *l* after a single vowel at the end of a base word. This is a spelling rule. When the suffix forms a new syllable, we divide the syllables between the double consonants.
- Leave a small space between syllables. Dictate the next syllable—*ling*. Underline *ng*.
- Read the word. Now you read the word.

<u>o</u> pen

He was excited to <u>open</u> the box.
- How many syllables does this word have? Dictate the first syllable.
- Leave a small space between syllables. Dictate the other syllable(s).
- Underline /ō/ because **o** says its name at the end of a syllable.
- Read the word. Now you read the word.

frigh ten

Did the story <u>frighten</u> you?
- How many syllables does this word have? Dictate the first syllable.
- Leave a small space between syllables. Dictate the other syllable(s).
- Underline the multi-letter phonogram(s).
- Read the word. Now you read the word. Blend /f/ and /r/ together when you read it, like this—/fr/.

sh <u>out</u> ✚<u>ed</u>

He will <u>shout</u> to get everyone's attention.
- How many syllables does this word have? Dictate the word until you get to the suffix.
- Underline the multi-letter phonogram(s).
- Which of its sounds is **ou** saying? It's saying its first sound, so we don't need to mark it! We only mark phonograms when they're saying a sound other than their first.
- Read the word. Now you read the word.
- ✚ Can we add our **ed** suffix to change this word? We can! Listen: Today, I **shout**. Yesterday, I **shouted**. Let's add **ed** to this word as a new syllable.
- The 1+1+1 rule does not apply because this word is one syllable, and it ends in one consonant, but it has two vowels! We add the suffix as usual.
- Phonogram **ed** forms a new syllable when the base word ends in /d/ or /t/.
- Leave a small space between syllables. Dictate the next syllable—**ed**. Underline **ed**.
- Now read the word again.

gat<u>e</u>

Close the <u>gate</u> behind you.
- How many syllables does this word have? Dictate the word.
- **A** says its name because of the silent **e**; underline the silent **e** twice, and draw a bridge between the silent **e** and the **a**.
- Read the word. Now you read the word.

<u>kni</u>f<u>e</u>

He used his pocket <u>knife</u> to open the package.
- How many syllables does this word have? Dictate the word.
- Underline the multi-letter phonogram(s).
- **I** says its name because of the silent **e**; underline the silent **e** twice, and draw a bridge between the silent **e** and the **i**.
- Read the word. Now you read the word.

<u>kni</u>✚v<u>e</u>s²

Mother has many sharp <u>knives</u> in the kitchen.
- How many syllables does this word have? Dictate the word until you get to the suffix.
- ⬤ STOP. The base word ends in **f**, so we change the **f** to **v** and add **e-s** to make this word plural.
- Dictate the next phonograms—**v-e-s**.
- Underline the multi-letter phonogram(s).
- **I** says its name because of the silent **e**; underline the silent **e** twice, and draw a bridge between the silent **e** and the **i**.
- Which of its sounds is **s** saying? It's saying its second sound, so put a small 2 above it.
- Read the word. Now you read the word.

## 62 New: ui; Compound Words

Some words are ***compound words***, which means that we put two words together to make one new word. Some words, like ***into***, make sense when we consider the original two words. We're going ***to*** the house, and we're going ***in***, so we're going ***into*** the house.

Other compound words make no sense at all! A ***butterfly*** is neither ***butter*** nor a ***fly***. But when the two words are put together, we have a brand new word that means something different than the words mean on their own.

**cam el** — The <u>camel</u> poked its nose into the tent.
- How many syllables does this word have? Dictate the first syllable.
- Leave a small space between syllables. Dictate the other syllable(s).
- This word has a lazy vowel. When we say it, we usually say /căm-əl/. We think to spell /căm-ĕl/.
- Read the word. Now you read the word.

**sn<u>ou</u>t** — The pig rooted in the dirt with its <u>snout</u>.
- How many syllables does this word have? Dictate the word.
- Underline the multi-letter phonogram(s).
- Which of its sounds is ***ou*** saying? It's saying its first sound, so we don't need to mark it! We only mark phonograms when they're saying a sound other than their first.
- Read the word. Now you read the word. Blend /s/ and /n/ together when you read it, like this—/sn/.

**fr<u>ui</u>t** — Which <u>fruit</u> do you like best?
- How many syllables does this word have? Dictate the word.
- Underline the multi-letter phonogram(s).
- Read the word. Now you read the word. Blend /f/ and /r/ together when you read it, like this—/fr/.

**s<u>ui</u>t** — He got a new <u>suit</u> for the party.
- How many syllables does this word have? Dictate the word.
- Underline the multi-letter phonogram(s).
- This word rhymes with ***fruit***.
- Read the word. Now you read the word.

**in side** — Because it's hot today, we're working <u>inside</u>.
- How many syllables does this word have? Dictate the first syllable.
- Leave a small space between syllables. Dictate the other syllable(s).
- ***I*** says its name because of the silent ***e***; underline the silent ***e*** twice, and draw a bridge between the silent ***e*** and the ***i***.
- This is a ***compound word***. That means that it's two words put together to become one word.
- Read the word. Now you read the word.

rat͟h er²

I would rather stay home today.
- How many syllables does this word have? Dictate the first syllable.
- Leave a small space between syllables. Dictate the other syllable(s).
- Underline the multi-letter phonogram(s).
- Which of its sounds is *th* saying? It's saying its second sound, so put a small 2 above it.
- Read the word. Now you read the word.

o͟r

You can have an apple or a banana, but not both.
- How many syllables does this word have? Dictate the word.
- Underline the multi-letter phonogram(s).
- Read the word. Now you read the word.

hump✚s

Some camels have one hump while others have two.
- How many syllables does this word have? Dictate the word until you get to the suffix.
- Read the word. Now you read the word. Blend /m/ and /p/ together when you read it, like this—/mp/.
✚ Now let's make it plural! Add /s/, /z/ and read the word again.

wall³

Humpty Dumpty briefly sat on a wall.
- How many syllables does this word have? Dictate the word.
- Which of its sounds is *a* saying? It's saying its third sound, so put a small 3 above it.
- We often double *l* after a single vowel at the end of a base word.
- Read the word. Now you read the word.

small³

Small acts of kindness make a big difference.
- How many syllables does this word have? Dictate the word.
- Which of its sounds is *a* saying? It's saying its third sound, so put a small 3 above it.
- We often double *l* after a single vowel at the end of a base word.
- This word rhymes with *wall*.
- Read the word. Now you read the word. Blend /s/ and /m/ together when you read it, like this—/sm/.

**Homonyms** are words that sound the same or are spelled the same, but they mean different things. We've talked about two different kinds of homonyms, **homophones** and **homographs**.

In Latin, the word **homo** means **same**, and the word **phone** means **sound**, so a homophone means **same sound**. Homophones sound alike, but they are spelled differently and have different meanings, like **blew** and **blue**. Homophones always sound the same, but they're spelled differently. When they're spelled the same, they're called **homographs**.

## The wind <u>blew</u> the clouds across the <u>blue</u> sky.

The Latin word **graph** means **writing** or **picture**, so homographs are words that have the **same writing**—they are spelled the same. Sometimes, they sound the same, too, but not always! Homographs are always spelled the same.

## <u>Does</u> he see the <u>does</u> with their fawns?

## The <u>crow</u> will be startled if the rooster begins to <u>crow</u>.

cr<u>ow</u>²

### The rooster will <u>crow</u> every morning.
- How many syllables does this word have? Dictate the word.
- Underline the multi-letter phonogram(s).
- Which of its sounds is **ow** saying? It's saying its second sound, so put a small 2 above it.
- This word is a **homograph**. **Homograph** means **same writing**, and this word has two meanings. It can be a verb, like the rooster will **crow**. But it can also be a noun, like the black bird called a **crow**. They are spelled the same and even sound the same, but they have different meanings.
- Read the word. Now you read the word. Blend /c/ and /r/ together when you read it, like this—/cr/.

<u>ear</u> l<u>y</u>

### We try to arrive <u>early</u> instead of late.
- How many syllables does this word have? Dictate the first syllable.
- Leave a small space between syllables. Dictate the other syllable(s).
- Underline the multi-letter phonogram(s).
- Underline **y** because **y** says /ē/ at the end of a multi-syllable word.
- Read the word. Now you read the word.

an gr<u>y</u>

### The man was <u>angry</u> when the rooster woke him.
- How many syllables does this word have? Dictate the first syllable.
- Leave a small space between syllables. Dictate the other syllable(s).
- Underline **y** because **y** says /ē/ at the end of a multi-syllable word.
- Read the word. Now you read the word. Blend /g/ and /r/ together when you read it, like this—/gr/.

hai̱r bru̱s̲h̲ ✚es    Oh, where is my hai̱rbru̱s̲h̲?
- How many syllables does this word have? Dictate the first syllable.
- Leave a small space between syllables. Dictate the word until you get to the suffix.
- Underline the multi-letter phonogram(s).
- This is a **compound word**. That means that it's two words put together to become one word.
- Read the word. Now you read the word. Blend /b/ and /r/ together when you read it, like this—/br/.

✚ Now let's make it plural! Does **hairbrush** end in a hiss? Yes, it does! To make it plural, we will add **e-s** as a new syllable.
- Leave a small space between syllables. Dictate the next syllable—**es**.
- Now read the word again.

co̱m̲b̲    We have both a co̱m̲b̲ and a brush.
- How many syllables does this word have? Dictate the word.
- Underline the multi-letter phonogram(s).
- Underline /ō/ because **o** says its name when followed by two consonants.
- Read the word. Now you read the word.

we̱e̲d ✚ing    The we̱e̲d grew happily in the garden, unnoticed by the gardener.
- How many syllables does this word have? Dictate the word until you get to the suffix.
- Underline the multi-letter phonogram(s).
- Read the word. Now you read the word.

✚ Can we add our **ing** suffix to change this word? We can! Listen: The gardener was **weeding** the garden. Let's add **ing** to this word as a new syllable.
- The 1+1+1 rule does not apply because this word is one syllable, and it ends in one consonant, but it has two vowels! We add the suffix as usual.
- Leave a small space between syllables. Dictate the next syllable—**ing**. Underline **ng**.
- Now read the word again.

ju̱i̲ c̲e̲₃    She made fresh-squeezed orange ju̱i̲c̲e̲.
- How many syllables does this word have? Dictate the word.
- Underline the multi-letter phonogram(s).
- **C** says /s/ because of the silent **e**; underline the **c**, and double underline the silent **e**. Put a small 3 next to the silent **e** to show that it is a type 3.
- Read the word. Now you read the word.

ju̱i̲ ✚c̲y̲    The oranges were very ju̱i̲c̲y̲.
- How many syllables does this word have? Dictate the word until you get to the suffix.

◯ STOP. We're going to add a suffix. The base word ends in silent **e**, so we drop the silent **e** before adding a vowel suffix.
- Leave a small space between syllables. Dictate the other syllable(s).
- Underline the multi-letter phonogram(s).
- Underline **c** because **c** says /s/ before **e**, **i**, and **y**. This is a spelling rule.
- Underline **y** because **y** says /ē/ at the end of a multi-syllable word.
- Read the word. Now you read the word.

**Spelling Rule:** *C* says /s/ before e, i, and y. Otherwise, *c* says /k/.

lo̲ t̲ion

## She put lo̲t̲ion on her arms.

- How many syllables does this word have? Dictate the first syllable.
- Leave a small space between syllables. Dictate the other syllable(s).
- Underline the multi-letter phonogram(s).
- Underline /ō/ because *o* says its name at the end of a syllable.
- Read the word. Now you read the word.

na̲ t̲ion

## Our na̲t̲ion is the United States of America.

- How many syllables does this word have? Dictate the first syllable.
- Leave a small space between syllables. Dictate the other syllable(s).
- Underline the multi-letter phonogram(s).
- Underline /ā/ because *a* says its name at the end of a syllable.
- Read the word. Now you read the word.

Reading & Spelling Through Literature Book 1

# 64

Remember that a base word is just a word without endings added to it. We call those endings *suffixes*. We can add *–s* or *–es* to make words plural—more than one

one *boy*, two *boys*          one *fox*, two *foxes*

We can add *ed* to show that something happened in the past, and we can add *ing* to show that something is continuing to happen.

Yesterday, I *helped* mother. Today, I *help* mother. I am still *helping* mother now.

We can add the suffix *ly* to words to change their meanings in different ways. The new word describes how things are done. Listen to these examples:

The boy *sadly* told the story.          The doctor gave the girl a *fatherly* smile.

### work✚ed²

First we <u>work</u>, and then we play.
- How many syllables does this word have? Dictate the word until you get to the suffix.
- Underline the multi-letter phonogram(s).
- Read the word. Now you read the word.
- ✚ Can we add our *ed* suffix to change this word? We can! Listen: Today, I *work*. Yesterday, I *worked*. Let's add *ed* to this word as a suffix.
- The 1+1+1 rule does not apply because this word is one syllable, and it has one vowel, but it ends in two consonants! We add the suffix as usual.
- *Ed* does not form a new syllable in this word, so we just add it to the word without leaving a space. Dictate the next phonogram—*ed*. Underline *ed*.
- Which of its sounds is *ed* saying? It's saying its second sound, so put a small 2 above it.
- Now read the word again.

### puff

The wolf will huff and <u>puff</u> and blow the house down.
- How many syllables does this word have? Dictate the word.
- We often double *f* after a single vowel at the end of a base word. This is a spelling rule.
- Read the word. Now you read the word.

**Spelling rule:** We often double *f* after a single vowel at the end of a base word.

### li ly

Little white <u>lily</u> sat by a stone, drooping and waiting till the sun shone.
(From "Little White Lily" by George MacDonald.)
- How many syllables does this word have? Dictate the first syllable.
- Leave a small space between syllables. Dictate the other syllable(s).
- Underline *y* because *y* says /ē/ at the end of a multi-syllable word.
- Read the word. Now you read the word.

### gone₅

The mother bird was <u>gone</u> from the nest when the egg hatched.
- How many syllables does this word have? Dictate the word.
- Double underline the silent *e*. Put a small 5 next to the silent *e* to show that it is a type 5—the miscellaneous silent *e*.
- Read the word. Now you read the word.

li l✚ies[2]

"Consider the lilies of the field, how they grow."
(From the Bible.)
- How many syllables does this word have? Dictate the first syllable.
- Leave a small space between syllables. Dictate the word until you get to the suffix.
- ⭕ STOP. We're going to add a suffix. The base word ends in the vowel *y*, so we change the *y* to *i* before adding a suffix. To make this word plural, we change the *y* to *i* and add *e-s*.
- Dictate the other phonogram(s)—*ie-s*.
- Underline the multi-letter phonogram(s). When we changed the *y* to *i* and added *e-s*, it formed the phonogram /ē/—2 letter /ē/.
- Which of its sounds is *s* saying? It's saying its second sound, so put a small 2 above it.
- Read the word. Now you read the word.

bud ✚ⓓing

The flower bud began to open.
- How many syllables does this word have? Dictate the word until you get to the suffix.
- Read the word. Now you read the word.
- ✚ Can we add our *ing* suffix to change this word? We can! Listen: The plants are *budding*. Let's add *ing* to this word as a new syllable.
- The 1+1+1 Rule: This word is one syllable, and it ends with one vowel following by one consonant, so we double the final consonant before adding the suffix.
- Leave a small space between syllables. Dictate the next syllable—*ding*. Underline *ng*.
- Circle the extra letter that we added before the suffix.
- Now read the word again.

rough[5] ✚ly

The bark of the tree felt rough.
- How many syllables does this word have? Dictate the word until you get to the suffix.
- Underline the multi-letter phonogram(s).
- Which of its sounds is *ough* saying? It's saying its fifth sound, so put a small 5 above it.
- Read the word. Now you read the word.
- ✚ Can we add the ending *ly* as a suffix to change this word? We can! Listen: Don't play so *roughly*. Let's add *ly* to this word as a new syllable.
- Leave a small space between syllables. Dictate the next syllable—*ly*.
- Underline *y* because *y* says /ē/ at the end of a multi-syllable word.
- Now read the word again.

stand

We stand to sing the national anthem.
- How many syllables does this word have? Dictate the word.
- Read the word. Now you read the word. Blend /s/ and /t/ together at the beginning when you read it, like this—/st/. Blend /n/ and /d/ together at the end of the word when you read it, like this—/nd/.

bur y
(ĕ)

The pirate will bury the treasure.
- How many syllables does this word have? Dictate the first syllable.
- Leave a small space between syllables. Dictate the other syllable(s).
- This word has an exception. The *u* is not making its regular sound. Instead, it sounds like /ĕ/, so put a small *e* over it to remind you what sound it is making.
- Read the word. Now you read the word.

*Reading & Spelling Through Literature Book 1*

bur $\overset{e}{\Box}$ied        They <u>buried</u> all the treasure.

- How many syllables does this word have? Dictate the word until you get to the suffix.
- ⬡ STOP. We're going to add a suffix *ed*. The base word ends in the vowel *y*, so we change the *y* to *i* before adding a suffix. We change the *y* to *i* and add *ed*.
- Leave a small space between syllables. Dictate the other syllable(s).
- When we changed the *y* to *i* and added *ed*, it formed the phonogram /ē/—2 letter /ē/. Let's underline *ie* to remind us of the sound it's making here.
- This word has an exception. The *u* is not making its regular sound. Instead, it sounds like /ĕ/, so put a small *e* over it to remind you what sound it is making.
- Read the word. Now you read the word.

# 65

# Review: Suffixes, 1+1+1 Rule

Let's review suffixes and the 1+1+1 rule. It's an important rule in spelling, so we'll keep talking about it until you understand it perfectly!

Verbs are what we do, like *spin*, *trip*, and *dim*. We can add suffixes to verbs to show different things about what we do. We can add *ed* to show that something happened in the past, and we can add *ing* to show that something is continuing to happen. We can even add *er* sometimes to turn a verb into a noun!

Today, I *farm*. Yesterday, I *farmed*. I am *farming*. I am a *farmer*.

We can also add suffixes to nouns. We add *s* or *e-s* to make plurals. And we can even add suffixes to describing words, like *big*!

My cat is *big*. My dog is *bigger*.

You've learned to spell many super short words that are one-syllable and end with one vowel followed by one consonant. Look at these one-syllable words and notice how each word ends in one vowel followed by one consonant. We can add an *s* to these words without any problem. But if we want to add a vowel suffix like *ed*, *er*, or *ing*, we have to double the final consonant before we add the ending. This is called the 1+1+1 rule because it has 1 syllable, 1 vowel, and 1 consonant at the end.

| spin | trip | big | dim |
| --- | --- | --- | --- |
| spins | trips | | dims |
| spinner | tripping | bigger | dimmed |

bil ly

The new story is about three <u>billy</u> goats.
- How many syllables does this word have? Dictate the first syllable.
- Leave a small space between syllables. Dictate the other syllable(s).
- Underline *y* because *y* says /ē/ at the end of a multi-syllable word.
- Read the word. Now you read the word.

troll

The grumpy <u>troll</u> lived under the bridge.
- How many syllables does this word have? Dictate the word.
- Underline /ō/ because *o* says its name when followed by two consonants.
- We often double *l* after a single vowel at the end of a base word.
- Read the word. Now you read the word. Blend /t/ and /r/ together when you read it, like this—/tr/.

gob ble

The troll wants to <u>gobble</u> the goats up.
- How many syllables does this word have? Dictate the first syllable.
- Leave a small space between syllables. Dictate the other syllable(s).
- Every syllable must have a written vowel; double underline the silent *e*. Put a small 4 next to the silent *e* to show that it is a type 4.
- Read the word. Now you read the word. Blend /b/ and /l/ together when you read it, like this—/bl/.

**gob bl✜ing**

## The troll would be gobbling up goats every day if he could!

- How many syllables does this word have? Dictate the first syllable.
- Leave a small space between syllables. Dictate the word until you get to the suffix.
- ⬭ STOP. We're going to add a suffix. The base word ends in silent **e**, so we drop the silent **e** before adding a vowel suffix.
- Dictate the other phonogram(s).
- Underline the multi-letter phonogram(s).
- Read the word. Now you read the word. Blend /b/ and /l/ together when you read it, like this—/bl/.

**trip ✜(p)ing**

## She will trip if she doesn't watch where she's going.

- How many syllables does this word have? Dictate the word until you get to the suffix.
- This word is a **homograph. Homograph** means **same writing**, and this word has two meanings. It can be a verb, like I **trip** over things. But it can also be a noun, when you take a **trip**, a journey. They are spelled the same and even sound the same, but they have different meanings.
- Read the word. Now you read the word. Blend /t/ and /r/ together when you read it, like this—/tr/.
- ✜ Can we add our **ing** suffix to change this word? We can! Listen: The girl is **tripping** over the toys on the floor. Let's add **ing** to this word as a new syllable.
- The 1+1+1 Rule: This word is one syllable, and it ends with one vowel followed by one consonant, so we double the final consonant before adding a vowel suffix.
- Leave a small space between syllables. Dictate the next syllable—**ping**. Underline **ng**.
- Circle the extra letter that we added before the suffix.
- Now read the word again.

**trap✜(p)ed³**

## It's a trap.

- **Trip-trap** appears in your story for this spelling list as an **onomatopoeia**, which is a word that we use to describe a sound. **Trip-trap** is the sound the Billy Goats Gruff make as they walk across the bridge.
- How many syllables does this word have? Dictate the word until you get to the suffix.
- Read the word. Now you read the word. Blend /t/ and /r/ together when you read it, like this—/tr/.
- ✜ Can we add our **ed** suffix to change this word? We can! Listen: Today, I **trap**. Yesterday, I **trapped**. Let's add **ed** to this word as a suffix.
- The 1+1+1 Rule: This word is one syllable, and it ends with one vowel followed by one consonant, so we double the final consonant before adding a vowel suffix.
- **Ed** does not form a new syllable in this word, so we just add it to the word without leaving a space. Dictate the next phonograms—**p-ed**.
- Underline the multi-letter phonogram(s).
- Which of its sounds is **ed** saying? It's saying its third sound, so put a small 3 above it.
- Circle the extra letter that we added before the suffix.
- Now read the word again.

trap ✚ⓟing

## The trip-trapping alerted the troll.
- How many syllables does this word have? Dictate the word until you get to the suffix.
- ✚ We're adding our *ing* suffix to this word.
- The 1+1+1 Rule: This word is one syllable, and it ends with one vowel followed by one consonant, so we double the final consonant before adding a vowel suffix.
- Leave a small space between syllables. Dictate the next syllable—*ping*. Underline *ng*.
- Circle the extra letter that we added before the suffix.
- Read the word. Now you read the word. Blend /t/ and /r/ together when you read it, like this—/tr/.

sec ond

## The second billy goat came next.
- How many syllables does this word have? Dictate the first syllable.
- Leave a small space between syllables. Dictate the other syllable(s).
- This word has a lazy vowel. When we say it, we usually say /sĕk-ənd/. We think to spell /sĕk-ŏnd/.
- Read the word. Now you read the word. Blend /n/ and /d/ together when you read it, like this—/nd/.

big ✚ⓖer

## The second billy goat was bigger than the first billy goat.
- How many syllables does this word have? Dictate the word until you get to the suffix.
- ✚ We're adding our *er* suffix to this word.
- The 1+1+1 Rule: This word is one syllable, and it ends with one vowel followed by one consonant, so we double the final consonant before adding a vowel suffix.
- Leave a small space between syllables. Dictate the next syllable—*ger*. Underline *er*.
- Circle the extra letter that we added before the suffix.
- Read the word. Now you read the word.

gruff

## The man was kind but gruff.
- How many syllables does this word have? Dictate the word.
- We often double *f* after a single vowel at the end of a base word.
- Read the word. Now you read the word. Blend /g/ and /r/ together when you read it, like this—/gr/.

*Reading & Spelling Through Literature Book 1*

# 66

# Review: Five Ways to Spell /er/

We have five different ways to spell the sound /er/, and we have two sentences that we can use to remember these ways.

## Oyst<u>er</u>s t<u>ur</u>n d<u>ir</u>t into p<u>ear</u>ls.

## M<u>er</u>maids t<u>ur</u>n and tw<u>ir</u>l with p<u>ear</u>ls.

Most of the time, we use the first way, /er/ as in **her**. This is the most common spelling of the sound. But today, you'll get to use one of the less common ways to spell /er/.

<u>see</u>d✚s²

## He planted a <u>seed</u> and watched it grow.

- How many syllables does this word have? *Dictate the word until you get to the suffix.*
- Underline the multi-letter phonogram(s).
- *Read the word. Now you read the word.*
- ✚ Now let's make it plural! Does **seed** end in a hiss? No, it doesn't! So we will make it plural in the regular way.
- Add **s** and read the word again. Put a small 2 above the **s** to show that it's saying its second sound.

<u>rai</u>n drop✚s

## She watched the <u>raindrop</u> slide down the window.

- How many syllables does this word have? *Dictate the first syllable.*
- Leave a small space between syllables. *Dictate the word until you get to the suffix.*
- Underline the multi-letter phonogram(s).
- This is a **compound word**. That means that it's two words put together to become one word.
- *Read the word. Now you read the word.* Blend /d/ and /r/ together when you read it, like this—/dr/.
- ✚ Now let's make it plural! Does **raindrop** end in a hiss? No, it doesn't! So we will make it plural in the regular way.
- Add **s** and read the word again.

m<u>igh</u>t ✚y

## We m<u>igh</u>t plant some sweet potatoes.

- How many syllables does this word have? *Dictate the word until you get to the suffix.*
- Underline the multi-letter phonogram(s).
- This word is a **homograph**. **Homograph** means **same writing**, and this word has two meanings. It can be a verb, like he **might** go to his friend's house. But it can also be a noun, like he ran with all his **might**. They are spelled the same and even sound the same, but they have different meanings.
- *Read the word. Now you read the word.*
- ✚ Can we add the ending **y** as a suffix to change this word? We can! Listen: The tiny acorn grew into a **mighty** oak. Let's add **y** to this word as a new syllable.
- Leave a small space between syllables. *Dictate the next syllable—y.*
- Underline **y** because **y** says /ē/ at the end of a multi-syllable word.
- Now read the word again.

he art

Your <u>heart</u> pumps blood throughout your body.
- How many syllables does this word have? Dictate the word.
- Double underline the silent **e**. This is not any of our normal types of silent **e** because those occur at the end of words. Some words just have silent letters.
- Underline the multi-letter phonogram(s).
- Read the word. Now you read the word.

ros<u>e</u>

The <u>rose</u> bush was in full bloom.
- How many syllables does this word have? Dictate the word.
- **O** says its name because of the silent **e**; underline the silent **e** twice, and draw a bridge between the silent **e** and the **o**.
- Which of its sounds is **s** saying? It's saying its second sound, so put a small 2 above it.
- This word is a **homograph**. **Homograph** means **same writing**, and this word has two meanings. It can be a verb, like she **rose** from the chair. But it can also be a noun, the flower called a **rose**. They are spelled the same and even sound the same, but they have different meanings.
- Read the word. Now you read the word.

<u>e</u> lev en

Ten, <u>eleven</u>, twelve
- How many syllables does this word have? Dictate the first syllable.
- Leave a small space between syllables. Dictate the other syllable(s).
- Underline /ē/ because **e** says its name at the end of a syllable.
- Read the word. Now you read the word.

twel<u>v</u><u>e</u>₂

Eleven, <u>twelve</u>, thirteen
- How many syllables does this word have? Dictate the word.
- English words do not end in **v**; underline the **v**, and double underline the silent **e**. Put a small 2 next to the silent **e** to show that it is a type 2.
- Read the word. Now you read the word. When you read this word, blend /t/ and /w/ together at the beginning, like this—/tw/, and blend /l/ and /v/ together at the end, like this—/lv/.

<u>th</u><u>ir</u> <u>teen</u>

Twelve, <u>thirteen</u>, fourteen
- How many syllables does this word have? Dictate the first syllable.
- Leave a small space between syllables. Dictate the other syllable(s).
- Underline the multi-letter phonogram(s).
- Read the word. Now you read the word.

<u>four</u> <u>teen</u>

Thirteen, <u>fourteen</u>, fifteen
- How many syllables does this word have? Dictate the first syllable.
- Leave a small space between syllables. Dictate the other syllable(s).
- Underline the multi-letter phonogram(s).
- Which of its sounds is **ou** saying? It's saying its second sound, so put a small 2 above it.
- Read the word. Now you read the word.

fif <u>teen</u>

Fourteen, <u>fifteen</u>, sixteen
- How many syllables does this word have? Dictate the first syllable.
- Leave a small space between syllables. Dictate the other syllable(s).
- Underline the multi-letter phonogram(s).
- Read the word. Now you read the word.

We're going to add a NEW suffix to a word today. Sometimes, we want to describe a noun to someone. **Adjectives** are words that describe nouns.

## a *pretty* flower          a *pleasant* day

We can talk about the **big** ball, the **fluffy** cat, and the **blue** sky. These are adjectives. But sometimes, that's not enough! We want to say that it's the most—the most pretty flower or the most pleasant day of all. We add the suffix **est** to words to show that something is the most—the **biggest** ball, the **fluffiest** cat, and the **bluest** sky.

## the *prettiest* flower          the *pleasantest* day

We usually don't use the word **pleasantest** these days. Instead, we usually say **most pleasant**. But the stories you're reading are old, written even before your mother was born! When we read old books, sometimes they include old words that we don't use anymore because language changes over time.

pleas ant est

### This is the pleasantest day of summer this year.
- How many syllables does this word have? Dictate the first syllable.
- Leave a small space between syllables. Dictate the other syllable(s).
- Underline the multi-letter phonogram(s).
- Which of its sounds is **ea** saying? It's saying its second sound, so put a small 2 above it.
- Which of its sounds is **s** saying? It's saying its second sound, so put a small 2 above it.
- Read the word. Now you read the word. When you read this word, blend /p/ and /l/ together at the beginning, like this—/pl/, and blend /n/ and /t/ together at the end, like this—/nt/.

air

### She took a deep breath of air after running.
- How many syllables does this word have? Dictate the word.
- Underline the multi-letter phonogram(s).
- Read the word. Now you read the word.

cat tle

### The cowboys were herding cattle.
- How many syllables does this word have? Dictate the first syllable.
- Leave a small space between syllables. Dictate the other syllable(s).
- Every syllable must have a written vowel; double underline the silent **e**. Put a small 4 next to the silent **e** to show that it is a type 4.
- Read the word. Now you read the word. Blend /t/ and /l/ together when you read it, like this—/tl/.

roof✚s

### No one likes a leaky roof. They're unpleasant.
- How many syllables does this word have? Dictate the word until you get to the suffix.
- Underline the multi-letter phonogram(s).
- Read the word. Now you read the word.
- ✚ Now let's make it plural! Some words that end with two vowels followed by **f** make their plural in the normal way. How will you know? Listen: One **roof**, two **roofs**. You hear /f/ instead of /v/ at the end of the plural word!
- Add **s** and read the word again.

coun try side

They enjoyed a pleasant drive through the countryside.
- How many syllables does this word have? Dictate the first syllable.
- Leave a small space between syllables. Dictate the other syllable(s).
- Underline the multi-letter phonogram(s).
- Which of its sounds is *ou* saying? It's saying its fourth sound, so put a small 4 above it.
- This is a **compound word.** That means that it's two words put together to become one word. So remember that even though **country** is not at the end of this multi-syllable word, **country** is actually a multi-syllable word all by itself, so we need to...
- Underline *y* because *y* says /ē/ at the end of a multi-syllable word.
- *I* says its name because of the silent *e*; underline the silent *e* twice, and draw a bridge between the silent *e* and the *i.*
- Read the word. Now you read the word. Blend /t/ and /r/ together when you read it, like this—/tr/.

six teen

Fifteen, sixteen, seventeen
- How many syllables does this word have? Dictate the first syllable.
- Leave a small space between syllables. Dictate the other syllable(s).
- Underline the multi-letter phonogram(s).
- Read the word. Now you read the word.

sev en teen

Sixteen, seventeen, eighteen
- How many syllables does this word have? Dictate the first syllable.
- Leave a small space between syllables. Dictate the other syllable(s).
- Underline the multi-letter phonogram(s).
- Read the word. Now you read the word.

eigh teen

Seventeen, eighteen, nineteen
- How many syllables does this word have? Dictate the first syllable.
- Leave a small space between syllables. Dictate the other syllable(s).
- Underline the multi-letter phonogram(s).
- Read the word. Now you read the word.

nine teen

Eighteen, nineteen, twenty
- How many syllables does this word have? Dictate the first syllable.
- Leave a small space between syllables. Dictate the other syllable(s).
- Underline the multi-letter phonogram(s).
- *I* says its name because of the silent *e*; underline the silent *e* twice, and draw a bridge between the silent *e* and the *i.*
- Read the word. Now you read the word.

twen ty

Nineteen, twenty, twenty-one
- How many syllables does this word have? Dictate the first syllable.
- Leave a small space between syllables. Dictate the other syllable(s).
- Underline *y* because *y* says /ē/ at the end of a multi-syllable word.
- Read the word. Now you read the word. Blend /t/ and /w/ together when you read it, like this—/tw/.

Reading & Spelling Through Literature Book 1

# 68

Today, you have a word in the spelling list that makes its plural in a different way. First, listen to these two phrases: one **calf**, two **calves**. Did you hear the difference in the sounds at the end of the words?

The phonograms **f** and **v** make very similar sounds, but **f** is soft while **v** is hard. Sometimes, when a word ends in **f**, the sound changes from /f/ to /v/, and the spelling changes, too. We change the **f** to **v** and add **e-s** to make words like **calf** and **scarf** plural.

When **f** changes to **v**, you can hear the difference! Remember the word **roof** from the last lesson? Some words that end with two vowels followed by **f** make their plural in the normal way, by just adding an **s**. How will you know? Listen: One **roof**, two **roofs**. You hear /f/ instead of /v/ at the end of the plural word!

---

**be̲ gin**

## Shall we be̲gin the next spelling list?

- How many syllables does this word have? Dictate the first syllable.
- Leave a small space between syllables. Dictate the other syllable(s).
- Underline /ē/ because **e** says its name at the end of a syllable.
- Read the word. Now you read the word.

---

**kiss ✚es**

## She gave her father a ki̲ss.

- How many syllables does this word have? Dictate the word until you get to the suffix.
- We often double **s** after a single vowel at the end of a base word.
- Read the word. Now you read the word.
- ✚ Now let's make it plural! Does **kiss** end in a hiss? Yes, it does! To make it plural, we will add **e-s** as a new syllable.
- Leave a small space between syllables. Dictate the next syllable—**es**.
- Now read the word again.

---

**go̲ld en**

## She threw the go̲lden apple to them.

- How many syllables does this word have? Dictate the first syllable.
- Leave a small space between syllables. Dictate the other syllable(s).
- Underline /ō/ because **o** says its name when followed by two consonants.
- Read the word. Now you read the word. Blend /l/ and /d/ together when you read it, like this—/ld/.

---

**ch̲eek✚s**

## Mother kissed him on the ch̲eek.

- How many syllables does this word have? Dictate the word until you get to the suffix.
- Underline the multi-letter phonogram(s).
- Read the word. Now you read the word.
- ✚ Now let's make it plural! Does **cheek** end in a hiss? If necessary, point out that this word BEGINS with a hiss, but it does not END with a hiss. No, it doesn't! So we will make it plural in the regular way.
- Add **s** and read the word again.

---

**sc̲arf**

## He wore a sc̲arf to keep him warm.

- How many syllables does this word have? Dictate the word.
- Underline the multi-letter phonogram(s).
- Read the word. Now you read the word. Blend /s/ and /c/ together when you read it, like this—/sc/

---

scar✛ve̲=s²₅

## She knit scarves for her family.
- How many syllables does this word have? Dictate the word until you get to the suffix.
- ⬡ STOP. The base word ends in *f*, so we change the *f* to *v* and add *e-s* to make this word plural.
  - Dictate the next phonograms—*v-e-s*.
  - Underline the multi-letter phonogram(s).
  - Double underline the silent *e*. Put a small 5 next to the silent *e* to show that it is a type 5—the miscellaneous silent *e*.
  - Which of its sounds is *s* saying? It's saying its second sound, so put a small 2 above it.
  - Read the word. Now you read the word.

il lu̲² sion̲²✛s

## In the desert, a person might see an illusion called a mirage.
- How many syllables does this word have? Dictate the first syllable.
- Leave a small space between syllables. Dictate the word until you get to the suffix.
- Underline the multi-letter phonogram(s).
- Underline /ö/ because *u* says its name at the end of a syllable.
- Sometimes, *u* is a little lazy. It drops the /y/ sound at the beginning of its name and only says /ö/ instead of /ū/.
- Which of its sounds is *si* saying? It's saying its second sound, so put a small 2 above it.
- Read the word. Now you read the word.
- ✛ Now let's make it plural! Does *illusion* end in a hiss? If necessary, point out that the final sound is actually the /n/ sound, not the /ẕh/ sound. No, it doesn't! So we will make it plural in the regular way.
  - Add *s* and read the word again. Put a small 2 above the *s* to show that it's saying its second sound.

vi si̲on²

## People with poor vision need glasses.
- How many syllables does this word have? Dictate the first syllable.
- Leave a small space between syllables. Dictate the other syllable(s).
- Underline the multi-letter phonogram(s).
- Which of its sounds is *si* saying? It's saying its second sound, so put a small 2 above it.
- Read the word. Now you read the word.

el e phant̲

## The elephant sprayed water with its trunk.
- How many syllables does this word have? Dictate the first syllable.
- Leave a small space between syllables. Dictate the other syllable(s).
- Underline the multi-letter phonogram(s).
- Read the word. Now you read the word. Blend /n/ and /t/ together when you read it, like this—/nt/.

fire̲✛s²

## They lit a fire to stay warm.
- How many syllables does this word have? Dictate the word until you get to the suffix.
- *I* says its name because of the silent *e*; underline the silent *e* twice, and draw a bridge between the silent *e* and the *i*.
- Read the word. Now you read the word.
- ✛ Now let's make it plural! Does *fire* end in a hiss? No, it doesn't! So we will make it plural in the regular way.
  - Add *s* and read the word again. Put a small 2 above the *s* to show that it's saying its second sound.

# New: ci; Verb Suffixes

Remember that nouns are naming words and verbs are what we do. We use suffixes to change verbs to say different things. We can add *ed* to show that something happened in the past, and we can add *ing* to show that something is continuing to happen.

Today, I will *help* mother. Yesterday, I *helped* mother. I am still *helping* mother now.

We also use suffixes to depending on who is doing something.

I *help* mother. He *helps* mother, too.

We add suffixes to make verbs into nouns! The suffix *er* is used for this purpose sometimes.

You are mother's *helper*.

And the suffix *tion* can be added to some verbs to make them nouns!

The man will *act*. He will take *action*.

---

por ridge

## They ate <u>por</u> <u>ridge</u> for breakfast.
- How many syllables does this word have? Dictate the first syllable.
- Leave a small space between syllables. Dictate the other syllable(s).
- Underline the multi-letter phonogram(s).
- Read the word. Now you read the word.

sup per

## They ate <u>sup</u> <u>per</u> together.
- How many syllables does this word have? Dictate the first syllable.
- Leave a small space between syllables. Dictate the other syllable(s).
- Underline the multi-letter phonogram(s).
- Read the word. Now you read the word.

boil ✚ing

## The water will <u>boil</u> when it's hot enough.
- How many syllables does this word have? Dictate the word until you get to the suffix.
- Underline the multi-letter phonogram(s).
- Read the word. Now you read the word.
- ✚ Can we add our *ing* suffix to change this word? We can! Listen: The water was *boiling* on the stove. Let's add *ing* to this word as a new syllable.
- The 1+1+1 rule does not apply because this word is one syllable, and it ends in one consonant, but it has two vowels! We add the suffix as usual.
- Leave a small space between syllables. Dictate the next syllable—*ing*. Underline *ng*.
- Now read the word again.

stov͡e̲

## Mother boiled water on the stove.

- How many syllables does this word have? Dictate the word.
- *O* says its name because of the silent *e*; underline the silent *e* twice, and draw a bridge between the silent *e* and the *o*.
- This is a type 1 silent *e* because it makes the vowel say its name. However, let's underline *v* as a reminder that English words do not end in *v*.
- Read the word. Now you read the word. Blend /s/ and /t/ together when you read it, like this—/st/.

spe ci̲al

## English words do not end in **u** or **i**, but **you** and **I** are special.

- How many syllables does this word have? Dictate the first syllable.
- Leave a small space between syllables. Dictate the other syllable(s).
- Underline the multi-letter phonogram(s).
- Read the word. Now you read the word. Blend /s/ and /p/ together when you read it, like this—/sp/.

gla̲ ci̲ er

## They saw a glacier when they visited Alaska.

- How many syllables does this word have? Dictate the first syllable.
- Leave a small space between syllables. Dictate the other syllable(s).
- Underline the multi-letter phonogram(s).
- Read the word. Now you read the word. Blend /g/ and /l/ together when you read it, like this—/gl/.

flo̲w̲² ✚ing

## They watched the water flow down the stream.

- How many syllables does this word have? Dictate the word until you get to the suffix.
- Underline the multi-letter phonogram(s).
- Which of its sounds is **ow** saying? It's saying its second sound, so put a small 2 above it.
- Read the word. Now you read the word. Blend /f/ and /l/ together when you read it, like this—/fl/.

✚ Can we add our *ing* suffix to change this word? We can! Listen: The water was *flowing* downhill. Let's add *ing* to this word as a new syllable.
- The 1+1+1 rule does not apply to this word because we do not double **x**, **w**, or **y** before adding a suffix. This is a spelling rule. We add the suffix as usual.
- Leave a small space between syllables. Dictate the next syllable—*ing*. Underline *ng*.
- Now read the word again.

pe̲r son

## A new person was there this week.

- How many syllables does this word have? Dictate the first syllable.
- Leave a small space between syllables. Dictate the other syllable(s).
- Underline the multi-letter phonogram(s).
- This word has a lazy vowel. When we say it, we usually say /per-sən/. We think to spell /per-sŏn/.
- Read the word. Now you read the word.

pe‿o‿ple‿₄

## Many people come to visit.
- This is an irregular noun. Listen: One **person**, two **people**.
- How many syllables does this word have? Dictate the first syllable.
- Leave a small space between syllables. Dictate the other syllable(s).
- Double underline the silent **o**.
- Underline /ē/ because **e** says its name at the end of a syllable.
- Every syllable must have a written vowel; double underline the silent **e**. Put a small 4 next to the silent **e** to show that it is a type 4.
- Read the word. Now you read the word. Blend /p/ and /l/ together when you read it, like this—/pl/.

turn✚ed²

## They will turn around at the end of the road.
- How many syllables does this word have? Dictate the word until you get to the suffix.
- Underline the multi-letter phonogram(s).
- Read the word. Now you read the word.
- ✚ Can we add our **ed** suffix to change this word? We can! Listen: Today, I **turn**. Yesterday, I **turned**. Let's add **ed** to this word as a suffix.
- The 1+1+1 rule does not apply because this word is one syllable, and it has one vowel, but it ends in two consonants! We add the suffix as usual.
- **Ed** does not form a new syllable in this word, so we just add it to the word without leaving a space. Dictate the next phonogram—**ed**. Underline **ed**.
- Which of its sounds is **ed** saying? It's saying its second sound, so put a small 2 above it.
- Now read the word again.

Today, one of your words is a name—*Johnny*. Nouns are naming words. A person's name is a **proper noun**. When we write someone's name, we begin the name with a capital letter. If you haven't learned to write capital letters yet, your instructor will show you how to write a capital *J*. Here are some various ways that people write capital *J* and lowercase *j*. Do you see your kind of writing?

Jj     Jj     Jj     𝒥𝒿     𝒥𝒿

**John ny**

### Johnny planted apples.
- This word is a **proper noun**, so it begins with a capital letter.
- How many syllables does this word have? Dictate the first syllable.
- Leave a small space between syllables. Dictate the other syllable(s).
- Double underline the silent *h*.
- Underline *y* because *y* says /ē/ at the end of a multi-syllable word.
- Read the word. Now you read the word.

**spade**

### He used a spade in the garden.
- How many syllables does this word have? Dictate the word.
- *A* says its name because of the silent *e*; underline the silent *e* twice, and draw a bridge between the silent *e* and the *a*.
- Read the word. Now you read the word. Blend /s/ and /p/ together when you read it, like this—/sp/.

**hoe**

### She used a hoe in the garden.
- How many syllables does this word have? Dictate the word.
- Underline the multi-letter phonogram(s).
- Read the word. Now you read the word.

**door**

### Close the door!
- How many syllables does this word have? Dictate the word.
- Underline the multi-letter phonogram(s).
- Which of its sounds is *oo* saying? It's saying its third sound, so put a small 3 above it.
- Read the word. Now you read the word.

**hav ✚ing**

### They are having lunch.
- How many syllables does this word have? Dictate the word until you get to the suffix.
- ⬡ STOP. We're going to add a suffix. The base word ends in silent *e*, so we drop the silent *e* before adding a vowel suffix.
- Leave a small space between syllables. Dictate the next syllable—*ing*. Underline *ng*.
- Read the word. Now you read the word.

**den**

### The fox hid in his den.
- How many syllables does this word have? Dictate the word.
- Read the word. Now you read the word.

roll➕ed²

## The toy car will roll down the ramp.

- How many syllables does this word have? Dictate the word until you get to the suffix.
- We often double *l* after a single vowel at the end of a base word.
- Underline /ō/ because *o* says its name when followed by two consonants.
- Read the word. Now you read the word.

➕ Can we add our *ed* suffix to change this word? We can! Listen: Today, I *roll*. Yesterday, I *rolled*. Let's add *ed* to this word as a suffix.

- The 1+1+1 rule does not apply because this word is one syllable, and it has one vowel, but it ends in two consonants! We add the suffix as usual.
- *Ed* does not form a new syllable in this word, so we just add it to the word without leaving a space. Dictate the next phonogram—*ed*. Underline *ed*.
- Which of its sounds is *ed* saying? It's saying its second sound, so put a small 2 above it.
- Now read the word again.

ly ing

## He is lying on the couch.

- How many syllables does this word have? Dictate the first syllable.
- Leave a small space between syllables. Dictate the other syllable(s).
- Underline the multi-letter phonogram(s).
- Underline *y* because *y* says /ī/ at the end of a one-syllable base word.
- This word is a *homograph*. *Homograph* means *same writing*, and this word has two meanings. It can be a verb, like he is *lying* on the couch. But it can also be another verb, like he is *lying* instead of telling the truth. They are spelled the same and even sound the same, but they have different meanings.
- *Lying* breaks the rules! It not only breaks the rule about telling the truth; it also breaks our spelling rules. We often change the *y* to *i* before adding a suffix, but in *lying*, we change the *i* to *y*!
- If your student is interested and at a point where they can understand, here's the reason. *Lie* is spelled *l-i-e*. Since it ends with a silent *e*, we would need to drop the silent *e* before adding a vowel suffix. But if we did that, we would have two letters *i* in a row, so we change the *i* to *y* to add our *ing* suffix.
- Read the word. Now you read the word.

woof²

## The dog said, "Woof!"

- *Woof* is an *onomatopoeia*, which is a word that we use to describe a sound.
- How many syllables does this word have? Dictate the word.
- Underline the multi-letter phonogram(s).
- Which of its sounds is *oo* saying? It's saying its second sound, so put a small 2 above it.
- Read the word. Now you read the word.

roost

## The rooster flew to a tree to roost.

- How many syllables does this word have? Dictate the word.
- Underline the multi-letter phonogram(s).
- Which of its sounds is *oo* saying? It's saying its first sound, so we don't need to mark it! We only mark phonograms when they're saying a sound other than their first.
- Read the word. Now you read the word. Blend /s/ and /t/ together when you read it, like this—/st/.

Today, one of your words is a name—*Mary*. Nouns are naming words. A person's name is a *proper noun*. When we write someone's name, we begin the name with a capital letter. If you haven't learned to write capital letters yet, your instructor will show you how to write a capital *M*. Here are some various ways that people write capital *M* and lowercase *m*. Do you see your kind of writing?

Mm     Mm     Mm     Mm     Mm

In today's spelling list, you will learn to spell the four compass points—*north, south, east*, and *west*. These words are nouns that name directions. And you'll learn a new suffix as well—*ern*. This suffix makes these nouns into adjectives, describing words. We use these to talk about the *northern* and *southern* hemispheres, the *eastern* states, or the *western* plains. They describe these nouns by telling in what direction they are.

Ma ry

## Mary had a little lamb whose fleece was white as snow.
- This word is a *proper noun*, so it begins with a capital letter.
- How many syllables does this word have? Dictate the first syllable.
- Leave a small space between syllables. Dictate the other syllable(s).
- Underline *y* because *y* says /ē/ at the end of a multi-syllable word.
- Read the word. Now you read the word.

ti ny

## The kitten is tiny.
- How many syllables does this word have? Dictate the first syllable.
- Leave a small space between syllables. Dictate the other syllable(s).
- Underline /ī/ because *i* says its name at the end of a syllable.
- Underline *y* because *y* says /ē/ at the end of a multi-syllable word.
- Read the word. Now you read the word.

much

## How much does it cost?
- How many syllables does this word have? Dictate the word.
- Underline the multi-letter phonogram(s).
- Read the word. Now you read the word.

south ✚ern

## The birds flew south for the winter.
- How many syllables does this word have? Dictate the word until you get to the suffix.
- Underline the multi-letter phonogram(s).
- Which of its sounds is *ou* saying? It's saying its fourth sound, so put a small 4 above it.
- Read the word. Now you read the word.
✚ Let's add *ern* as a suffix to change this word into an adjective. The suffix *ern* forms a new syllable.
- Note: Technically, the final syllable in southern and northern is *thern* rather than *ern*—sou-thern and nor-thern. However, we're keeping it simple.
- Leave a small space between syllables. Dictate the next syllable—*ern*.
- Underline the multi-letter phonogram(s).
- Now read the word again. Notice that *th* says its second sound when we add the suffix!

nor<u>th</u> ✚<u>ern</u>

## The birds flew <u>north</u> again in the spring.

- How many syllables does this word have? Dictate the word until you get to the suffix.
- Underline the multi-letter phonogram(s).
- Read the word. Now you read the word.

✚ Let's add *ern* as a suffix to change this word into an adjective. The suffix *ern* forms a new syllable.
- Leave a small space between syllables. Dictate the next syllable—*ern*.
- Underline the multi-letter phonogram(s).
- Now read the word again. Notice that *th* says its second sound when we add the suffix!

<u>ea</u>st ✚<u>ern</u>

## The early cities in the United States were in the <u>east</u>.

- How many syllables does this word have? Dictate the word until you get to the suffix.
- Underline the multi-letter phonogram(s).
- Read the word. Now you read the word. Blend /s/ and /t/ together when you read it, like this—/st/.

✚ Let's add *ern* as a suffix to change this word into an adjective. The suffix *ern* forms a new syllable.
- Leave a small space between syllables. Dictate the next syllable—*ern*.
- Underline the multi-letter phonogram(s).
- Now read the word again.

west ✚<u>ern</u>

## The pioneers headed <u>west</u>.

- How many syllables does this word have? Dictate the word until you get to the suffix.
- Read the word. Now you read the word. Blend /s/ and /t/ together when you read it, like this—/st/.

✚ Let's add *ern* as a suffix to change this word into an adjective. The suffix *ern* forms a new syllable.
- Leave a small space between syllables. Dictate the next syllable—*ern*.
- Underline the multi-letter phonogram(s).
- Now read the word again.

sp<u>i</u>n ✚ⓝ<u>ing</u>

## He likes to <u>spin</u> in circles.

- How many syllables does this word have? Dictate the word until you get to the suffix.
- Read the word. Now you read the word. Blend /s/ and /p/ together when you read it, like this—/sp/.

✚ Can we add our *ing* suffix to change this word? We can! Listen: I am *spinning*. Let's add *ing* to this word as a new syllable.
- The 1+1+1 Rule: This word is one syllable, and it has one vowel following by one consonant, so we double the final consonant before adding the suffix.
- Leave a small space between syllables. Dictate the next syllable—*ning*. Underline *ng*.
- Circle the extra letter that we added before the suffix.
- Now read the word again.

nic̲e̲ ✚ly̲

## The children like her because she's <u>nice</u> and friendly.

- How many syllables does this word have? Dictate the word until you get to the suffix.
- *I* says its name because of the silent *e*; underline the silent *e* twice, and draw a bridge between the silent *e* and the *i*.
- *C* says /s/ because of the silent *e*; underline the *c*. This is a spelling rule. We do NOT put a small 3 next to the silent *e* to show that it is a type 3, though, because the main job of silent *e* in this word is to make *i* say its name, which makes it a type 1 silent *e*.
- Read the word. Now you read the word.
- ✚ Can we add the ending *ly* as a suffix to change this word? We can! Listen: The children were playing *nicely*. Let's add *ly* to this word as a new syllable.
- Leave a small space between syllables. Dictate the next syllable—*ly*.
- Underline *y* because *y* says /ē/ at the end of a multi-syllable word.
- Now read the word again.

dr<u>ea</u>m

## Last night I had the strangest <u>dream</u>.

- How many syllables does this word have? Dictate the word.
- Which of its sounds is *ea* saying? It's saying its first sound, so we don't need to mark it! We only mark phonograms when they're saying a sound other than their first.
- Underline the multi-letter phonogram(s).
- Read the word. Now you read the word. Blend /d/ and /r/ together when you read it, like this—/dr/.

# Common and Proper Nouns

Nouns are naming words. They name a person, place, thing, or idea. Most nouns are *common nouns*, like *librarian*, *zoo*, *toy*, and *loyalty*.

But some nouns are special because they name a specific person, place, thing, or idea. These are called *proper nouns*. A person's name is a proper noun, so when we write someone's name, we begin the name with a capital letter. Names of places, things, and ideas can also be proper nouns, too, and they also begin with capital letters!

Proper names of places include cities like *Dallas* and *Oklahoma City*, states like *Texas* and *Hawaii*, and countries like the *United States of America* and *England*. And it also includes the names of stores, parks, and zoos!

A thing like *book* is not a proper name, but the title of your favorite book is, like *The Wonderful Wizard of Oz*. And some toys also have proper names, like *Ty Beanie Babies*.

Even ideas can have proper names, like holidays such as *Thanksgiving* or *Christmas*.

Your new story contains a number of names, so you will have many capital letters in today's spelling list!

| Cc | Cc | Cc | Cc | Cc |
|----|----|----|----|----|
| Dd | Dd | Dd | Dd | Dd |
| Gg | Gg | Gg | Gg | Gg |
| Hh | Hh | Hh | Hh | Hh |
| Ll | Ll | Ll | Ll | Ll |
| Pp | Pp | Pp | Pp | Pp |
| Ww | Ww | Ww | Ww | Ww |

gan d<u>er</u>

## Mother Goose was married to Father <u>Gander</u>.

- How many syllables does this word have? Dictate the first syllable.
- Leave a small space between syllables. Dictate the other syllable(s).
- Underline the multi-letter phonogram(s).
- Read the word. Now you read the word.

$\overset{2}{\text{fea}}$ $\overset{2}{\text{th}}$ er✚$\overset{2}{\text{s}}$

## The bird's nest had a <u>feather</u> in it.

- How many syllables does this word have? Dictate the first syllable.
- Leave a small space between syllables. Dictate the word until you get to the suffix.
- Underline the multi-letter phonogram(s).
- Which of its sounds is *ea* saying? It's saying its second sound, so put a small 2 above it.
- Which of its sounds is *th* saying? It's saying its second sound, so put a small 2 above it.
- Read the word. Now you read the word.
- ✚ Now let's make it plural! Add /s/, /z/ and read the word again. Put a small 2 above the *s* to show that it's saying its second sound.

**fool**

A jester was also called a <u>fool</u>.
- How many syllables does this word have? Dictate the word.
- Underline the multi-letter phonogram(s).
- Read the word. Now you read the word.

**chim ney**²

The bird built a nest in the <u>chimney</u>.
- How many syllables does this word have? Dictate the first syllable.
- Leave a small space between syllables. Dictate the other syllable(s).
- Underline the multi-letter phonogram(s).
- Which of its sounds is *ey* saying? It's saying its second sound, so put a small 2 above it.
- Read the word. Now you read the word.

**Do ver**

<u>Dover</u> is the name of a town.
- This word is a *proper noun*, so it begins with a capital letter.
- How many syllables does this word have? Dictate the first syllable.
- Leave a small space between syllables. Dictate the other syllable(s).
- Underline the multi-letter phonogram(s).
- Underline /ō/ because *o* says its name at the end of a syllable.
- Read the word. Now you read the word.

**Cock y Lock y**

<u>Cocky Locky</u> is a rooster.
- This name is two rhyming words. We'll dictate the words separately and then mark both words at the same time.
- Names are *proper nouns*, so both names begin with a capital letter.
- First name.
- How many syllables does this word have? Dictate the first syllable.
- Leave a small space between syllables. Dictate the other syllable(s).
- Second name. Leave a small space between the names.
- How many syllables does this word have? Dictate the first syllable.
- Leave a small space between syllables. Dictate the other syllable(s).
- Underline the multi-letter phonogram(s).
- The phonogram *ck* is used only after a single vowel that says its short sound.
- Underline *y* because *y* says /ē/ at the end of a multi-syllable word.
- Read the word. Now you read the word.

**Hen ny Pen ny**

<u>Henny Penny</u> is a hen.
- This name is two rhyming words. We'll dictate the words separately and then mark both words at the same time.
- Names are *proper nouns*, so both names begin with a capital letter.
- First name.
- How many syllables does this word have? Dictate the first syllable.
- Leave a small space between syllables. Dictate the other syllable(s).
- Second name. Leave a small space between the names.
- How many syllables does this word have? Dictate the first syllable.
- Leave a small space between syllables. Dictate the other syllable(s).
- Underline *y* because *y* says /ē/ at the end of a multi-syllable word.
- Read the word. Now you read the word.

Reading & Spelling Through Literature Book 1

**Du<u>ck</u> y Lu<u>ck</u> <u>y</u>**  <u>Ducky Lucky</u> is a duck. There's a theme here.

- This name is two rhyming words. We'll dictate the words separately and then mark both words at the same time.
- Names are *proper nouns*, so both names begin with a capital letter.
- First name.
- How many syllables does this word have? Dictate the first syllable.
- Leave a small space between syllables. Dictate the other syllable(s).
- Second name. Leave a small space between the names.
- How many syllables does this word have? Dictate the first syllable.
- Leave a small space between syllables. Dictate the other syllable(s).
- Underline the multi-letter phonogram(s).
- The phonogram *ck* is used only after a single vowel that says its short sound.
- Underline *y* because *y* says /ē/ at the end of a multi-syllable word.
- Read the word. Now you read the word.

**Fox <u>y</u> Wox <u>y</u>**  Can you guess what <u>Foxy Woxy</u> is? A fox!

- This name is two rhyming words. We'll dictate the words separately and then mark both words at the same time.
- Names are *proper nouns*, so both names begin with a capital letter.
- First name.
- How many syllables does this word have? Dictate the first syllable.
- Leave a small space between syllables. Dictate the other syllable(s).
- Second name. Leave a small space between the names.
- How many syllables does this word have? Dictate the first syllable.
- Leave a small space between syllables. Dictate the other syllable(s).
- Underline *y* because *y* says /ē/ at the end of a multi-syllable word.
- Read the word. Now you read the word.

**Gan <u>dy</u> Pan <u>dy</u>**  This one is a little tricky. <u>Gandy Pandy</u> is a gander, a male goose.

- This name is two rhyming words. We'll dictate the words separately and then mark both words at the same time.
- Names are *proper nouns*, so both names begin with a capital letter.
- First name.
- How many syllables does this word have? Dictate the first syllable.
- Leave a small space between syllables. Dictate the other syllable(s).
- Second name. Leave a small space between the names.
- How many syllables does this word have? Dictate the first syllable.
- Leave a small space between syllables. Dictate the other syllable(s).
- Underline *y* because *y* says /ē/ at the end of a multi-syllable word.
- Read the word. Now you read the word.

Today, one of your words is a name—*Hansel*. Nouns are naming words. A person's name is a ***proper noun***. When we write someone's name, we begin the name with a capital letter. If you haven't learned to write capital letters yet, your instructor will show you how to write a capital *H*. Here are some various ways that people write capital *H* and lowercase *h*. Do you see your kind of writing?

Hh        Hh        Hh        Hh        Hh

Han sel

## Hansel is a little boy.
- This word is a ***proper noun***, so it begins with a capital letter.
- How many syllables does this word have? Dictate the word.
- Leave a small space between syllables. Dictate the other syllable(s).
- Read the word. Now you read the word.

curl ✚y

## A curl fell across her forehead.
- How many syllables does this word have? Dictate the word until you get to the suffix.
- Underline the multi-letter phonogram(s).
- Read the word. Now you read the word.
✚ Can we add the ending *y* as a suffix to change this word? We can! Listen: Her hair is *curly*. Let's add *y* to this word as a new syllable.
- Leave a small space between syllables. Dictate the next syllable—*y*.
- Underline *y* because *y* says /ē/ at the end of a multi-syllable word.
- Now read the word again.

th orn ✚y

## He caught his shirt on a thorn.
- How many syllables does this word have? Dictate the word until you get to the suffix.
- Underline the multi-letter phonogram(s).
- Read the word. Now you read the word.
✚ Can we add the ending *y* as a suffix to change this word? We can! Listen: The bush is *thorny*. Let's add *y* to this word as a new syllable.
- Leave a small space between syllables. Dictate the next syllable—*y*.
- Underline *y* because *y* says /ē/ at the end of a multi-syllable word.
- Now read the word again.

bu<sub>3</sub>sh ✚es

## The thorn was on a rose bush.
- How many syllables does this word have? Dictate the word until you get to the suffix.
- Underline the multi-letter phonogram(s).
- Which of its sounds is *u* saying? It's saying its third sound, so put a small 3 above it.
- Read the word. Now you read the word.
✚ Now let's make it plural! Does *bush* end in a hiss? Yes, it does! To make it plural, we will add *e-s* as a new syllable.
- Leave a small space between syllables. Dictate the next syllable—*es*.
- Now read the word again.

**straight**

He used a ruler to draw a <u>straight</u> line.
- How many syllables does this word have? Dictate the word.
- Underline the multi-letter phonogram(s).
- Read the word. Now you read the word. Blend /s/, /t/, and /r/ together when you read it, like this—/str/.

**spi̲ de̲r**

We watched the <u>spider</u> clean her web.
- How many syllables does this word have? Dictate the first syllable.
- Leave a small space between syllables. Dictate the other syllable(s).
- Underline the multi-letter phonogram(s).
- Underline /ī/ because *i* says its name at the end of a syllable.
- Read the word. Now you read the word. Blend /s/ and /p/ together when you read it, like this—/sp/.

**crab**

The <u>crab</u> skittered across the rocks.
- How many syllables does this word have? Dictate the word.
- Read the word. Now you read the word. Blend /c/ and /r/ together when you read it, like this—/cr/.

**thr²e̲ad**

She used <u>thread</u> to sew her dress.
- How many syllables does this word have? Dictate the word.
- Underline the multi-letter phonogram(s).
- Which of its sounds is *ea* saying? It's saying its second sound, so put a small 2 above it.
- Read the word. Now you read the word. Blend /th/ and /r/ together when you read it, like this—/<u>thr</u>/.

**sci²s ²so̲²rs**

He cut some paper with the <u>scissors</u>.
- How many syllables does this word have? Dictate the first syllable.
- Leave a small space between syllables. Dictate the other syllable(s).
- Underline the multi-letter phonogram(s).
- Each letter *s* makes its second sound, so put a small 2 above each one. Remember, though, that the word begins with the phonogram *sc*, not the letter *s*!
- Read the word. Now you read the word.

**se̲w⊕²ed**

She can hand-<u>sew</u>, but I use a machine.
- How many syllables does this word have? Dictate the word until you get to the suffix.
- Underline the multi-letter phonogram(s).
- This word has an exception. The *ew* is not making its regular sound. Instead, it sounds like /ō/, so put a small *o* over it to remind you what sound it is making.
- Read the word. Now you read the word.
- ⊕ Can we add our *ed* suffix to change this word? We can! Listen: Today, I *sew*. Yesterday, I *sewed*. Let's add *ed* to this word as a suffix.
- The 1+1+1 rule does not apply to this word because we do not double *x*, *w*, or *y* before adding a suffix. This is a spelling rule. We add the suffix as usual.
- *Ed* does not form a new syllable in this word, so we just add it to the word without leaving a space. Dictate the next phonogram—*ed*. Underline *ed*.
- Which of its sounds is *ed* saying? It's saying its second sound, so put a small 2 above it.
- Now read the word again.

We're on the **penultimate** lesson! This is a fun word. **Penultimate** means the second to the last. The **ultimate** lesson is the last one. In these two lessons, we're going to review the concepts you've learned in this book. If you don't know the answers, that's okay. You'll learn all of these answers as you continue to read and practice spelling.

[Instructor: Give the student a chance to answer, but simply read the answer if they do not know it.]

What is a contraction? A contraction is two words put together to form one new word, and we replace the missing letters with an apostrophe, for example, **has not** becomes **hasn't**.

What is a suffix? A suffix is an ending that we add to words to change them, like **s**, **ed**, and **ing**.

Which sounds do **a**, **e**, **o**, and **u** usually say at the end of a syllable? They usually say their second sounds, their names, at the end of a syllable!

When a word ends in silent **e**, how do we add a vowel suffix? We drop the silent **e** before we add the suffix.

When a word ends in the vowel **y**, how do we add a vowel suffix? We change the **y** to **i** unless the vowel suffix begins with **i**.

When a word ends in **f**, how do we make it plural? There are two ways. If we hear the /v/ sound in the plural, we change the **f** to **v** and add **e-s**, like **loaves**. If a word ends in two vowels plus **f**, and we hear the /f/ sound in the plural, we can just add an **s**, like **roofs**.

Can you remember the 1+1+1 rule? When a word is one syllable, and it ends in one vowel followed by one consonant, we double the final consonant before adding a vowel suffix.

---

la<u>mb</u> kin

### The <u>lambkin</u> went to granny's house to get fat.
- How many syllables does this word have? Dictate the first syllable.
- Leave a small space between syllables. Dictate the other syllable(s).
- Underline the multi-letter phonogram(s).
- Read the word. Now you read the word.

---

drum kin

### I'm not sure what a <u>drumkin</u> is, but the word is in the story.
- I think the **drumkin** in the story is a drum. The story uses an **onomatopoeia**, which is a word that we use to describe a sound. **Tum-pa, tum-too** might be the sound of a drum.
- How many syllables does this word have? Dictate the first syllable.
- Leave a small space between syllables. Dictate the other syllable(s).
- Read the word. Now you read the word. Blend /d/ and /r/ together when you read it, like this—/dr/.

---

gran n<u>y</u>

### Will <u>granny</u> feed the lambkin?
- How many syllables does this word have? Dictate the first syllable.
- Leave a small space between syllables. Dictate the other syllable(s).
- Underline **y** because **y** says /ē/ at the end of a multi-syllable word.
- Read the word. Now you read the word. Blend /g/ and /r/ together when you read it, like this—/gr/.

---

<sup>4</sup>
<u>bough</u>

### A <u>bough</u> is a branch of a tree.
- How many syllables does this word have? Dictate the word.
- Underline the multi-letter phonogram(s).
- Which of its sounds is **ough** saying? It's saying its fourth sound, so put a small 4 above it.
- Read the word. Now you read the word.

**bin**

The <u>bin</u> was used to store corn.
- How many syllables does this word have? Dictate the word.
- Read the word. Now you read the word.

**skin**

The grass tickled where it touched her <u>skin</u>.
- How many syllables does this word have? Dictate the word.
- This word rhymes with *bin*.
- Read the word. Now you read the word. Blend /s/ and /k/ together when you read it, like this—/sk/.

**jac<u>k</u> al**

The <u>jackal</u> wanted to eat lambkin.
- How many syllables does this word have? Dictate the first syllable.
- Leave a small space between syllables. Dictate the other syllable(s).
- Underline the multi-letter phonogram(s).
- The phonogram *ck* is used only after a single vowel that says its short sound.
- This word has a lazy vowel. When we say it, we usually say /jăk-əl/. We think to spell /jăk-ăl/.
- Read the word. Now you read the word.

**ten d<u>er</u> ✚<u>ly</u>**

Mother's touch is <u>tender</u>.
- How many syllables does this word have? Dictate the first syllable.
- Leave a small space between syllables. Dictate the word until you get to the suffix.
- Underline the multi-letter phonogram(s).
- This word is a **homograph. Homograph** means **same writing**, and this word has two meanings. It's an **adjective**, a word that describes nouns. **Tender** can mean fond or loving. But it can also mean easy to chew, like lambkin! They are spelled the same and even sound the same, but they have different meanings.
- Read the word. Now you read the word.
- ✚ Can we add the ending **ly** as a suffix to change this word? We can! Listen: Mother touched his head **tenderly**. Let's add **ly** to this word as a new syllable.
- Leave a small space between syllables. Dictate the next syllable—**ly**.
- Underline **y** because **y** says /ē/ at the end of a multi-syllable word.
- Now read the word again.

**t<u>i</u> g<u>er</u>**

A white <u>tiger</u> is a rare sight.
- How many syllables does this word have? Dictate the first syllable.
- Leave a small space between syllables. Dictate the other syllable(s).
- Underline the multi-letter phonogram(s).
- Underline /ī/ because *i* says its name at the end of a syllable.
- Read the word. Now you read the word.

**pro mis<u>e</u>₅**

He made a <u>promise</u> to do his chores.
- How many syllables does this word have? Dictate the first syllable.
- Leave a small space between syllables. Dictate the other syllable(s).
- Double underline the silent **e**. Put a small 5 next to the silent **e** to show that it is a type 5—the miscellaneous silent **e**.
- This type 5 silent **e** is there to keep the word **promise** from looking like it's a plural word. Without silent **e, promise** would end in an **s**.
- Read the word. Now you read the word. Blend /p/ and /r/ together when you read it, like this—/pr/.

We're on the *ultimate* lesson! The *ultimate* lesson is the last one. *Penultimate* means the second to the last. If you don't know the answers, that's okay. You'll learn all of these answers as you continue to read and practice spelling.

An irregular plural doesn't follow the normal rules of making a plural by adding *s* or *e-s*, such as one *child* but two *children*.

An irregular verb doesn't follow the normal rules to show that something happened in the past. For instance, today, I *think*. Instead of adding *ed* to the word to show that thinking happened in the past, we say that yesterday, I *thought*.

[Instructor: Give the student a chance to answer, but simply read the answer if they do not know it.]

Can you remember all five types of silent *e*?

Type 1 silent *e* makes a vowel say its name, like the words *hide* and *safe*.

Type 2 silent *e* is there because English words do not end in *v* or *u*. So if a word would otherwise end in *v* or *u*, it will have a silent *e* on the end, like the words *give* and *blue*.

Type 3 silent *e* is there to make *g* say /j/ or *c* say /s/, like the words *bulge* and *voice*.

Type 4 silent *e* is there because every syllable must have a written vowel, like the words *little* and *apple*. Without the silent *e*, the second syllable would not have a vowel.

And type 5 silent *e* is our *miscellaneous* type. This means that there can be other reasons for a silent *e*, reasons that are not as common, like the words *were* and *come*.

Can you remember what a *verb* is? Verbs are what we do, like *talk, run, sleep*.

Can you remember what a *noun* is? Nouns are naming words. Nouns name people, places, things, and ideas, like *librarian, zoo, toy*, and *kindness*.

Can you remember what an *adjective* is? Adjectives are words that describe *nouns*, like the *kind* librarian.

## The children joyfully watched the snowflakes fall.

- How many syllables does this word have? Dictate the first syllable.
- Leave a small space between syllables. Dictate the word until you get to the suffix.
- Underline the multi-letter phonogram(s).
- Which of its sounds is *ow* saying? It's saying its second sound, so put a small 2 above it.
- *A* says its name because of the silent *e*; underline the silent *e* twice, and draw a bridge between the silent *e* and the *a*.
- This is a *compound word*. That means that it's two words put together to become one word.
- Read the word. Now you read the word. When you read this word, blend /s/ and /n/ together at the beginning, like this—/sn/, and blend /f/ and /l/ together in the middle, like this—/fl/.
- ✚ Now let's make it plural! Add /s/, /z/ and read the word again.

fil ✚ling

## They were filling the bags with the groceries.

- How many syllables does this word have? Dictate the word until you get to the suffix.
- ⭕ STOP. We're going to add a suffix. We often double *l* after a single vowel at the end of a base word. This is a spelling rule. When the suffix forms a new syllable, we divide the syllables between the double consonants.
- Leave a small space between syllables. Dictate the next syllable—*ling*. Underline *ng*.
- Read the word. Now you read the word.

shăk ✚ing

## The kitten was cold and shaking.

- How many syllables does this word have? Dictate the word until you get to the suffix.
- ⬭ STOP. We're going to add a suffix. The base word ends in silent *e*, so we drop the silent *e* before adding a vowel suffix.
- Leave a small space between syllables. Dictate the next syllable—*ing*.
- Underline the multi-letter phonogram(s).
- *A* says its name because of the silent *e* that we dropped when we added the vowel suffix. Draw a tiny bridge over the *a* as a reminder.
- Read the word. Now you read the word.

swift ✚ly

## The race is to the swift.

- How many syllables does this word have? Dictate the word until you get to the suffix.
- Read the word. Now you read the word. When you read this word, blend /s/ and /w/ together at the beginning, like this—/sw/, and blend /f/ and /t/ together at the end, like this—/ft/.
- ✚ Can we add the ending *ly* as a suffix to change this word? We can! Listen: We ran *swiftly* to the house. Let's add *ly* to this word as a new syllable.
- Leave a small space between syllables. Dictate the next syllable—*ly*.
- Underline *y* because *y* says /ē/ at the end of a multi-syllable word.
- Now read the word again.

sky

## The sky is partly cloudy.

- How many syllables does this word have? Dictate the word.
- Underline *y* because *y* says /ī/ at the end of a one-syllable base word.
- Read the word. Now you read the word. Blend /s/ and /k/ together when you read it, like this—/sk/.

de ceive₂

## To deceive means to lie.

- How many syllables does this word have? Dictate the first syllable.
- Leave a small space between syllables. Dictate the other syllable(s).
- Underline the multi-letter phonogram(s).
- Underline /ē/ because *e* says its name at the end of a syllable.
- English words do not end in *v*; underline the *v*, and double underline the silent *e*. Put a small 2 next to the silent *e* to show that it is a type 2.
- Read the word. Now you read the word.

re ceive₂

## He will receive an award

- How many syllables does this word have? Dictate the first syllable.
- Leave a small space between syllables. Dictate the other syllable(s).
- Underline the multi-letter phonogram(s).
- Underline /ē/ because *e* says its name at the end of a syllable.
- English words do not end in *v*; underline the *v*, and double underline the silent *e*. Put a small 2 next to the silent *e* to show that it is a type 2.
- This word rhymes with *deceive*.
- Read the word. Now you read the word.

dol phin

The <u>dol</u>phin swam back to its pod.
- How many syllables does this word have? Dictate the first syllable.
- Leave a small space between syllables. Dictate the other syllable(s).
- Underline the multi-letter phonogram(s).
- Read the word. Now you read the word.

gn<u>u</u>

<u>Gnu</u> is another name for wildebeest.
- How many syllables does this word have? Dictate the word.
- Underline the multi-letter phonogram(s).
- Underline /ö/ because *u* says its name at the end of a syllable.
- Sometimes, *u* is a little lazy. It drops the /y/ sound at the beginning of its name and only says /ö/ instead of /ū/.
- English words do not end in *u*. However, *gnu* is a word that English adopted! When English adopts new words from other languages, the spelling might not follow our normal rules.
- Read the word. Now you read the word.

z<u>e</u> br<u>a</u>

The stripes of a <u>zebra</u> act as camouflage.
- How many syllables does this word have? Dictate the first syllable.
- Leave a small space between syllables. Dictate the other syllable(s).
- Underline /ē/ because *e* says its name at the end of a syllable.
- Underline *a* because *a* said its third sound at the end of a word. This is a spelling rule.
- Read the word. Now you read the word. Blend /b/ and /r/ together when you read it, like this—/br/.

Part 3

Elson Readers
Book 1

All the pret-ty things put by,

Wait up-on the child-ren's eye,

Sheep and shep-herds, trees and crooks,

In the pic-ture story-books.

Robert Louis Stevenson.

## 30. Lit-tle Gus-ta-va

Once there was a lit-tle girl.

Her name was Gus-ta-va.

One day she heard a lit-tle bird.

It sang and sang and sang.

"Oh, spring has come!" said Gus-ta-va.

"Moth-er, do you hear the bird?

I am so hap-py! I love the spring."

Her moth-er gave her some bread and milk.

She sat in the warm sun to eat it.

Lit-tle Gray Kit-ten saw her there.

She ran to Gus-ta-va. "Mew, mew," said the kit-ten.

"What have you to eat?"

"I have bread and milk," said Gus-ta-va.

"Will you have some?

I will give you some of my good milk."

"Mew, mew," said Gray Kit-ten.

"It is good. Give me some more."

"Oh, I am so hap-py," said Gus-ta-va.

"Spring is here, Gray Kit-ten."

"I like spring, too," said Gray Kit-ten.


Soon lit-tle Brown Hen came by.

"Good day, Brown Hen," said Gus-ta-va.

"I am glad to see you.

Here is some bread for you. Eat all you want.

Spring is here, Brown Hen. Are you not glad?

I am so glad that win-ter is o-ver.

Do take some more bread."

"Cluck, cluck," said lit-tle Brown Hen.

"Spring makes me hap-py, too."


"Coo, coo. Coo, coo," said the doves.

"Oh, I hear my white doves," said Gus-ta-va.

They flew down to her.

"I am so glad to see you," she said.

"How pret-ty your white wings are!

Win-ter is o-ver, White Doves.

Now you can find food.

But I will give you some bread to-day."

She threw them some bread.

"Oh, spring has come," said Gus-ta-va.

"We are all so hap-py."

"We like spring, too," said the doves.


Soon her lit-tle dog came by.

"Bow-wow, bow-wow," he said.

"Don't you want me, too?"

"Oh, yes, Lit-tle Dog," said Gus-ta-va.

"You must have some food, too.

Spring is here, Lit-tle Dog.

We are so glad that win-ter is o-ver.

Take some of this milk. I have not had an-y yet.

But take all you want.

I will put it on the floor for you.

I like to see you eat."

Then Gus-ta-va sat down on the floor .

Lit-tle Dog, Gray Kit-ten, Brown Hen,

and the White Doves sat a-round her.

Just then her moth-er came out.

"Oh, Gus-ta-va!" she said. "You have no din-ner.

I will get you some more bread and milk."

"I gave it all a-way," said Gus-ta-va.

"Spring made me so hap-py."

## 31. Who Took the Bird's Nest?

"Tweet-tweet, tweet-tweet!" said Yel-low Bird.

"I made a pret-ty lit-tle nest.

I made it in the lit-tle tree. I put four eggs in it.

Then I flew to the brook. How hap-py I was!

But now I can-not find my nest.

What shall I do? What shall I do?

I will see if White Cow took it."

"Tweet-tweet, tweet-tweet!" said Yel-low Bird.

"White Cow, did you take a-way my nest?"

"Oh, no!" said "White Cow. "Not I!

I did not take a-way your nest.

I would not do such a thing.

I gave you some hay for your nest.

I saw you put your nest in the lit-tle tree.

You sang and sang and sang.

It was a beau-ti-ful lit-tle nest.

I am sor-ry you can-not find it.

But I did not take it," said White Cow.

"Oh, no! I would not do such a thing."


"Tweet-tweet, tweet-tweet!" said Yel-low Bird.

"Who took my lit-tle nest?

Oh! Here comes Brown Dog.

Brown Dog, did you take a-way my nest?

I put it in the lit-tle tree. There were four eggs in it."

"Oh, no!" said Brown Dog. "Not I!

I would not do such a thing.

I gave you some hairs for your nest.

I am sor-ry you can-not find it.

But I did not take it. Oh, no!

I would nev-er do such a thing!"


"Tweet-tweet, tweet-tweet!" said Yel-low Bird.

"Who took my lit-tle nest?

Oh! Here comes Black Sheep.

Black Sheep, did you take a-way my nest?

I put it in the lit-tle tree. Then I flew to the brook."

"Oh, no!" said Black Sheep. "Not I.

I would nev-er do such a thing.

I gave you wool to make your nest soft.

It was the pret-ti-est nest I ev-er saw.

Oh, no! I did not take it a-way.

I would nev-er do such a thing."


"Moo, moo!" said White Cow.

"Bow-wow!" said Brown Dog.

"Baa, baa!" said Black Sheep.

"Who took Yel-low Bird's nest?

We think a lit-tle boy took it.

We wish we could find him."


A lit-tle boy heard them. He hung his head.

Then he ran in-to the house and hid be-hind the bed.

He would not eat his din-ner. Can you guess why?

The lit-tle boy felt ver-y sor-ry.

Soon he came out of the house a-gain.

He took the nest back to the lit-tle tree.

"Dear Yel-low Bird," he said, "I am sor-ry.

I took your nest from the lit-tle tree.

But I will nev-er do such a thing a-gain."

"Tweet-tweet, tweet-tweet!" sang Yel-low Bird.

"I am as hap-py as can be."

# 32. The Mouse, the Crick-et, and the Bee

Once there was a lit-tle mouse.

One spring day she sat in the sun.

A crick-et and a bee came a-long.

"Win-ter is o-ver," said the lit-tle mouse.

"Let us make a house. We are so lit-tle.

We can all live in one lit-tle house.

We can be so hap-py there."

"That is a good plan," said the crick-et.

"I like that plan, too," said the bee.

"Where shall we make a house?" said the bee.

"Let us find a ver-y dark place," said the crick-et.

"I like the dark. It is dark un-der the barn.

The sun can-not find us there.

I like to chirp in the dark. I do not like the light."

"Oh, dear! Oh, dear!" said the mouse.

"I do not like to live in the dark.

I am not hap-py in the dark.

The warm sun is the place for me.

Let us try to find a light place."

"Yes, yes!" said the bee. "Yes, yes!

I like the sun-shine, too.

I know a good place for a house.

It is up in a tall tree. It is ver-y light there.

The tree is in a pret-ty mead-ow.

The mead-ow has flow-ers in it.

The sun will keep us warm. The wind will sing to us.

I like to buzz in the sun-shine.

I am ver-y hap-py in the sun-shine."

"Oh, dear! Oh, dear!" said the crick-et.

"I nev-er chirp in the sun-shine, and I can-not fly.

I can-not live in a tall tree.

Oh, dear, no! That place would not do for me.

What shall I do? What shall I do?"

"Let us try my place," said the mouse.

"I know a good place for a house.

It is on the ground. It is in the sun-shine, too.

I like to live in a corn field. We can eat the corn.

We can run and play in the sun-shine.

That will be such fun.

I can make a warm home for us.

There we can be ver-y hap-py."

"Oh, dear! Oh, dear!" said the bee.

"I can-not eat corn. That place would not do for me.

We can-not live to-geth-er."

So the bee flew to the tall tree.

"Buzz, buzz," she sang in the sun-shine.

"See how high I am. My home is best."

The crick-et ran un-der the barn.

"Chirp, chirp," he sang in the dark.

"I have a good hid-ing place. My home is best."

The mouse ran in-to the field.

She made a soft, warm nest.

"Squeak, squeak," she said in the corn.

"My home is best." She went to sleep in the sun-shine.

# 33. Bob-bie's Yel-low Chick-en

Bob-bie's grand-moth-er lived on a farm.

One sum-mer he went to see her.

He saw man-y cows and sheep there.

He saw man-y hors-es and pigs, too.

Bob-bie lived on the farm all sum-mer.

He was as hap-py as he could be.

One day he said, "Grand-moth-er,

I wish I could live here al-ways.

I have great fun here."

One day Grand-moth-er went to the barn.

Bob-bie went with her.

She said, "See this lit-tle yel-low chick-en, Bob-bie."

"May I have her?" said Bob-bie.

"She is the pret-ti-est chick-en I ev-er saw."

"Yes, Bob-bie," said Grand-moth-er.

"You may have her.

You must give her food ev-er-y day.

Some day she will lay an egg for you."

Bob-bie gave her food all sum-mer.

She grew and grew and grew.

One day Grand-moth-er said,

"Bob-bie, your moth-er wants you to come home.

You may come a-gain next sum-mer."

Bob-bie felt sor-ry to leave the farm.

He went to the barn.

"Good-bye, lit-tle yel-low chick-en," he said.

"I must go home to moth-er.

Please do not for-get me.

I will see you a-gain next sum-mer."

"I will not for-get you, Bob-bie,"

said the lit-tle yel-low chick-en.

"When you come back, I will lay an egg for you."

Bob-bie went home to his moth-er.

His moth-er was wait-ing for him.

How glad she was to see him!

Bob-bie was glad to see her, too.

"Oh, Moth-er!" he cried,

"Grand-moth-er gave me a lit-tle yel-low chick-en.

I gave it food and wa-ter ev-er-y day.

It is my own lit-tle chick-en.

Next sum-mer it will lay big white eggs for me.

Do you think it will know me when I go back?"


The next sum-mer Bob-bie went

back to Grand-moth-er's.

He ran at once to the barn.

He looked and looked and looked,

but he could not see his lit-tle chick-en.

Just then he saw a big brown hen jump off her nest.

Grand-moth-er laughed.

"There is your lit-tle yel-low chick-en," she said.

"You did not know her when you saw her."

"Oh, see the egg in her nest!" said Bob-bie.

"I did not know my lit-tle yel-low chick-en.

But she did not for-get to lay an egg for me."

How proud the big brown hen was!

## 34. The Go-to-Sleep Stor-y

"I must go to bed," said lit-tle dog Pen-ny.

"But first I must say good night to Ba-by Ray.

He is kind to me.

He gives me some of his bread and milk.

I will see if he is a-sleep."

So lit-tle dog Pen-ny found Ba-by Ray.

His moth-er was tell-ing him a Go-to-Sleep stor-y.

Lit-tle dog Pen-ny heard it.

This is what he heard:

The dog-gie that was giv-en

him to keep, keep, keep,

Went to see if Ba-by Ray was

a-sleep, sleep, sleep.

"We must go to bed, too," said the two kit-tens.

"But first we must say good night to Ba-by Ray.

He gives us milk for our din-ner.

Let us see if he is a-sleep."

So the lit-tle kit-tens found Ba-by Ray.

They heard the Go-to-Sleep stor-y.

This is what they heard:

One dog-gie that was giv-en

him to keep, keep, keep.

Two cun-ning lit-tle kit-ty cats,

creep, creep, creep,

Went to see if Ba-by Ray was

a-sleep, sleep, sleep.

"We must go to bed, too," said the three bun-nies.

"But first we must say good night to Ba-by Ray.

He gives us green leaves for our din-ner.

Let us see if he is a-sleep."

So the bun-nies found Ba-by Ray.

They heard the Go-to-Sleep stor-y.

This is what they heard:

One dog-gie that was giv-en

him to keep, keep, keep,

Two cun-ning lit-tle kit-ty cats,

creep, creep, creep.

Three pret-ty lit-tle bun-nies

with a leap, leap, leap,

Went to see if Ba-by Ray was

a-sleep, sleep, sleep.


"We must go to bed," said the four white geese.

"But first we must say good night to Ba-by Ray.

He gives us corn. Let us see if he is a-sleep."

So the four geese found Ba-by Ray.

They heard the Go-to-Sleep stor-y.

This is what they heard:

One dog-gie that was giv-en

him to keep, keep, keep.

Two cun-ning lit-tle kit-ty cats,

creep, creep, creep,

Three pret-ty lit-tle bun-nies

with a leap, leap, leap,

Four geese from the duck pond,

deep, deep, deep,

Went to see if Ba-by Ray was

a-sleep, sleep, sleep.


"We must go to bed," said the five lit-tle chicks.

"But first we must say good night to Ba-by Ray.

He gives us bread. Let us see if he is a-sleep."

So the five lit-tle chicks found Ba-by Ray.

He was just go-ing to sleep.

They heard all of the Go-to-Sleep stor-y.

This is what they heard:

One dog-gie that was giv-en

him to keep, keep, keep,

Two cun-ning lit-tle kit-ty cats,

creep, creep, creep.

Three pret-ty lit-tle bun-nies,

with a leap, leap, leap,

Four geese from the duck pond,

deep, deep, deep,

Five down-y lit-tle chicks, cry-ing

peep, peep, peep,

All saw that Ba-by Ray was

a-sleep, sleep, sleep.

## 35. A Lul-la-by

Lul-la-by, oh, lul-la-by!

Flow-ers are closed² and lambs are sleep-ing;

Lul-la-by, oh, lul-la-by!

Stars are up; the moon is peep-ing;²

Lul-la-by, oh, lul-la-by!

Sleep, my ba-by, fall a-sleep-ing,³

Lul-la-by, oh, lul-la-by!

## 36. The Ant and the Dove

"I want some wa-ter," an ant

once said.

"I will go to the brook.

I can get some wa-ter there."

So she went to the brook.

But she tum-bled in-to the wa-ter.

"Help! Help!" she cried. "The wa-ter is cold!"

A dove heard the ant.

"I will help you!" cried the dove.

So she threw a leaf in-to the brook.

The ant got on the leaf.

Reading & Spelling Through Literature Book 1

"Ooo-oo-o-o!" blew the wind.

It blew the leaf to the land.

Then the ant got off the leaf.

"Thank you, kind dove," she said.

"Some-time I will help you."


Soon a man came by. He saw the pret-ty dove.

He said, "I will catch her." So he kept ver-y still.

He came ver-y near to the dove.

"Coo, coo!" said the pret-ty dove.

She did not see the man. But the ant saw him.

She said, "I will help the good dove."

So she bit the man and made him jump.

The man cried out, "Oh! Oh!"

Then the dove saw the man. A-way she flew!

She was safe, and the ant was hap-py.

## 37. The Proud Leaves

A big tree grew in a mead-ow.

Green leaves grew on the tree.

One day they said to the sun,

"How beau-ti-ful we are!

We make the tree beau-ti-ful.

What would the tree be if it

had no leaves?

We make a cool shade, too.

Boys and girls play in our shade.

They swing and laugh and sing.

All the birds fly in-to the tree.

Reading & Spelling Through Literature Book 1

They sing to us, 'Tweet-tweet, tweet-tweet.'

See their lit-tle nests all a-round us!

The wind sings through us.

It says, 'Oo-oo-oo! Oo-oo-oo! Oo-oo-oo!'"

So the leaves felt ver-y proud.


All at once they heard a soft lit-tle voice far be-low.

It said, "Leaves, we help the tree, too."

"Who are you?" said the leaves.

"We are the roots," said the voice.

"We get food for you. You are beau-ti-ful, but you die.

New leaves come ev-er-y spring.

But we live on and on.

If we should die, the great tree would die, too."

The leaves said, "You do help the tree, kind roots.

We will not for-get you a-gain."

## 38. The Dog and His Shad-ow

Once there was a big dog.

When he got a bone, he al-ways hid it.

He nev-er gave a bit to an-y oth-er dog.

If he saw a lit-tle dog with a bone, he would say,

"Bow-wow! Give me that bone!"

Then he would take the bone.

One day he took a bone from a lit-tle dog.

"The lit-tle dog shall not find this bone," he said.

"I will take it far a-way.

I will go a-cross the brook and hide it."

So the big dog ran to the brook.

There was a lit-tle bridge o-ver the brook.

The dog ran out on the bridge.

He looked down in-to the wa-ter and

thought he saw an-oth-er dog there.

He thought the dog had a bone, too.

"I will take that bone," said the big dog.

"Then I shall have two bones.

Bow-wow! Bow-wow!" said the big dog.

Then his own bone fell out of his mouth.

It fell in-to the brook.

The big dog could not get it out.

There was no dog in the wa-ter at all!

The big dog had seen his own shad-ow.

## 39. The Kite and the But-ter-fly

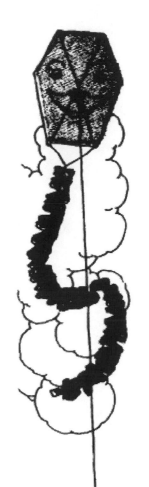

A kite flew far up in-to the clouds.

It play ed with the wind.

It looked at the sun.

The kite saw a but-ter-fly far be-low.

"Look at me!" said the kite.

"See how high I am!

I can see far, far a-way.

May-be I shall fly to the sun.

Don't you wish you were a kite?

Then you could fly with me."

"Oh, no!" said the but-ter-fly.

"I do not fly ver-y high.

But I go where I please.

You fly ver-y high.

But you are tied to a string!"

# 40. The Cat and the Fox

One day a cat met a fox in the woods.

They were looking for food.

The cat want-ed a fat mouse.

The fox want-ed a fat rab-bit.

They had looked and looked.

But all the fat rab-bits and

all the fat mice were hid-ing.

The fox was ver-y cross.

When he want-ed a rab-bit,

he want-ed it!

The cat was not cross at all.

When she want-ed a mouse,

she could wait for it.

She said, "Good morn-ing, Mr. Fox.

I am glad to see you. How are you get-ting on?"

The fox looked at the cat and laughed.

"You fool-ish lit-tle cat!" he said.

"I can al-ways get a-long all right.

I know so man-y tricks.

How man-y tricks do you know?"

"I know just one trick," said the cat.

"Ha, ha!" laughed the fox.

"Just one lit-tle trick! What is that?"

"I can jump up in-to a tree," said the cat.

"When the dogs come—jump! I am safe!"

"Ha, ha!" laughed the fox.

"Just one lit-tle trick! I know man-y tricks.

They are all bet-ter than your trick, too.

Let me tell you some of them.

Then the dogs will nev-er catch you."

"All right!" said the cat.

Just then they heard a great noise.

It was a hunt-er on his horse.

His dogs were run-ning and bark-ing.

Jump! The cat was safe in a tree!

But the dogs got Mr. Fox!

"I am just a fool-ish lit-tle cat," said the cat.

"I know on-ly one trick.

But one trick is some-times bet-ter than man-y."

## 41. A Wish

May: Oh, see the pret-ty birds!

How fast they fly!

They look so hap-py.

I wish I had wings.

Then I could fly, too.

But I have on-ly legs.

My legs are short, and

they are slow, too.

Wings can go fast.

When I go home, I must walk.

It will take me a long time.

I must go through the mead-ow.

Then there is such a hill to go up!

I do not like to like to go up high hills.

Oh, if I were on-ly a bird!

How fast I would fly home to moth-er!

Bird: Are you sure you would like to be a bird?

I eat worms for my din-ner.


May: Oh, dear! I did not think of that!

I should not like to eat worms.

I like bread and milk for my din-ner.


Bird: Would you like to sleep up in a tree?

My lit-tle ones like a tree-top bed.


May: Oh, no! That would not do at all!

The wind some-times shakes the tree.

It would shake me out of the nest.

My lit-tle white bed is best for me.

Bird: What would you do when the hawk came?

My lit-tle birds hide from the hawk.


May: I am so big the hawk would see me.

Oh, I am so glad I am not a bird!

It is best for me to be a girl.

## 42. Mol-ly and the Pail of Milk

Mol-ly lived on a farm.

A lit-tle cow lived on the farm, too.

The cow gave good milk.

One day Mol-ly's moth-er said,

"You may have this pail of milk, Mol-ly.

Go to town and sell it.

You may have all the mon-ey you get."

"Oh, thank you, Moth-er!" said Mol-ly.

She put the pail of milk on her head

and walked down the road.

"When I sell this milk, I shall get some mon-ey,"

she said. "Then I will buy some eggs.

I will put the eggs un-der our hens.

The hens will sit on the eggs.

Soon lit-tle chick-ens will be hatched.


"I will sell the chick-ens.

With the mon-ey I will buy more eggs.

I will buy man-y, man-y eggs.

Soon I shall have man-y lit-tle chick-ens.

They will grow big and fat. I will sell them all.

What shall I do with all that mon-ey?

Oh, I know! I will buy some geese.

Then I will buy some ducks.

I will buy a pig. I will buy a horse.

I will buy a cow. I will buy a farm.

I will build a lit-tle house on the farm.

I will live in the lit-tle house.

How hap-py I shall be there!

This lit-tle pail of milk will do it all."


It made Mol-ly hap-py just to think of it.

She be-gan to jump and sing.

Down came the pail of milk!

Poor Mol-ly! She did not sell the milk.

She could not buy an-y eggs.

She could not buy ducks and geese,

a pig, a horse, a cow, and a lit-tle farm.

She could not build a lit-tle house.

She count-ed her chick-ens too soon.

Next time she will wait un-til they are hatched.

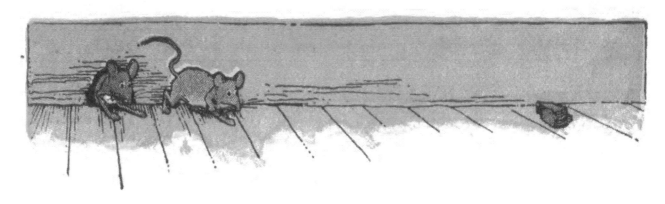

## 43. The Fine Plan

Once some mice lived in a big house.

They ran all o-ver the house.

Pat-ter, pat-ter, pat-ter, went their feet!

The house was full of mice.

A cat lived in the big house, too. He was a big cat.

He liked to catch the mice.

He caught some ev-er-y day.

The mice were a-fraid of him.

They said, "What shall we do?

This big cat will catch us all. He will eat us up.

Oh, what shall we do?"

"I know what to do," said a lit-tle mouse.

"The cat makes no noise when he walks.

We can-not hear him. I have a fine plan.

We must hang a bell on his neck.

The bell will make a noise.

Ting-a-ling! Ting-a-ling! it will go.

We shall hear the bell. Then we shall

know that the cat is com-ing.

We will run a-way. The cat can-not catch us."


"What a fine plan!" said the oth-er mice.

"Yes! Yes! The cat must have a bell on his neck!

Then he can-not catch us."

The mice jumped for joy.

The lit-tle mouse was ver-y proud.

"How wise I am!" he said. "Now we shall be safe."

But Old Gray Mouse laughed.

He was wis-er than the lit-tle mouse.

"Ha, ha!" he laughed, "Ha, ha, ha!

That is a fine plan, lit-tle mouse.

But who will hang the bell on the cat?

Will you, lit-tle mouse?"

"Oh, no, no! He would eat me up!"

But some-one must put the bell on the cat!

The lit-tle mouse had not thought of that.

He ran a-way as fast as he could go.

He cried "Squeak! Squeak!" all the way home.

# 44. The Race

One day a lit-tle hare was in

a mead-ow.

A lit-tle tor-toise was

there, too.

He was creep-ing to the riv-er for a swim.

"How slow you are!" said the hare.

"You can-not hop. You can on-ly creep.

Look at me! See how fast I hop!"

And the lit-tle hare gave a great hop.

"I am slow," said the tor-toise. "But I am sure.

Would you like to run a race with me?"

"Run a race!" cried the hare.

"How fool-ish that would be! I hop and you creep.

How can we run a race?"

"Let us try," said the tor-toise.

"Let us race to the riv-er.

We shall see who gets there first."

"The riv-er is a long way off," said the hare.

"But I shall soon be there. Good-bye!"

Off went the lit-tle hare, hop, hop, hop!

Off went the tor-toise, creep, creep, creep.

Soon the hare was near-ly to the riv-er.

It was a warm day. "I will rest a lit-tle," he said.

So the hare rest-ed and ate some leaves.

Then he felt sleep-y.

"It is ver-y warm," he said. "I will sleep a lit-tle.

That fool-ish old tor-toise is slow.

I shall wake up be-fore he creeps here.

Then I can hop to the riv-er.

I shall be there long be-fore he comes."

So the lit-tle hare went to sleep.

The lit-tle tor-toise came creep-ing on.

He did not stop to eat. He did not stop to sleep.

He went on and on, creep, creep, creep.

By and by he came to the riv-er.

The lit-tle hare slept a long time.

Then he woke up with a jump.

"Dear me! I must hop a-long," he said.

"Where can that slow tor-toise be?

He is not here yet."

The lit-tle hare hopped on to the riv-er.

There was the lit-tle tor-toise wait-ing for him!

"Creep and creep beats hop and sleep!"

said the tor-toise.

## 45. The Roos-ter and the Fox

One morn-ing a roos-ter flew to the top of the barn.

He flapped his wings and called,

"Cock-a-doo-dle-doo!"

Now a fox heard the roos-ter. So he came to the barn.

He want-ed to get the roos-ter and eat him.

But the fox could not reach him.

Reading & Spelling Through Literature Book 1

So he called up to the roos-ter, "Come down, friend!

Have you heard the news?

The beasts and the birds are go-ing to live to-geth-er.

They will not hurt each oth-er an-y-more.

They will not eat each oth-er up.

They will all be friends.

Come down, friend roos-ter!

Let us talk a-bout the news."


But the roos-ter knew the fox had man-y tricks.

So he stayed on top of the barn.

He looked far, far a-way.

"What do I see? What do I see?" said he.

"Well, what do you see?" asked the fox.

The roos-ter looked far, far a-way.

"Oh! The dogs are com-ing!

The dogs are com-ing!" he said.


The fox got up in great haste.

"Good-bye," he said. "I must go!"

"Oh, no, friend," said the roos-ter. "Don't go.

The dogs won't hurt you, will they?

You said the beasts and the birds were

go-ing to live to-geth-er and be friends.

Let us talk a-bout the great news."

"No, no! I must run a-way," said the fox.

"May-be the dogs have not heard the news."

So he ran off as fast as he could go.

That time the roos-ter was wis-er than the fox.

# 46. Thanks-giv-ing in the Hen House

Brown Hen: This is Thanks-giv-ing Day. How cold it is!

It has snowed all day.

Gray Goose: In-deed it has.

I do not like this day at all.

I wish Jack would come. It is time for our din-ner.

May-be he will for-get us to-day.

Lit-tle Chick: Peep, peep! I am hun-gry, too.

All the lit-tle chicks are hun-gry.

Red Roos-ter: Cheer up, Brown Hen.

Cheer up, Gray Goose. Cheer up, Lit-tle Chick.

This is Thanks-giv-ing Day.

We must all be hap-py to-day.


Brown Hen: We can-not be hap-py, Red Roos-ter,

when we are hun-gry.

We want some wa-ter, too.

We don't like to eat snow.


Gray Goose: How cold it is out-side!


Red Roos-ter: But it is warm in here.

Jack has filled all the cracks to keep us warm.

The wind can-not hurt us now.

And the fox can-not get us.

I am hun-gry, too, but I won't be sad to-day.

This is the best day of the year.


Big Tur-key: Red Roos-ter, you are right.

Brown Hen and Gray Goose are too cross.

We should all be hap-py to-day.


Red Roos-ter: Let us sing a glad Thanks-giv-ing song.

Will you sing first, Brown Hen? You have a fine voice.


Brown Hen: Cut—cut—ca—da—cut!


Red Roos-ter: Now let us all sing to-geth-er.

Sing loud. There! That is fine.


Moth-er: What a noise in the hen house!

The poor chick-ens want their Thanks-giv-ing din-ner.

Fa-ther: Jack, you for-got them!

Take them some food.


Jack: Yes, in-deed I will.

I will give them a bas-ket of corn and wheat.


Hol-ly: And I will take them some wa-ter.

Poor chick-ens! They have not had

an-y Thanks-giv-ing din-ner.

Let us run to the hen house.


Gray Goose: Here come Jack and Mol-ly.

Jack has a bas-ket of corn and wheat.


Brown Hen: And Mol-ly is bring-ing

a pail of wa-ter, too.

Reading & Spelling Through Literature Book 1

Red Roos-ter: Hur-rah! I guess the chil-dren

liked our Thanks-giv-ing song.

Let us all sing a-gain. One, two, three, sing!


Jack: How hap-py they all are in

the hen house this eve-ning!


Hol-ly: They like Thanks-giv-ing Day, too.

## 47. Th<u>e</u> <u>Ch</u>rist-mas F<u>air</u>-y

It w<sup>3</sup>a<sup>2</sup>s <u>th e</u> da<u>y</u> be-f<u>or e</u> <u>Ch</u>rist-mas.

T<u>wo</u><sup>3</sup> lit-tl<u>e</u> <u>ch</u>il-dren went to<sup>3</sup> <u>th e</u> w<u>oo</u><sup>2</sup>ds.

<u>Th</u> <u>ey</u> want-<u>ed</u><sup>3</sup> to f<u>i</u>nd<sup>3</sup> <u>a</u> <u>Ch</u>rist-mas tr<u>ee</u>.

P<u>oo</u>r lit-tle <u>ch</u>il-dren!

<u>Th</u> <u>ey</u> had nev-<u>er</u> had <u>a</u> <u>Ch</u>rist-mas tr<u>ee</u>.

"<u>O</u><u>h</u>, d<u>ear</u>!" s<u>ai</u><sup>e</sup>d <u>th e</u> lit-tl<u>e</u> g<u>ir</u>l.

"W<u>e</u> ha<u>v</u><u>e</u> no<u>th</u>-in<u>g</u><sup>3</sup> to<sup>3</sup> put on <u>th e</u> tr<u>ee</u>."

"W<u>e</u> must f<u>i</u>nd <u>a</u> tr<u>ee</u> wi<u>th</u> man-<u>y</u> con<u>e</u>s on it,"

s<u>ai</u><sup>e</sup>d <u>th e</u> lit-tl<u>e</u> boy.

Reading & Spelling Through Literature Book 1

"Cones will make our tree beau-ti-ful."

"Yes, yes!" said the lit-tle girl.

"We must find a tree with cones on it."


The chil-dren walked on and on.

But they could not find a tree with cones on it.

By and by night came.

The chil-dren were ver-y, ver-y tired.

They could not find their way home.

So they sat down to rest.

Soon the lit-tle girl fell a-sleep.

The lit-tle boy was tired, too,

but he did not close his eyes.

"I must take care of sis-ter," he said.

"I will put my coat a-round her to keep her warm."

He sat there a long time un-til he shook with the cold.

By and by he saw a ver-y bright light.

It woke his lit-tle sis-ter.

Soon the chil-dren saw a beau-ti-ful fair-y.

She came right up to them.

"Who are you?" asked the lit-tle boy.

"I am the Christ-mas Fair-y," said the fair-y.

"I am al-ways in the woods at Christ-mas time.

I make the woods bright at night.

Then good lit-tle boys and girls can find

the pret-ti-est trees. Come, chil-dren!

I will take you to a beau-ti-ful tree."


The fair-y took them to a beau-ti-ful tree.

It had man-y, man-y cones on it.

"Here is your tree," said the fair-y.

Then she said, "Lit-tle cones, light the tree."

The lit-tle cones be-gan to shine like gold.

"Oh, what a won-der-ful Christ-mas tree!"

said the chil-dren.

"It will light you all the way home," said the fair-y.

"It will shine for you on Christ-mas Day, too."

The chil-dren took the beau-ti-ful tree.

It light-ed them all the way home.

They were ver-y, ver-y hap-py.

## 48. Ba-by's Stock-ing

Hang up the ba-by's stock-ing,

Be sure you don't for-get.

The dear lit-tle ba-by dar-ling

Has nev-er seen Christ-mas yet.

Write , "This is the ba-by's stock-ing

That hangs in the corn-er here .

You have nev-er seen her, San-ta,

For she on-ly came this year.

But she is the pret-ti-est ba-by!

And now be-fore you go,

Just fill her stock-ing with good-ies

From the top way down to the toe."

## 49. The Big Man and the Lit-tle Birds

One day a tall man went for a ride.

He was go-ing a-long a coun-try road.

Some friends were with him.

Near the road was an ap-ple tree.

He saw two lit-tle ba-by birds in the road.

They had just tum-bled out of their

nest in the ap-ple tree.

The moth-er bird was fly-ing a-bout, near them.

But she could not put them in-to the nest.

"Tweet-tweet, tweet-tweet!" she cried.

She want-ed the men to help her.

"Let us help the bird," said the tall man.

"No, we can-not stop," said his friends.

But the tall man jumped from his horse.

He put the lit-tle birds back in-to the nest.

"Tweet-tweet, tweet-tweet!" said the moth-er bird.

She was try-ing to thank the man.

Then the tall man jumped up on his horse.

He soon caught up with his friends.

"I had to help the bird," he said.

"I could not have slept to-night

if I had not helped her."

The tall man was named A-bra-ham Lin-coln.

## 50. O̲ur Flag

Ther̲e a̲r̲e man-y flags in man-y lands,

    Ther̲e a̲r̲e flags of ev-er̲-y hu̲e,

But the̲re is no̲ flag in an-y land

    Lik̲e o̲ur o̲wn Red, Whit̲e, and Blu̲e.

Then "Hur-rah for the Flag!" our coun-try's flag.

Its stripes and white stars, too;

There is no flag in an-y land

Like our own Red, White, and Blue.


# A-mer-i-ca

My coun-try, 'tis of thee,

Sweet land of Lib-er-ty,

Of thee I sing;

Land where my fa-thers died,

Land of the pil-grims' pride;

From ev-er-y moun-tain side

Let Free-dom ring.

## 51. The Par-ade on Wash-ing-ton's Birth-day

Grand-fa-ther and Grand-moth-er had a flag.

It was an old, old flag.

It was near-ly as old as Fa-ther.

They gave the flag to Fa-ther. He loved the old flag.

Pat-ty and Ned loved it, too.

They hung it out of the win-dow ev-er-y Flag Day.

One day Fa-ther said, "There will be a par-ade

on George Wash-ing-ton's Birth-day.

It will be a fine par-ade.

I will take Pat-ty and Ned to see it."

"That will be great fun," said Ned.

The chil-dren jumped for joy.

"Hur-rah! Hur-rah!" they cried.

The great day came at last.

But Fa-ther could not take Ned

and Pat-ty to the par-ade.

Their Grand-moth-er was sick.

Fa-ther and Moth-er had to go to see her.

Pat-ty and Ned felt ver-y sad.

But they did not cry. Oh, no!

Pat-ty said, "We can-not see the par-ade.

But we can hang our flag out of the win-dow."

"Yes," said Ned.

"Fa-ther and Moth-er would like us to do that."

So they hung the flag out of the win-dow.

Soon they heard a great noise.

"Oh, it is the par-ade!" said Ned.

It is com-ing down our street.

I am so glad our flag is out."

The par-ade went right by the house.

Ev-er-y one saw the old, old flag.

They said, "Hur-rah for the old, old flag!"

Pat-ty and Ned felt ver-y proud.


Soon Fa-ther and Moth-er came home.

Pat-ty and Ned told them a-bout the par-ade.

"Oh! We had a won-der-ful day!" said Pat-ty.

"Hur-rah for the old, old flag!" said Ned.

"Hur-rah for George Wash-ing-ton!" said Fa-ther.

## 52. The Lit-tle Red Hen

A lit-tle red hen once found a grain of wheat.

"Who will help plant this wheat?" she asked.

"Not I," said the dog.

"Not I," said the cat.

"Not I," said the pig.

"Not I," said the tur-key.

"Then I will," said the lit-tle red hen. "Cluck! Cluck!"

So she plant-ed the grain of wheat.

Soon the wheat be-gan to grow.

By and by it grew tall and ripe.

"Who will help reap this wheat?"

asked the lit-tle red hen.

"Not I," said the dog.

"Not I," said the cat.

"Not I," said the pig.

"Not I," said the tur-key.

"I will, then," said the lit-tle red hen. "Cluck! Cluck!"

So she reaped the wheat.


"Who will help thresh this wheat?"

said the lit-tle red hen.

"Not I," said the dog.

"Not I," said the cat.

"Not I," said the pig.

"Not I," said the tur-key.

"I will, then," said the lit-tle red hen. "Cluck! Cluck!"

So she threshed the wheat.


"Who will help take this wheat to the mill to

have it ground?" asked the lit-tle red hen.

"Not I," said the dog.

"Not I," said the cat.

"Not I," said the pig.

"Not I," said the tur-key.

"I will, then," said the lit-tle red hen. "Cluck! Cluck!"

So she took the wheat to the mill.


By and by she came back with the flour.

"Who will help bake a loaf of bread with this flour?"

asked the lit-tle red hen.

"Not I," said the dog, the cat, the pig, and the tur-key.

"I will, then," said the lit-tle red hen. "Cluck! Cluck!"

So she baked a loaf of bread with the flour.

"Who will help eat this bread?"

asked the lit-tle red hen.

"I will," said the dog.

"I will," said the cat.

"I will," said the pig.

"I will," said the tur-key.

"No, you won't," said the lit-tle red hen.

"My lit-tle chicks and I are go-ing

to do that. Cluck! cluck!"

So she called her four lit-tle chicks,

and they ate up the loaf of bread.

## 53. The Lost Egg

Bob-bie had a pret-ty hen named Brown-ie.

Brown-ie had a soft nest in the barn.

Can you guess why she

sat there so long?

There were ten white

eggs un-der her.

By and by Brown-ie heard a "Peep-peep!"

The shells of the eggs were break-ing.

Lit-tle chicks were com-ing out of the shells.

Soon Brown-ie had nine lit-tle chicks.

She kept them un-der her wings where it was warm.

"Peep, peep, peep!" said the nine chicks.

"Where is my oth-er chick?" said Brown-ie.

"I had ten eggs. I see on-ly nine chicks."

"Cluck-cluck, cluck-cluck,"

said Brown-ie to her lit-tle chick-ens.

"Let us take a walk."

She took them in-to the gar-den

to find Bob-bie and his moth-er.


"Oh, Moth-er," cried Bob-bie,

"look at Brown-ie's lit-tle chicks!"

"How man-y has she?" asked his moth-er.

"I will count them," said Bob-bie.

"One, two, three, four, five, six, sev-en, eight, nine.

There are nine lit-tle chick-ens."

"Why, Bob-bie," said his moth-er, "she had ten eggs.

Where is the oth-er chick-en?"

Then his moth-er count-ed them.

She count-ed nine chick-ens, too.

"I will run to the barn," said Bob-bie.

"I may find it there."

A-way he ran as fast as he could go.

There was the egg, right in the nest!

Bob-bie took it up to look at it.

But the egg fell to the ground.


Hark! What did he hear? "Peep-peep! Peep-peep!"

He looked at the egg and saw a big crack in the shell.

Then Bob-bie saw an-oth-er lit-tle chick-en.

He gave it to Brown-ie,

and she put it un-der her wing.

All the oth-er lit-tle chick-ens ran

a-bout and flapped their wings.

They were so hap-py! Brown-ie was hap-py, too.

She had found the lost chick.

# 54. The Goats in the Tur-nip Field

Once a boy had three fine goats.

Ev-er-y morn-ing he took them to the hill

so that they could eat the green grass.

The goats were ver-y hap-py on the hill.

When eve-ning came, the boy would take them home.

Once they ran in-to a tur-nip field.

The boy could not get them out.

What do you think he did?

He sat down and cried.

A-long came a rab-bit, hop, hop, hop.

"Why are you cry-ing?" asked the rab-bit.

"Oh, oh! I can-not get my goats out of

the tur-nip field," said the boy.

"I will do it for you," said the rab-bit.

So he ran af-ter the goats.

But he could not get them out.

Then the rab-bit sat down and cried.


Soon a fox came a-long.

"Rab-bit, why are you cry-ing?" asked the fox.

"I cry be-cause the boy cries," he said.

"The boy cries be-cause he can-not get

his goats out of the tur-nip field."

"I will do it for him," said the fox.

So the fox ran af-ter the goats.

Reading & Spelling Through Literature Book 1

But he could not get them out.

Then the fox sat down and cried.


As they were cry-ing, a wolf came by.

"Fox, why are you cry-ing?" said the wolf.

"I cry be-cause the rab-bit cries," said the fox.

"The rab-bit cries be-cause the boy cries.

The boy cries be-cause he can-not get

his goats out of the tur-nip field."

"I will do it for him," said the wolf.

So the wolf ran af-ter the goats.

But he could not get them out.

Then the wolf sat down and cried, too.


A lit-tle bee saw them all cry-ing.

"Wolf, why are you cry-ing?" said the bee.

"I cry be-cause the fox cries," said the wolf.

"The fox cries be-cause the rab-bit cries.

The rab-bit cries be-cause the boy cries.

The boy cries be-cause he can-not get

his goats out of the tur-nip field."


"I will do it for him," said the bee.

Then they all stopped cry-ing and be-gan to laugh.

"Ha, ha! Ha, ha, ha!" they said.

"How can a lit-tle bee like you do it?"

But the bee flew in-to the tur-nip field.

He flew right to a big goat's back.

"Buzz-z-z!" he said, and out the goats ran!

Do you know why they ran out so fast?

They ran all the way home, too.

The boy laughed and ran af-ter them.

Norwegian Folk Tale.

Reading & Spelling Through Literature Book 1

## 55. The Kind Cranes

Six hun-gry lit-tle birds once sat by the sea.

"Let us cross the sea," said one.

"We can get fat worms o-ver there."

"But the sea is so wide!" said an-oth-er.

"How can we get a-cross?"

Soon a fish came a-long.

"Fish, will you take us a-cross the sea?"

asked the lit-tle birds.

"I will take you down in-to the sea!" said the fish.

"We will go just like this!"

And he swam down, down, down, in-to the sea.

"Dear, dear!" said the lit-tle birds.

"Dear, dear! Let us wait."

So the hun-gry lit-tle birds wait-ed.

By and by a sheep came walk-ing a-long.

"Sheep, will you take us a-cross the sea?"

asked the lit-tle birds.

"I nev-er swim," said the sheep, "and I can-not fly.

Why don't you wait for the cranes?"

"Who are they?" asked the lit-tle birds.

"They are great, big birds," said the sheep.

"Their wings are so strong that they

can fly a-cross the sea.

They have long beaks and long necks.

They have long legs and big backs.

The cranes are ver-y kind.

Ev-er-y year they take oth-er

lit-tle birds a-cross the sea.

They will take you, too."

Reading & Spelling Through Literature Book 1

So the hun-gry lit-tle birds wait-ed.

By and by four cranes came fly-ing a-long.

The lit-tle birds called to the first crane,

"Will you take us a-cross the sea?

We can get some fat worms o-ver there."

"My back is full of lit-tle birds now,"

said the first crane.

"Ask the last crane. He can take you a-cross."

So the lit-tle birds called to the last crane,

"Will you take us a-cross the sea?"

"Yes, I will take you," he said.

"My back is near-ly full.

See all the lit-tle birds on it!

But you are so lit-tle that I can find

a place for you. Hop on!"

The six lit-tle birds hopped on-to his back.

The oth-er birds made a place for them.

"Are you all right?" asked the crane.

"Here we go, lit-tle birds."

The lit-tle birds held on with their

beaks and their claws.

A-way they flew, a-cross the wide, wide sea.

They found all the worms they could eat.

And the six lit-tle birds got fat-ter and fat-ter.

Old Tale.

## 56. The North Wind

"The North Wind is cold,"

    The Rob-ins say;

"And that is the rea-son

    We fly a-way."


"The North Wind is cold;

    He is com-ing, hark!

I must haste a-way,"

    Says the Mead-ow Lark.

The North Wind is cold

    And brings the snow,"

Says Jen-ny Wren,

    "And I must go."


"The North Wind is cold

    As cold can be,

But I'm not a-fraid,"

    Says the Chick-a-dee.


So the Chick-a-dee stays

    And sees the snow,

And likes to hear

    The North Wind blow.

Rebecca B. Foresman.

## 57. What Does Lit-tle Bird-ie Say?

What does lit-tle bird-ie say,

    In her nest at peep of day?

Let me fly, says lit-tle bird-ie,

    Moth-er, let me fly a-way.


Bird-ie, rest a lit-tle long-er

    Till the lit-tle wings are strong-er.

So she rests a lit-tle long-er,

    Then she flies a-way.

What does lit-tle ba-by say,

    In her bed at peep of day?

Ba-by says, like lit-tle bird-ie,

    Let me rise and fly a-way.


Ba-by, sleep a lit-tle long-er,

    Till the lit-tle limbs are strong-er.

If she sleeps a lit-tle long-er,

    Ba-by too shall fly a-way.

Alfred, Lord Tennyson.

## 58. The Hen and the Squir-rel

One day a hen met a squir-rel.

"Friend Hen," said the squir-rel,

"do you see that tall oak tree?

It is full of good a-corns. Let us get some to eat."

"All right, friend Squir-rel," said the hen.

So they ran to the tree.

The squir-rel ran right up the tree and ate an a-corn.

"How good it is!" he said.

The hen tried to fly up to get an a-corn.

But she could not fly so high.

So she called up to the squir-rel,

"Friend Squir-rel, give me an a-corn."

The squir-rel found a big a-corn.

He threw it down to her.

The a-corn hit the hen and cut her head.

So she ran to an old wo-man and said,

"Old Wo-man, please give me a soft cloth.

Then I can tie up my poor head."

"First give me two hairs," said the old wo-man.

"Then I will give you a soft cloth."


The hen ran to a dog.

"Good Dog, give me two hairs," she said.

"I will give them to the old wo-man.

The old wo-man will give me a soft cloth.

Reading & Spelling Through Literature Book 1

Then I can tie up my poor head."

"First give me some bread," said the dog.

"Then I will give you two hairs."


The hen went to a bak-er and said,

"Oh, Good Bak-er, give me some bread.

I will give the bread to the dog.

The dog will give me two hairs.

I will give the hairs to the old wo-man.

The old wo-man will give me a soft cloth.

Then I can tie up my poor head."

"First get me some wood," said the bak-er.

"Then I will give you some bread."


The hen went to the for-est and said,

"Oh, Good For-est, give me some wood.

I will give the wood to the bak-er.

The bak-er will give me some bread.

I will give the bread to the dog.

The dog will give me two hairs.

I will give the hairs to the old wo-man.

The old wo-man will give me a soft cloth.

Then I can tie up my poor head."

"First give me some wa-ter," said the for-est.

"Then I will give you wood."


The hen went to a brook.

"Brook, give me some wa-ter.

I will give it to the for-est.

The for-est will give me wood.

I will give the wood to the bak-er.

The bak-er will give me bread.

I will give the bread to the dog.

The dog will give me two hairs.

Reading & Spelling Through Literature Book 1

I will give them to the old wo-man.

The old wo-man will give me a soft cloth.

Then I can tie up my poor head."


The brook gave the hen wa-ter.

She gave the wa-ter to the for-est.

The for-est gave her some wood.

She gave the wood to the bak-er.

The bak-er gave her some bread.

She gave the bread to the dog.

The dog gave her two hairs.

She gave the two hairs to the old wo-man.

The old wo-man gave her a soft cloth.

So the hen tied up her poor head.

Old Tale.

## 59. The Pine Tree and Its Nee-dles

A lit-tle pine tree lived in

the woods.

It had leaves like long

green nee-dles.

But the lit-tle pine tree was

not hap-py.

"I do not like my green

nee-dles," it said.

"I wish I had beau-ti-ful leaves.

How hap-py I should be

if I on-ly had gold leaves!"

Night came.

Then the Fair-y of the Trees walked in the woods.

"Lit-tle pine tree," she said, "you may have your wish."

In the morn-ing the lit-tle pine tree had leaves of gold.

"How beau-ti-ful I am!" it said.

"See how I shine in the sun! Now I am hap-py!"


Night came.

Then a man walked in the woods.

He took all the gold leaves and put them in-to a bag.

The lit-tle tree had no leaves at all.

"What shall I do?" it said.

"I do not want gold leaves a-gain.

I wish I had glass leaves.

Glass leaves would shine in the sun, too.

And no one would take glass leaves."


Night came.

The Fair-y walked in the woods a-gain.

"Lit-tle pine tree," she said, "you may have your wish."

In the morn-ing the tree had glass leaves.

"How beau-ti-ful I am!" it said.

"See how I shine in the sun! Now I am hap-py."


Night came.

Then the wind came through the woods.

Oh, how it blew!

It broke all the beau-ti-ful glass leaves.

"What shall I do now?" said the tree.

"I do not want glass leaves a-gain.

The oak tree has big green leaves.

I wish I had big green leaves, too."


Night came.

Then the Fair-y of the Trees walked

in the woods a-gain.

"Lit-tle pine tree," she said,

"you may have your wish."

In the morn-ing the lit-tle pine

tree had big green leaves.

"How beau-ti-ful I am!" it said.

"Now I am like the oth-er trees. At last I am hap-py."


Night came.

A goat came through the woods.

He ate all the big green leaves.

"What shall I do?" said the tree.

"A man took my leaves of gold.

The wind broke my leaves of glass.

A goat ate my big green leaves.

I wish I had my long nee-dles a-gain."

Night came.

The Fair-y walked in the woods a-gain.

"Lit-tle pine tree," she said,

"you may have your wish."

In the morn-ing the lit-tle pine tree

had its long nee-dles a-gain.

"Now I am hap-py," said the tree.

"I do not want an-y oth-er leaves.

Lit-tle pine nee-dles are best for lit-tle pine trees."

Old Tale.

# 60. How Gos-ling Learned to Swim

One day Lit-tle Gos-ling

went in-to a pond.

"Why do you go in-to the pond?"

asked the chick-en.

"I am go-ing to learn to swim,"

said Lit-tle Gos-ling.

"Then I will peep," said the chick-en.

So the chick-en peeped.

"Why do you peep?"

asked the duck-ling.

"Lit-tle Gos-ling swims, so I peep,"

said the chick-en.

"Then I will quack," said the duck-ling.

So the duck-ling quacked.

"Why do you quack?" asked the rab-bit.

"Lit-tle Gos-ling swims, the chick-en peeps,

so I quack," said the duck-ling.

"Then I will leap," said the rabbit.

So the rab-bit leaped.


"Why do you leap?" asked the black colt.

"Lit-tle Gos-ling swims, the chick-en peeps,

the duck-ling quacks, so I leap," said the rab-bit.

"Then I will run," said the black colt.

So the black colt ran.


"Why do you run?" asked the white dove.

"Lit-tle Gos-ling swims, the chick-en peeps,

the duck-ling quacks, and the rab-bit leaps,

so I run," said the black colt.

"Then I will coo," said the white dove.

So the white dove cooed.


"Why do you coo?" asked the brown dog.

"Lit-tle Gos-ling swims, the chick-en peeps,

the duck-ling quacks, and the rab-bit leaps.

The black colt runs, so I coo," said the white dove.

"Then I will bark," said the brown dog.

So the brown dog barked.


"Why do you bark?" said the yel-low calf.

"Lit-tle Gos-ling swims, the chick-en peeps,

the duck-ling quacks and the rab-bit leaps.

The black colt runs, and the white dove coos,

so I bark," said the brown dog.

"Then I will moo," said the yel-low calf.

So Lit-tle Gos-ling swam, and the chick-en peeped,

The duck-ling quacked, and the rab-bit leaped,

The black colt ran, and the white dove cooed,

The brown dog barked, and the yel-low calf mooed.

And Lit-tle Gos-ling learned to swim.

English Folk Tale.

## 61. I Don't Care

A horse and a brown colt once lived in a mead-ow.

One day the gate was o-pen.

"I will run out of the gate," said the brown colt.

"No, no!" said the horse.

"You must stay in the mead-ow."

"Why?" asked the brown colt.

"I do not know," said the horse.

"But the old white horse told me to stay.

So I shall stay."

"I don't care!" said the colt. "I do not like it here.

If I run down the road, I shall have more fun."

So off he ran, down the road.


By and by he met the old white horse.

"Why are you here?" asked the old horse.

"I want some fun," said the colt.

"I am tired of stay-ing in the mead-ow."

"The mead-ow is the best place for you,"

said the old white horse.

"You are safe in the mead-ow.

You are too lit-tle to see the world."

"I don't care!" said the brown colt.

He shook his head and ran on.

By and by he met a mule.

The mule was pul-ling a big cart.

"Why are you here?" he asked the colt.

"You should be in the mead-ow. The town is close by,

and it is no place for a lit-tle colt like you."

"I don't care! I want some fun," said the brown colt.


The colt ran on un-til he came to the town.

He had nev-er seen a town be-fore.

What a noise the carts made!

The lit-tle colt was fright-ened.

He want-ed to run back to the mead-ow.

Then some men and boys ran af-ter him.

They shout-ed at him and tried to catch him.

Soon he came to a big glass win-dow.

He saw his shad-ow in the win-dow,

and he thought it was an-oth-er colt.

"Oh, there is an-oth-er colt just like me!"

said the lit-tle brown colt.

"I will ask him the way to the mead-ow."

But it was not an-oth-er colt.

It was on-ly his shad-ow he saw in the glass.

The lit-tle brown colt ran in-to the win-dow and broke

the glass. The glass cut him, and he fell down.

Then some men caught him.

They took the lit-tle colt back to the

mead-ow and shut him in.

Now he does not want to run a-way.

He nev-er says, "I don't care" an-y-more.

Gertrude Sellon.

## 62. The Cam-el and the Pig

One day a cam-el and a pig were talk-ing.

The cam-el was proud be-cause he was tall.

But the pig was proud be-cause he was short.

"Just look at me!" said the cam-el.

"See how tall I am! It is bet-ter to be tall, like me."

"Oh, no!" said the pig.

"Just look at me! See how short I am!

It is bet-ter to be short, like me."

"If I am not right, I will give up my hump,"

said the cam-el.

"If I am not right, I will give up my snout,"

said the pig.


Soon they came to a gar-den.

All a-round it was a wall.

There was no gate in the wall.

The cam-el was so tall that

he could see o-ver the wall.

He could see fine, ripe fruit in the gar-den.

His neck was so long that he could reach o-ver the

wall and get the fruit. He ate all he want-ed.

But the poor pig was short.

He could not reach o-ver the wall.

He could not get in-side be-cause there was no gate.

"Ha, ha, ha!" laughed the cam-el.

"Now would you rath-er be tall or short?"


Soon they came to an-oth-er gar-den.

All a-round it was a high wall.

It was so high that the cam-el could not see o-ver it.

But there was a gate in the wall.

The pig went through the gate.

This gar-den was full of fine, ripe fruit, too.

The pig ate all he want-ed.

But the cam-el was so tall that he

could not get through the gate.

"Ha, ha, ha!" laughed the pig.

"Now would you rath-er be tall or short?"

So the cam-el kept his hump,

and the pig kept his snout.

For they said,

"Some-times it's bet-ter to be tall,

And some-times it's bet-ter to be small ."

A Tale from India.

# 63. The Lit-tle Roos-ter

Once there was a man who

had a lit-tle roos-ter.

The lit-tle roos-ter liked to crow.

One night the man said, "How

sleep-y I am! I will go to bed

and have a good sleep."

So he went to bed and slept.

Next morn-ing the lit-tle

roos-ter got up ver-y ear-ly and ran to the house.

He flapped his wings and crowed,

"Cock-a-doo-dle-doo!"

He crowed so loud that he woke the man.

"That must be the lit-tle roos-ter," said the man.

The man was so an-gry that he threw his

hair-brush at the lit-tle roos-ter.

The roos-ter ran a-way as fast as he could.

Then the man said, "Now that I am up,

I will plant my gar-den." So he plant-ed his gar-den.


That night he put the lit-tle roos-ter in-to the hen yard.

He said, "Now I will have a long sleep."

He went to bed and slept.

But the lit-tle roos-ter got up

ver-y ear-ly the next morn-ing.

He flew out of the hen yard and ran to the house.

"Cock-a-doo-dle-doo!" he crowed.

The man woke up and said,

"There is that lit-tle roos-ter a-gain."

He was so an-gry that he threw

his comb at the roos-ter.

But th͟e lit-tl͟e r͟oos-ter had a͟ co͟mb.

So͟ he ran a͟-way² as fast as² he cou͟ld.⁵

Then th͟e man saͥid, "Now that I am up,

I will weͤed my gar-den." So͟ he weed-ed² his gar-den.

That night th͟e man tieͩ͡d² th͟e lit-tl͟e r͟oos-ter

in th͟e hen ya͟rd with͟ a͟ string.

He saͥid, "Now I will hav͟e a͟ long sleͤep."

So͟ he went to³ bed and slept.

Th͟e lit-tl͟e r͟oos-ter got up ver-y

ear-ly th͟e next mo͟rn-ing.

He bit th͟e string in two³ and fleͤw ou͟t of th͟e hen yaͮ͟rd.

He ran to³ th͟e ho͟use³ and flapped³ his wings.²

"Cock-a-do͟o-dl͟e-do͟o!" he crow͟ed²̇.²

Th͟e lit-tl͟e r͟oos-ter crow͟ed² so͟ loud²

that th͟e man wok͟e⌢ up.

"There is that lit-tle roos-ter a-gain!"

said the man. "How can I sleep?"

He was as an-gry as he could be.

So he caught the lit-tle roos-ter and gave him a-way.

That night the man went to sleep ear-ly.

He had a long sleep.

The next night he had a long sleep.

And the next night.

And the next.

And the next.

But the weeds grew up and filled his gar-den.

Charles Battell Loomis, Adapted.

## 64. North Wind at Play

North Wind went out one sum-mer day.

"Now I will have a good play," he said.

He saw an ap-ple tree full of ap-ples.

"Oh, ap-ple tree, come and play with me!

We can have fun to-geth-er," said North Wind.

"Oh, no!" said the ap-ple tree.

"I can-not play with you. I must work.

I am help-ing my ap-ples to grow.

By and by they will grow big and red.

Then lit-tle chil-dren can eat them.

Oh, no! I can-not play with you."

"We will see a-bout that," said North Wind.

"I will make you play with me. Puff! Puff!"

he said, and all the ap-ples fell to the ground.


Then North Wind saw a field of corn.

"Oh, corn, come and play with me!" he said.

"No, no, North Wind!" said the corn.

"I can-not play with you just now.

I must stand still and grow.

Look un-der my long, green leaves.

Do you see the white grains un-der them?

They must grow big and yel-low.

Then they can be ground at the mill.

Lit-tle chil-dren can have corn bread to eat.

No, no! I can-not play with you."

"Puff! Puff!" said North Wind.

All the corn fell to the ground.

By and by North Wind saw a lil-y.

"Oh, lil-y, come and play with me.

We can have fun to-geth-er," he said.

"Oh, no, North Wind!" said the lil-y.

"I can-not play with you to-day.

I must take care of my buds.

They will o-pen soon,

and then they will be beau-ti-ful lil-ies.

Then lit-tle chil-dren will come to see me.

Oh, no! I can-not play with you."

"Puff! Puff!" said North Wind.

The lil-y hung her head.

She could not look up a-gain.


At night North Wind went home.

"What did you do to-day?" said his fa-ther.

"I went out to play," said North Wind.

"But no one want-ed to play with me.

So I shook the ap-ple tree,

and all the ap-ples fell to the ground.

Then I shook the corn, and it fell, too.

I blew un-til the lil-y hung her head.

I did not want to hurt them, Fa-ther.

I was on-ly play-ing."


"You are too rough," said his fa-ther.

"I know you do not want to be rough.

You must stay at home in sum-mer.

You must wait un-til the ap-ples

and the corn and the lil-ies are gone.

You may go out to play in win-ter.

Then you can puff all you want to."

Old Tale.

## 65. Three Bil-ly Goats Gruff

Once there were three bil-ly goats.

They were all named Gruff.

Ev-er-y day they went up a hill

to eat the grass and grow fat.

They had to go o-ver a lit-tle brook

be-fore they came to the hill.

O-ver the brook was a bridge.

A Troll lived un-der the bridge.

He was so big and cross that

ev-er-y-one was a-fraid of him.


One day the three bil-ly goats were

go-ing up the hill to get fat.

Lit-tle Bil-ly Goat Gruff was the

first to cross the bridge.

Trip-trap! Trip-trap! went the bridge.

"Who is that trip-trap-ping on my bridge?"

called the Troll.

"Oh, it is just Lit-tle Bil-ly Goat Gruff.

I am go-ing up the hill to get fat,"

said the lit-tle bil-ly goat.

"Well, I am com-ing to gob-ble you up!"

said the Troll.

"Oh, no!" said Lit-tle Bil-ly Goat.

"Do not take me! I am too lit-tle.

Wait for Sec-ond Bil-ly Goat. He is big-ger than I am."

"Well, be off with you!" said the Troll.


Soon Sec-ond Bil-ly Goat Gruff came to the bridge.

Trip-trap! Trip-trap! Trip-trap! went the bridge.

"Who is that trip-trap-ping on my bridge!"

called the Troll.

"Oh, it is just Sec-ond Bil-ly Goat Gruff.

I am go-ing up the hill to get fat,"

said the sec-ond bil-ly goat.

"Well, I am com-ing to gob-ble you up!"

said the Troll.

"Oh, no!" said Sec-ond Bil-ly Goat.

"Do not take me. I am not ver-y big.

Wait for Big Bil-ly Goat. He is big-ger than I am."

"Well, be off with you!" said the Troll.


Just then Big Bil-ly Goat Gruff came to the bridge.

Trip-trap! Trip-trap! Trip-trap! Trip-trap!

went the bridge.

"Who is that trip-trap-ping on my bridge?"

called the Troll.

"Oh, it is just Big Bil-ly Goat Gruff.

I am go-ing up the hill to get fat."

"Well, I am com-ing to gob-ble you up!"

said the Troll.

"Come a-long, then, Troll!" said Big Bil-ly Goat Gruff.

So the Troll came a-long.

Big Bil-ly Goat Gruff flew at him.

He caught the Troll on his horns

and threw him in-to the brook.

The Troll was fright-ened.

He jumped out of the wa-ter and ran a-way.

The three bil-ly goats nev-er saw him a-gain.

They go up the hill ev-er-y day,

and now they are as fat as they can be.

## 66. The Lit-tle Plant

In the heart of a seed

Bur-ied deep, so deep,

A dear lit-tle plant

Lay fast a-sleep.


"Wake!" said the sun-shine,

"And creep to the light,"

"Wake!" said the voice

Of the rain-drops bright.


The lit-tle plant heard,

And it rose to see

What the won-der-ful

Out-side world might be.

Kate Louise Brown.

Reading & Spelling Through Literature Book 1

## 67. The Swing

How do you like to go up in a swing,

Up in the air so blue?

Oh, I do think it the pleas-ant-est thing

Ev-er a child can do!


Up in the air and o-ver the wall,

Till I can see so wide,

Riv-ers and trees and cat-tle and all

O-ver the coun-try-side.

Till I look down on the gar-den green,

Down on the roof so brown—

Up in the air I go fly-ing a-gain,

Up in the air and down!

Robert Louis Stevenson.

## 68. The Sleep-ing Ap-ple

A lit-tle ap-ple hung high up on an ap-ple tree.

It slept and grew, and slept and grew.

At last it was big and ripe, but it still slept on.

One day a lit-tle girl came walk-ing

un-der the tree and saw the ap-ple.

"Why does the ap-ple sleep so long?"

said the lit-tle girl.

"The world is so beau-ti-ful!

I wish the ap-ple would wake up and see.

May-be I can wake it."

So she called out, "Oh, ap-ple, wake up!

Do not sleep so long.

Wake up, wake up, and come with me!"

But the sleep-ing ap-ple did not wake.


"Oh, Sun, beau-ti-ful Sun!" said the girl.

"Will you kiss the ap-ple and make it wake?

That is the way moth-er wakes me."

"Oh, yes," said the sun, "in-deed I will."

So he kissed the ap-ple un-til it was a gold-en yel-low.

It was as gold-en as the sun.

But still the ap-ple slept on.


By and by a rob-in flew to the tree.

"Dear Rob-in," said the lit-tle girl,

"can you help me wake the sleep-ing ap-ple?

I can-not wake it, and the sun can-not wake it.

We have tried and tried. It will sleep too long."

"Oh, yes, lit-tle girl, I can wake the ap-ple,"

said the rob-in.

"I will sing to it just as I sing

to my lit-tle bird-ies in their nest.

I wake my bird-ies ev-er-y morn-ing with a song."

"Cheer up! Wake up! Cheer up! Wake up!"

sang the rob-in in the ap-ple tree.

But the sleep-ing ap-ple did not wake.


"Oo—oo—oo! Oo—oo—oo!"

"Who is that com-ing through the trees?"

said the lit-tle girl.

"Oh, it is my friend, the Wind.

Oh, Wind, you wake me some-times at night.

Can you not wake this beau-ti-ful ap-ple?

It has slept so long."

"In-deed I can," said the wind.

"It is time for all ap-ples to wake up.

Sum-mer will soon be o-ver."

"Oo—oo—oo!" he said, and he shook the tree.

The ap-ple woke and fell down,

down, down to the ground.

The lit-tle girl kissed its gold-en cheeks.

"Oh, thank you, kind wind," she said.

"If you had not come, the ap-ple would

have slept all the sum-mer long."

Folk Tale.

## 69. Sweet Por-ridge

Once there was a lit-tle girl

who lived with her moth-er.

They were ver-y poor.

Some-times they had no sup-per.

Then they went to bed hun-gry.

One day the lit-tle girl went in-to the woods.

She want-ed wood for the fire.

She was so hun-gry and sad!

"Oh, I wish I had some sweet por-ridge!" she said.

"I wish I had a pot full for moth-er and me.

We could eat it all up."

Just then she saw an old wo-man

with a lit-tle black pot.

She said, "Lit-tle girl, why are you so sad?"

"I am hun-gry," said the lit-tle girl.

"My moth-er is hun-gry, too.

We have noth-ing to eat.

Oh, I wish we had some sweet

por-ridge for our sup-per!"

"I will help you," said the old wo-man.

"Take this lit-tle black pot.

When you want some sweet por-ridge,

you must say, 'Lit-tle pot, boil!'

The lit-tle pot will boil and boil and boil.

Reading & Spelling Through Literature Book 1

You will have all the sweet por-ridge you want.

When the lit-tle pot is full,

you must say, 'Lit-tle pot, stop!'

Then the lit-tle pot will stop boil-ing."


The lit-tle girl thanked the old wo-man

and ran home with the lit-tle black pot.

Then she made a fire with the wood

and put the lit-tle black pot on the fire.

"Lit-tle pot, boil!" she said.

The lit-tle pot boiled and boiled and boiled

until it was full of sweet por-ridge.

Then the lit-tle girl said, "Lit-tle pot, stop!"

The lit-tle pot stopped boil-ing.

She called her moth-er, and they ate all

the sweet por-ridge they want-ed.

The lit-tle girl told her moth-er a-bout the old wo-man.

"Now," they said, "we are hap-py.

We shall not be hun-gry an-y-more."


The next day the lit-tle girl went

in-to the woods a-gain.

She was gone a long time.

"She will be hun-gry when she comes home,"

said her moth-er.

"I will boil the sweet por-ridge."

So she put the lit-tle black pot on the fire.

"Lit-tle pot, boil!" she said.

The lit-tle pot boiled and boiled un-til

it was full of sweet por-ridge.

The moth-er want-ed the pot to stop boil-ing.

But she for-got what to say.

The pot boiled and boiled.

The por-ridge boiled o-ver on-to the stove.

It ran all o-ver the stove.

Then it ran all o-ver the floor.

It flowed in-to the street.

It flowed on and on and on.


The peo-ple all ran out of their houses.

"Oh! Oh! Oh!" they cried.

"The sea has turned to por-ridge!

It is flow-ing o-ver the world! What shall we do?"

No one knew how to make the lit-tle

black pot stop boil-ing.


Af-ter a long time the lit-tle girl came home.

The pot was boil-ing and boil-ing.

"Lit-tle pot, stop!" said the lit-tle girl.

And the lit-tle pot stopped.

But for man-y days af-ter that,

the street was full of sweet por-ridge.

When peo-ple want-ed to get to the oth-er side,

they had to eat their way a-cross.

Folk Tale.

# 70. John-ny Cake

Once there were a lit-tle old man,

a lit-tle old wo-man, and a lit-tle boy.

One day the old wo-man made

a round John-ny cake.

She put it in-to the stove to bake.

She said to the lit-tle boy,

"You must bake the John-ny cake for us.

We will eat it for sup-per."

Then the lit-tle old man took a spade,

and the lit-tle old wo-man took a hoe.

They went to work in the gar-den.

The lit-tle boy was all a-lone in the house.

He for-got a-bout the John-ny cake.

All at once he heard a great noise.

The stove door flew o-pen,

and John-ny cake rolled out.

Out of the house he rolled.


The lit-tle boy ran to the gar-den.

"Fa-ther! Moth-er!" he called.

"John-ny cake is roll-ing a-way."

The lit-tle old man threw down his spade,

and the lit-tle old wo-man threw down her hoe.

Then they all ran as fast as they could af-ter

John-ny cake. But they could not catch him.

John-ny cake laughed and said,

"I am having some fun;

I roll and they run;

I can beat ev-er-y-one."

He rolled on and on.


Soon he came to a hen.

"John-ny cake, where are you go-ing?" asked the hen.

"Oh, I am out roll-ing," he said.

"I have rolled a-way from

A lit-tle old man,

A lit-tle old wo-man,

A lit-tle boy,

And I can roll a-way from you, too!"

"You can, can you?" said the hen.

"We will see a-bout that!

I think I will just eat you up!"

So the hen ran as fast as she could.

But she could not catch John-ny cake.

John-ny cake laughed and said,

"I am having some fun;

I roll and they run;

I can beat ev-er-y-one."

He rolled on and on.


By and by he came to a cow.

"John-ny cake, where are you go-ing?" asked the cow.

"Oh, I am out roll-ing," he said.

"I have rolled a-way from

A lit-tle old man,

A lit-tle old wo-man,

A lit-tle boy,

And a hen.

I can roll a-way from you, too!"

"You can, can you?" said the cow.

"I think I will just eat you up!"

The cow ran as fast as she could.

But she could not catch him.

John-ny cake laughed and said,

"I am having some fun;

I roll and they run;

I can beat ev-er-y-one."

He rolled on un-til he came to a pig.

The pig was ly-ing down.

"Where are you go-ing?" asked the pig.

"Oh, I am out roll-ing," said John-ny cake.

"I have rolled a-way from

A lit-tle old man,

A lit-tle old wo-man,

A lit-tle boy,

A hen,

And a cow.

I can roll a-way from you, too!"

"Woof, woof! I am sleep-y," said the pig.

John-ny cake went near to him.

"I will make you hear me!" he said.

"I have rolled a-way from

A lit-tle old man,

A lit-tle old wo-man,

A lit-tle boy,

A hen,

And a cow.

I can roll a-way from you, too!"

Reading & Spelling Through Literature Book 1

"Woof, woof!" said the pig.

"I am sleep-y. Go a-way!" He shut his eyes.

John-ny cake got as near to the pig as he could.

He shout-ed at him.

"Do you hear me?" he called.

"I have rolled a-way from

A lit-tle old man,

A lit-tle old wo-man,

A lit-tle boy,

A hen,

And a cow.

I can roll a-way from you, too!"

The pig o-pened his eyes.

He o-pened his mouth, too.

He caught John-ny cake and ate him up.

English Folk Tale.

# 71. Ma-ry and the Lark

Ma-ry: Good morn-ing, pret-ty lark.

Have you an-y bird-ies in that nest?


Lark: Oh, yes. I have three bird-ies here.

They are ver-y beau-ti-ful,

and they are ver-y good, too.


Ma-ry: May I see them, pret-ty lark?

Lark: Oh, yes. Come here, lit-tle ones.

This is Ti-ny Beak, this is Light Wing,

and this is Bright Eyes.


Ma-ry: How beau-ti-ful they are!

There are three chil-dren in our home, too,

Al-ice, Ned, and I. Moth-er says we are ver-y good.

We know how much she loves us.


Bright Eyes: Moth-er loves us, too.


Ma-ry: I am sure she does.

Pret-ty lark, may I take Ti-ny Beak

home to play with me?


Lark: Yes, you may take Ti-ny Beak home with you

if you will bring ba-by Al-ice to us.

Ma-ry: Oh, no, no! I can-not do that.

Ba-by Al-ice can-not leave moth-er. She is so lit-tle!

She would not like to live out of doors,

and she is too big for your lit-tle nest.

Lark: But Ti-ny Beak can-not leave his moth-er.

He is such a lit-tle bird.

He is too lit-tle for your big house.

He loves his lit-tle round nest the best.

Ti-ny Beak: Chirp, chirp, chirp! So I do!

Ma-ry: Poor lit-tle Ti-ny Beak!

I will not take you.

I see that your lit-tle round nest is best for you.

Lark: North and south and east and west,

Each one loves his own home best.

Ma-ry: Good-bye, bird-ies! Good-bye!

Light Wing: Good-bye, Ma-ry!

Come to see us a-gain soon.

## 72. The Hen Who

## Went to High Do-ver

Once a hen was in the woods.

When night came she flew up

in-to an oak tree and went to sleep.

Soon she had a dream.

She dreamed that she would find a nest

of gold-en eggs if she went to High Do-ver.

She woke up with a jump.

"I must go to High Do-ver," she said.

"I must find the nest of gold-en eggs."

So she flew out of the tree and went up the road.

When she had gone a lit-tle way, she met a roos-ter.

"Good-day, Cock-y Lock-y!" said the hen.

"Good-day, Hen-ny Pen-ny!

Where are you go-ing so ear-ly?" said the roos-ter.

"I am go-ing to High Do-ver.

I shall find a nest of gold-en eggs there,"

said the hen.

"Who told you that, Hen-ny Pen-ny?"

asked the roos-ter.

"I sat in the oak tree last night and dreamed it,"

said the hen.

"I will go with you," said the roos-ter.


So they went a long way to-geth-er

un-til they met a duck.

"Good-day, Duck-y Luck-y!" said the roos-ter.

"Good-day, Cock-y Lock-y!

Where are you go-ing so ear-ly?" asked the duck.

"I am go-ing to High Do-ver.

I shall find a nest of gold-en eggs there,"

said the roos-ter.

"Who told you that, Cock-y Lock-y?" asked the duck.

"Hen-ny Pen-ny!" said the roos-ter.

"Who told you that, Hen-ny Pen-ny?" asked the duck.

"I sat in the oak tree last night and dreamed it,"

said the hen.

"I will go with you!" said the duck.


So they went a long way to-geth-er

un-til they met a gan-der.

"Good-day, Gan-dy Pan-dy!" said the duck.

"Good-day, Duck-y Luck-y!" said the gan-der.

"Where are you go-ing so ear-ly?"

"I am go-ing to High Do-ver.

I shall find a nest of gold-en eggs there,"

said the duck.

"Who told you that, Duck-y Luck-y?"

asked the gan-der.

"Cock-y Lock-y."

"Who told you that, Cock-y Lock-y?"

"Hen-ny Pen-ny."

"How do you know that, Hen-ny Pen-ny?"

asked the gan-der.

"I sat in the oak tree last night and dreamed it,"

said the hen.

"I will go with you!" said the gan-der.

So they went a long way to-geth-er

un-til they met a fox.

"Good-day, Fox-y Wox-y!" said the gan-der.

"Good-day, Gan-dy Pan-dy!

Where are you go-ing so ear-ly?" asked the fox.

"I am go-ing to High Do-ver.

I shall find a nest of gold-en eggs there,"

said the gan-der.

"Who told you that, Gan-dy Pan-dy?"

"Duck-y Luck-y."

"Who told you that, Duck-y Luck-y?" asked the fox.

"Cock-y Lock-y."

"Who told you that, Cock-y Lock-y?"

"Hen-ny Pen-ny."

"How do you know that, Hen-ny Pen-ny?"

"I sat in the oak tree last night and dreamed it,

Fox-y Wox-y," said the hen.

"How fool-ish you are!" said the fox.

"There is no nest of gold-en eggs at High Do-ver.

You are cold and tired.

Come with me to my warm den."


So they all went with the fox to his den.

They all got warm and sleep-y.

The duck and the gan-der went to sleep in a corn-er.

But the roos-ter and the hen slept on a roost.

When they were a-sleep,

the fox ate the gan-der and the duck.

Just then the hen woke up.

She saw Cock-y Lock-y near her.

She looked for Gan-dy Pan-dy and Duck-y Luck-y.

She could not see them,

but she saw feath-ers on the floor!

"I must fool the fox," she said.

So she looked up the chim-ney.

"Oh! Oh!" she called to the fox.

"Look at the geese fly-ing by!"

The fox ran out to see the geese.

He want-ed some geese to eat.


Then Hen-ny Pen-ny woke up Cock-y Lock-y.

She told him what she had seen.

"Fly! Fly!" she cried.

"Let us get out of here!"

So Cock-y Lock-y and Hen-ny Pen-ny

flew up the chim-ney.

They went to High Do-ver and found

the nest of gold-en eggs.

Norwegian Folk Tale.

## 73. Han-sel's Coat

Sheep: Where is your coat, lit-tle Han-sel?

It is cold this spring morn-ing.


Han-sel: I have no coat.

Moth-er can-not get me a coat till win-ter comes.

I wish I could have one now.


Sheep: I will help you, Han-sel.

Take some of my wool. There!

Now you can make a warm coat.

Han-sel: Oh, thank you!

But how can I make a coat from this curl-y wool?

Thorn Bush: Come here, Han-sel.

Pull the curl-y wool o-ver my long thorns.

They will comb it and make it straight.

Han-sel: Oh, thank you!

How straight and soft you have made it!

But this is not a coat yet. What shall I do now?

Spi-der: Give me the wool, Han-sel.

I will spin the threads and make them

in-to cloth for you. There it is.

Crab: What have you there, Han-sel?

Han-sel: This is cloth for a coat.

Crab: My claws are like scis-sors.

I will cut it out for you. There it is!

Han-sel: Thank you, kind Crab. I wish I could sew.

Then I could make my coat.

Bird: I will sew your coat for you.

I sew my nest to-geth-er ev-er-y spring.

See, I take a thread in my beak.

Then I pull it through and through the cloth.

There is your coat, Han-sel.

Han-sel: Oh, thank you all!

How hap-py moth-er will be to see my nice warm coat.

Folk Tale.

## 74. The Lamb-kin

Once up-on a time was a wee, wee Lamb-kin.

The Lamb-kin jumped a-bout on his lit-tle legs.

He ate the green grass and had a fine time.

One day he thought he would go to see his Gran-ny.

"I shall have a fine time!" he said.

"I shall have such good things to

eat when I get there!"

The Lamb-kin jumped a-bout on his lit-tle legs.

He was as hap-py as he could be.


As he was go-ing a-long the road, he met a jack-al.

Now the jack-al likes to eat ten-der lit-tle lamb-kins.

So the jack-al said, "Lamb-kin! Lamb-kin! I'll eat you!"

But the Lamb-kin jumped a-bout

on his lit-tle legs and said,

"To Gran-ny's house I go,

Where I shall fat-ter grow;

Then you can eat me so."

The jack-al likes fat lambs,

so he let Lamb-kin go on to get fat.


By and by Lamb-kin met a ti-ger.

Then he met a wolf. Then he met a dog.

They all like good things to eat.

They like ten-der lamb-kins, so they all called out,

"Lamb-kin! Lamb-kin! We'll eat you!"

But Lamb-kin jumped a-bout on his lit-tle legs and said,

"To Gran-ny's house I go,

Where I shall fat-ter grow;

Then you can eat me so."

The ti-ger and the wolf and

the dog all like fat lamb-kins.

So they let Lamb-kin go on to his Gran-ny's to get fat.

At last Lamb-kin got to his Gran-ny's house.

Gran-ny came to the door to see him.

"Oh, Gran-ny, dear!" he said.

"I have prom-ised to get ver-y fat.

I must keep my prom-ise.

Please put me in-to the corn bin."

So his Gran-ny put him in-to the corn bin.

Lamb-kin stayed there sev-en days

and ate and ate and ate.

At last he grew ver-y fat.

"How fat you are, Lamb-kin," said his Gran-ny.

"You must go home."

"Oh, no!" said Lamb-kin. "The ti-ger might eat me up."

"But you must go home, Lamb-kin," said his Gran-ny.

"Well, then," said Lamb-kin.

"I will tell you what to do.

You must take a goat skin and make a lit-tle Drum-kin.

I can sit in-side and roll home."

So she made a Drum-kin.

Lamb-kin got in-to it, and his Gran-ny sewed it up.

Then Lamb-kin be-gan to roll

a-long the road to his home.


Soon he met the ti-ger.

The ti-ger called out,

"Drum-kin! Drum-kin! Have you seen Lamb-kin?"

Lamb-kin, in his soft nest, called back,

  "Lost in the for-est, and so are you!

  On, lit-tle Drum-kin! Tum-pa, tum-too!"

The ti-ger was an-gry.

"Now I shall have no fat Lamb-kin to eat," he said.

"Why didn't I eat him when I had him?"


By and by Lamb-kin met the dog and the wolf.

They called to him, "Drum-kin! Drum-kin!

Have you seen Lamb-kin?"

And Lamb-kin, in his soft, warm nest,

call<u>ed</u> ba<u>ck</u> to <u>th</u>em,

"Lost in <u>the</u> for-est, and s<u>o</u> ar<u>e</u> you!

On, lit-tl<u>e</u> Drum-kin! Tum-p<u>a</u>, tum-t<u>oo</u>!"

<u>The</u> dog and <u>the</u> wolf w<u>ere</u> ver-<u>y</u> an-gry

b<u>e</u>-c<u>au</u>se <u>th</u>ey had n<u>o</u> fat Lamb-kin to <u>eat</u>.

But La<u>mb</u>-kin r<u>o</u>ll<u>ed</u> <u>a</u>-long, l<u>augh</u>-ing and sing-ing,

"Tum-p<u>a</u>, tum-t<u>oo</u>! Tum-p<u>a</u>, tum-t<u>oo</u>!"

At last La<u>mb</u>-kin met <u>the</u> ja<u>ck</u>-al, <u>who</u> s<u>ai</u>d,

"Drum-kin! Drum-kin! Hav<u>e</u> you s<u>ee</u>n La<u>mb</u>-kin?"

La<u>mb</u>-kin, in his soft nest, call<u>ed</u> ba<u>ck</u>,

"Lost in <u>the</u> for-est, and s<u>o</u> ar<u>e</u> you!

On, lit-tl<u>e</u> Drum-kin! Tum-p<u>a</u>, tum-t<u>oo</u>!"

N<u>ow</u> <u>the</u> ja<u>ck</u>-al was wis<u>e</u>.

H<u>e</u> kn<u>ew</u> La<u>mb</u>-kin's v<u>oi</u>c<u>e</u>. S<u>o</u> he call<u>ed</u> <u>out</u>,

"Lamb-kin! Lamb-kin! Come out of that Drum-kin!"

"Come and make me!" shout-ed Lamb-kin.

The jack-al ran af-ter Drum-kin.

But Drum-kin rolled fast-er and fast-er,

and soon rolled a-way from him.

The last thing the jack-al heard was,

    "Lost in the for-est, and so are you!

    On, lit-tle Drum-kin! Tum-pa, tum-too!"

A Tale from India.

# 75. Snow-flakes

Child: Lit-tle white feath-ers

Fil-ling the air—

Lit-tle white feath-ers!

How came you there?

Snow-flakes: We came from the cloud birds,

Fly-ing so high,

Shak-ing their white wings

Up in the sky.

Child: Lit-tle white feath-ers,

Swift-ly you go!

Lit-tle white snow-flakes,

I love you so!

Snow-flakes : We are swift be-cause

    We have work to do;

But look up at us,

    And we will kiss you.

Mary Mapes Dodge.

## The Clouds

White sheep, white sheep,

    On a blue hill,

When the wind stops,

    You all stand still.

When the winds blow,

    You walk a-way slow;

White sheep, white sheep,

    Where do you go?

Christina G. Rossetti.

Appendix A

Alphabetical List of Spelling Words in RSTL

This list of spelling words is in alphabetical order and shows in which lesson each word is analyzed.

RSTL Primer: Lists 1-29
RSTL Book 1: Lists 30-75

Alphabetical List of Spelling Words in RSTL

Alphabetical List of Spelling Words in RSTL

Alphabetical List of Spelling Words in RSTL

Appendix B

Flashcards

- The flashcards include both basic and advanced phonograms. A number of basic phonograms also have advanced **sounds**, and these are included on the flashcards *on a separate line* so you can decide whether you want to teach only the basic sounds or whether you want to include the advanced sounds as well. For new readers, I advise only teaching the basic sounds. Fluent readers can learn the advanced sounds.

- The single-letter phonograms (the alphabet) and *qu* are arranged in the order that they appear in the optional *RSTL Primer Workbook A*. The multi-letter phonograms are arranged in the order that they are introduced in the spelling lists.

- Three advanced phonograms appear in the spelling lists in the *Primer* and *Book 1*. These three advanced phonograms are included with the basic phonograms in the order that they appear in the spelling lists. All other advanced phonograms are included after the basic phonograms in alphabetical order.

- To review, simply go through the flashcards in this order until you get to an unknown phonogram.

- Each phonogram is labeled as either *Primer*, *Book 1*, or *Advanced Phonogram*.
  - If you are beginning in the Primer, teach the first 26 phonograms (*a* to *z*) before beginning the spelling lists.
  - If you are beginning in Book 1, teach all of the phonograms taught in the Primer before beginning the spelling lists.
  - If you are beginning in Book 2 or higher, teach all of the phonograms taught in the Primer and Book 1 before beginning the spelling lists.

---

RSTL Primer

# C

## /k/, /s/

/k/ — cat                 /s/ — city

# a

## /ă/, /ā/, /ä/

/ă/ — at        /ā/ — acorn        /ä/ — wasp

---

# d

## /d/

/d/ — dog

# g

## /g/, /j/

/g/ — garden          /j/ — gem

---

# o

## /ŏ/, /ō/, /ö/

/ŏ/ — pot          /ō/ — go          /ö/ — to

# /t/

/t/ — tap

---

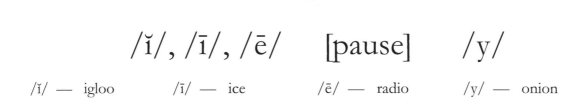

# /ĭ/, /ī/, /ē/    [pause]    /y/

/ĭ/ — igloo     /ī/ — ice     /ē/ — radio     /y/ — onion

These sounds are the same as those of **y**, only the order is different. To improve memory retention, pause before the /y/ sound to separate it from the others.

/j/

/j/ — jam

---

/m/

/m/ — mat

/n/

/n/ — no

/r/

/r/ — run

/l/

/l/ — lot

/h/

/h/ — hat

/k/

/k/ — kite

/b/

/b/ — but

# /p/

/p/ — put

---

# u

## /ŭ/, /ū/, /ü/

/ŭ/ — umbrella          /ū/ — unit          /ü/ — put

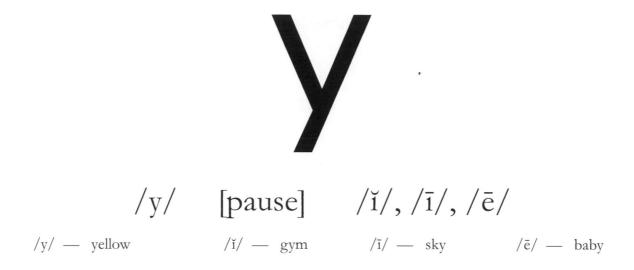

# y

/y/     [pause]     /ĭ/, /ī/, /ē/

/y/ — yellow          /ĭ/ — gym          /ī/ — sky          /ē/ — baby

These sounds are the same as those of *i*, only the order is different. To improve memory retention, pause after the /y/ sound to separate it from the others.

---

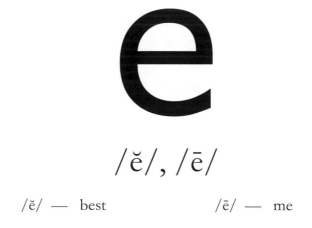

# e

/ĕ/, /ē/

/ĕ/ — best          /ē/ — me

/f/

/f/ — four

---

/v/

/v/ — vowel

# W

## /w/

/w/ — water

---

## /kw/

## Advanced: /kw/, /k/

/kw/ — queen          /k/ — croquet

# S

## /s/, /z/

/s/ — sass          /z/ — has

---

# X

## /ks/, /z/

/ks/ — fox          /z/ — xylophone

/z/

## Advanced: /z/, /s/

/z/ — zoo          /s/ — quartz

---

/th/, /TH/

## Advanced: /th/, /TH/, /t/

/th/ — think (motor off)          /TH/ — that (motor on)          /t/ — thyme

# aw

/ä/ — 2 letter /ä/ that we CAN use at the end of English words

/ä/ — p<u>aw</u>

---

# ir

/er/ as in d<u>ir</u>t

/er/ — d<u>ir</u>t

The four spellings of /er/: Oyst<u>er</u>s t<u>ur</u>n d<u>ir</u>t into p<u>ear</u>ls.       M<u>er</u>maids t<u>ur</u>n and tw<u>ir</u>l with p<u>ear</u>ls.

# or

/or/

/or/ — c<u>or</u>d

# ew

/ö/, /ū/

/ö/ — d<u>ew</u>          /ū/ — f<u>ew</u>

# ai

/ā/ — 2 letter /ā/ that we CANNOT use at the end of English words

Advanced: /ā/, /ī/, /ă/

/ā/ — h<u>ai</u>l     /ī/ — <u>ai</u>sle     /ă/ — pl<u>ai</u>d

---

# ay

/ā/ — 2 letter /ā/ that we CAN
use at the end of English words

Advanced: /ā/, /ī/

/ā/ — pl<u>ay</u>     /ī/ — c<u>ay</u>enne

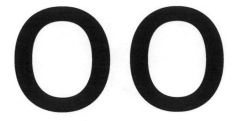

/ö/, /ü/, /ō/

/ö/ — f<u>oo</u>d     /ü/ — h<u>oo</u>k     /ō/ — fl<u>oo</u>r

---

/er/ as in h<u>er</u>

/er/ — h<u>er</u>

The four spellings of /er/: Oyst<u>er</u>s t<u>ur</u>n d<u>ir</u>t into p<u>ear</u>ls.     M<u>er</u>maids t<u>ur</u>n and tw<u>ir</u>l with p<u>ear</u>ls.

# ou

## /ow/, /ō/, /ö/, /ŭ/, /ü/

/ow/ — <u>ou</u>r      /ō/ — f<u>ou</u>r      /ö/ — t<u>ou</u>r
/ŭ/ — fam<u>ou</u>s      /ü/ — c<u>ou</u>ld

[Note: The fifth sound of **ou** occurs only in three base words, followed by a silent **l**—could, would, should.]

---

# ar

## /är/

/är/ — c<u>ar</u>

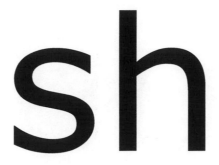

/sh/

/sh/ — s̲h̲ell

---

/ā/, /ē/

Advanced: /ā/, /ē/, /ī/

/ā/ — th<u>ey</u>        /ē/ — k<u>ey</u>        /ī/ — g<u>ey</u>ser

# ck

/k/ — 2 letter /k/

/k/ — ba<u>ck</u>

# wh

/wh/

/wh/ — <u>wh</u>eel

/ē/ — double /ē/

/ē/ — t<u>ee</u>

---

/ed/, /d/, /t/

/ed/ — wad<u>ed</u>          /d/ — wash<u>ed</u>          /t/ — pick<u>ed</u>

[Note: *Ed* is the ending used to form the past tense of regular verbs. *Ed* forms a new syllable when the base word ends in *d* or *t*. Otherwise, *ed* says /d/ or /t/.]

# gu

/g/, /gw/

/g/ — g<u>u</u>est          /gw/ — lang<u>u</u>age

---

# ie

/ē/ — 2 letter /ē/

/ē/ — th<u>ie</u>f

# ng

/ng/

/ng/ — di<u>ng</u> (nasal sound)

---

# ow

/ow/, /ō/

/ow/ — pl<u>ow</u>          /ō/ — gl<u>ow</u>

# oy

/oi/ that we CAN use at the end of English words

/oi/ — <u>toy</u>

---

# ea

/ē/, /ĕ/, /ā/

/ē/ — b<u>ea</u>t          /ĕ/ — br<u>ea</u>d          /ā/ — br<u>ea</u>k

# ei

/ā/, /ē/, /ī/

Advanced: /ā/, /ē/, /ī/, /ĭ/, /ĕ/

/ā/ — th<u>ei</u>r     /ē/ — prot<u>ei</u>n     /ī/ — f<u>ei</u>sty
/ĭ/ — forf<u>ei</u>t     /ĕ/ — h<u>ei</u>fer

---

# oa

/ō/ — 2 letter /ō/

/ō/ — b<u>oa</u>t

# ch

/ch/, /k/, /sh/

/ch/ — <u>ch</u>at       /k/ — <u>ch</u>asm       /sh/ — <u>ch</u>ef

---

# ear

/er/ as in p<u>ear</u>l

/er/ — p<u>ear</u>l

The four spellings of /er/: Oyst<u>er</u>s t<u>ur</u>n d<u>ir</u>t into p<u>ear</u>ls.       M<u>er</u>maids t<u>ur</u>n and tw<u>ir</u>l with p<u>ear</u>ls.

# igh

/ī/ — 3 letter /ī/

/ī/ —  s<u>igh</u>t

---

# ur

/er/ as in t<u>ur</u>n

/ur/ —  t<u>ur</u>n

The four spellings of /er/: Oyst<u>er</u>s t<u>ur</u>n d<u>ir</u>t into p<u>ear</u>ls.      M<u>er</u>maids t<u>ur</u>n and tw<u>ir</u>l with p<u>ear</u>ls.

Advanced: /ä/

/ä/ — bl<u>ah</u>

---

/n/ — 2 letter /n/ that we use only at the beginning of a base word

/n/ — <u>kn</u>ow

# eigh

## /ā/, /ī/

/ā/ — eight          /ī/ — height

---

# eau

## Advanced: /ō/, /ū/, /ŏ/

/ō/ — bureau          /ū/ — beauty          /ŏ/ — bureaucracy

# augh

/ä/, /ăf/

/ä/ — caught          /ăf/ — laugh

# mb

/m/ — 2 letter /m/

/m/ — comb

/ch/

/ch/ — clu<u>tch</u>

---

/oi/ that we CANNOT use at the end of English words

/oi/ — t<u>oi</u>l

# ough

/ŏ/, /ō/, /ö/,
/ow/, /ŭff/, /ŏff/

/ŏ/ — bought     /ō/ — dough     /ö/ — through
/ow/ — bough     /ŭff/ — rough     /ŏff/ — cough

---

# dge

/j/ — 3 letter /j/

/j/ — dodge

# wor

/wer/

/wer/ — worm

---

# wr

/r/ — 2 letter /r/

/r/ — wreck

# bu

/b/ — 2 letter /b/

/bu/ — b<u>u</u>ild

---

# oe

/ō/, /ö/

Advanced: /ō/, /ö/, /ē/

/ō/ — d<u>oe</u>        /ö/ — sh<u>oe</u>        /ē/ — subp<u>oe</u>na

# ph

/f/ — 2 letter /f/

/f/ — <u>ph</u>onics

---

# au

/ä/ — 2 letter /ä/ that we CANNOT use at the end of English words

Advanced: /ä/, /ō/, /ā/, /ow/

/ä/ — p<u>au</u>per     /ō/ — ch<u>au</u>ffeur     /ā/ — g<u>au</u>ge     /ow/ — s<u>au</u>erkr<u>au</u>t

# gn

/n/ — 2 letter /n/ that we can use at the beginning or the end of a word

/gn/ —  gnarl, sign

---

# ti

/sh/ — tall /sh/

"tall" because it begins with a tall letter
/sh/ —  nation

# ui

## /ö/

/ö/ — fr<u>ui</u>t

---

# si

## /sh/, /zh/

/sh/ — transgre<u>ssi</u>on          /zh/ — vi<u>si</u>on

/sh/ — short /sh/

"short" because it begins with a short letter
/sh/ — fa<u>ci</u>al

---

RSTL Book 1—Advanced Phonogram

# sc

Advanced: /s/ — 2 letter /s/

/s/ — <u>sc</u>ience

/sē/

/sē/ — re<u>cei</u>ve

---

RSTL Advanced Phonogram

Advanced: /ā/, /ē/, /ĕ/

/ā/ — <u>ae</u>rial      /ē/ — alg<u>ae</u>      /ĕ/ — <u>ae</u>sthetic

Advanced: /ch/

/ch/ — cappu<u>cc</u>ino

---

Advanced: /sh/

/sh/ — o<u>ce</u>an

# cu

## Advanced: /k/, /kw/

/k/ — bis<u>cu</u>it　　　　　/kw/ — <u>cu</u>isine

---

# et

## Advanced: /ā/

/ā/ — ball<u>et</u>

# eu

## Advanced: /ö/, /ū/

/ö/ — n<u>eu</u>tral          /ū/ — f<u>eu</u>d

---

# ge

## Advanced: /j/, /zh/

/j/ — sur<u>ge</u>on          /zh/ — mira<u>ge</u>

## Advanced: /g/

/g/ — <u>gh</u>ost

---

# ot

## Advanced: /ō/

/ō/ — dep<u>ot</u>

# our

## Advanced: /er/ as in journey

/er/ — journey

Advanced sentences for the five spellings of /er/:
Oysters turn dirt into pearls courageously.          Mermaids turn and twirl on an earthly journey.

---

# pn

## Advanced: /n/ — 2 letter /n/

/n/ — pneumonia

# ps

## Advanced: /s/ — 2 letter /s/

/s/ — psalm

---

# pt

## Advanced: /t/

/t/ — pterodactyl

# rh

Advanced: /r/ — 2 letter /r/

/r/ — <u>rh</u>yme

# sci

Advanced: /ch/

/ch/ — con<u>sci</u>ence

Advanced: /ū/

/ū/ — deb<u>ut</u>

---

Advanced: /ēr/, /er/

/ēr/ — l<u>yr</u>ic          /er/ — s<u>yr</u>up

Made in the USA
Coppell, TX
06 October 2022

84096434R00219